COMICS, TRAUMA, AND THE NEW ART OF WAR

COMICS, TRAUMA, AND THE NEW ART OF WAR

Harriet E. H. Earle

University Press of Mississippi / Jackson

www.upress.state.ms.us

The University Press of Mississippi is a member
of the Association of American University Presses.

Copyright © 2017 by University Press of Mississippi
All rights reserved

First printing 2017
∞

Names: Earle, Harriet, author.
Title: Comics, trauma, and the new art of war / Harriet Earle.
Description: Jackson : University Press of Mississippi, [2017] | Includes
bibliographical references and index.
Identifiers: LCCN 2016053354 (print) | LCCN 2016058047 (ebook) | ISBN
9781496812469 (hardback) | ISBN 9781496812476 (epub single) | ISBN
9781496812483 (epub institutional) | ISBN 9781496812490 (pdf single) |
ISBN 9781496812506 (pdf institutional)
Subjects: LCSH: Graphic novels—History and criticism. | Comic books, strips,
etc.—History and criticism. | Psychic trauma in literature. | War in
literature. | BISAC: LITERARY CRITICISM / Comics & Graphic Novels. |
SOCIAL SCIENCE / Popular Culture. | PSYCHOLOGY / Psychopathology /
Post-Traumatic Stress Disorder (PTSD). | SOCIAL SCIENCE / Violence in
Society.
Classification: LCC PN6714 .E36 2017 (print) | LCC PN6714 (ebook) | DDC
741.5/3—dc23
LC record available at https://lccn.loc.gov/2016053354

British Library Cataloging-in-Publication Data available

Contents

List of Figures and Tables   vii

Acknowledgments   ix

Introduction   3

1 Representing the Traumatic   29

2 Rituals, Mourning, and Grief   55

3 Trauma Invading Sleep   75

4 The Search for Identity   97

5 Moving in Four Dimensions   123

6 Postmodernism vs. Comics and Trauma   149

Excursus   171

Conclusion   189

Notes   197

Bibliography   207

Index   225

List of Figures and Tables

Introduction

Figure x.1 *Guernica*, Pablo Picasso, 1937.

Chapter Three

Table 1 "Who Develops PTSD Nightmares and Who Doesn't," Ernest Hartmann, 1997, p. 107.
Figure 3.1 "Three Day Pass," in *The 'Nam*, Doug Murray and Mike Golden, 1987, p. 12.
Figure 3.2 *American Widow*, Alissa Torres, 2008, p. 125.

Chapter Four

Figure 4.1 *You'll Never Know*, C. Tyler, 2009, n.p.
Figure 4.2 *You'll Never Know*, C. Tyler, 2009, n.p.
Figure 4.3 *Vietnamerica*, GB Tran, 2011, p. 268.

Chapter Five

Figure 5.1 *Vietnamerica*, GB Tran, 2011, p 71.
Figure 5.2 "Beginning of the End" in *The 'Nam Volume 3*, Murray and Golden, 2011, p. 93.

Chapter Six

Table 2 Précised from *The Dismemberment of Orpheus*, Ihab Hassan, 1971, p. 269.
Figure 6.1 *Yossel*, Joe Kubert, 2003, p. 43.
Figure 6.2 *Judenhass*, Dave Sim, 2008, pp. 18–20.

Excursus

Figure 7.1 A Response to the Angoulême *Grand Prix* 2016, Florence Cestac, 2016.
Figure 7.2 *Jobnik! An American Girl's Adventures in the Israeli Army*, 2008, p. 78.
Figure 7.3 *Jobnik! An American Girl's Adventures in the Israeli Army*, 2008, p. 23.

Conclusion

Figure xx.2 *X-Men Guernica*, Cynthia Sousa, 2012.

Acknowledgments

This book has affectionately become known as "My Firstborn"; its gestation has been a wonderful, terrifying, incomparable experience, and I am indebted to a great many people.

It is impossible to overstate my gratitude to my academic colleagues, whose support and strong words have guided me throughout the writing period. In particular, I'd like to thank Dr. James Peacock and Dr. Tim Lustig, who have supported me throughout my whole educational journey and continue to provide encouragement and sound advice as I moved on into the weird world of Academia. I would also like to extend my deepest gratitude to Professors Ian Bell and Oliver Harris at Keele and Dr. Isabel Davis and Dr. Joseph Brooker at Birkbeck for their support.

The editorial team at the University Press of Mississippi deserve many, many thanks for their support and guidance in the "realizing" of this book. I would especially like to thank Vijay Shah, Lisa McMurtray, and Peter Tonguette, who fielded my frantic emails and were an oasis of calm in my inbox, and Dr. Dorothea Fischer-Hornung, who first suggested the Press and kindly assisted with my proposal.

I am indebted to my brilliant friends, without whom I would be lost. Kudos to Hannah Bayley and Dr. Becky Bowler, who are almost certainly the world's best proofreaders and who are probably never going to open an email from me ever again. Thank you to Joe Duffin, for the use of her kettle and kitchen table; to Dr. Anna Hartnell, for the loan of her office as a cocoon of inspiration; and to the "Hive Mind" on Facebook, a constant source of advice and support. Special thanks to Emma Watson, Dr. Siân Jones, Marta Werbanowsky, Bryan Banker, Dr. Grace Halden, Sue Waind, Dr. Sam Knowles, Dr. Nick Bentley, Claire Mackie, Dr. Lise Tannahill, Laurike In 'T Veld, Dr. Alex Valente, Dr. Jo Taylor, Catherine Flay, Dr. Laura Seymour, Eszter Szép, Dr. Robin Hadley, David Whitaker, Dr. Carsten Fuhs, Lola Resano, Dr. Judith Muskett, Dr. Rebecca Darley, and Dr. Rebecca Whiting.

Various institutions around the UK have generously opened their doors to me to use their books, their desks, and their other facilities. Thank you to Keele University, Birkbeck College, the British Library, and Glasgow University. Many of the artists I discuss in this book have kindly given their permission to use their artwork and for this I am very grateful.

Sometimes help comes from strange places and I would like to offer my sincerest thanks to the many strangers I have met on public transport or in cafes and libraries who offered a friendly word of encouragement or piece of advice (and, one time, a word suggestion) when it was sorely needed. They will likely not remember our interaction but I do and their kindness will not be forgotten.

The biggest thanks go to the three people who have really made this book happen. First, Charmaine Simpson, my best friend, who has an uncanny knack for knowing what to say and what to do in any given situation. As we sat on the tarmac in PE at school, I told her that I'd write a book and I have—told you! Finally, the two people who are perhaps most to blame are my parents. Even when they despair and wonder what on earth I'm doing, they stay there, right behind me, supporting me always. And that is the most wonderful thing in the world. I can't thank them enough.

COMICS, TRAUMA, AND THE NEW ART OF WAR

Introduction
Reading Comics with Picasso

> Comics lull you into a false sense of security. You think, this will be funny or at least unserious. Then we hit you with the explosions and the dismemberment. That contrast lends a sharpening effect to the awfulness and violence.
> —**David Axe,** *War is Boring* (2010)

On Monday, April 26, 1937, at the height of the Spanish Civil War, the German *Luftwaffe* "Condor Legion" and Italian *Aviazione Legionaria* bombed the Basque town of Gernika in northern Spain. During the course of the three-hour raid, a total of thirty-one tons of munitions—explosives, fragmentation bombs, and incendiary devices—were dropped. Pilots also used machine guns to fire at individual targets on the ground. Alberto de Onaindía, a Basque priest, witnessed the bombing:

> I left the car by the side of the road and took refuge with five milicianos in a sewer. The water came up to our ankles. From our hiding-place we could see everything that happened without being seen. The aeroplanes came low, flying at two hundred metres. As soon as we could leave our shelter . . . We heard the bullets ripping through branches, and the sinister sound of splintering wood. Women, children and old men were falling in heaps, like flies, and everywhere we saw lakes of blood . . . The aeroplanes were dropping incendiary bombs to try to convince the world that the Basques had fired their own city. (de Onaindía in Payne, 1962: 34)

George Speer wrote in the *Times* that "Guernica flamed from end to end" (Speer in Patterson, 2007: 54). The town was firebombed and left to burn. The number of victims of the bombing is disputed; in 1937, the Basque government reported that 1,654 people had been killed, although modern reports suggest between 150 to 400 civilians died; these numbers may not include victims who later died of their injuries or whose bodies were discovered buried in the rubble (Maier, 1975: 13).

The bombing has been considered one of the first raids in the history of modern military aviation on a defenseless civilian population—an air raid carried out with no regard for women, children, or the elderly and vulnerable.[1] Jörg Diehl, writing in the German periodical *Der Spiegel*, reported:

> Three years before the destruction of Coventry and eight years before the bombing of Dresden, the pilots of Germany's Condor Legion broke with the basic military precept of doing no harm to civilians. Since then, it has been clear that the Germans saw the Spanish Civil War merely as a gigantic training camp. Some 19,000 soldiers—officially all were volunteers—were cycled through the war zone by the Nazis. "Two years of combat experience are more useful than ten years of peacetime training," a German general summarized. (Diehl, 2007: n.p.)

It was this horrific bombing of a civilian population that became the inspiration for Pablo Picasso's most famous painting, *Guernica* (1937).

On commission from the Spanish Republican government, Picasso created the enormous mural to hang in the Spanish pavilion at the *Exposition Internationale des Arts et Techniques dans la Vie Moderne* at the 1937 World's Fair in Paris. Inspired by George Speer's account and spurred on by sympathy for the Republican cause in Spain, he abandoned his original idea and began work on the mural, which was completed in early June. The painting itself is by no means easy to look at. The harsh monochromatic palette and angular forms are captivating and disturbing, both emotions being exacerbated by the huge physical size of the piece. An enormous horse, its abdomen gaping from a large wound, fills the center of the painting. A deformed yet stoic bull stands to the left of the horse, next to a woman cradling her dead child. The right of the painting depicts a burning woman and two witnesses, one bearing a lamp. The painting is chaotic, ably representing the pandemonium of the bombing. Although the mural hung in Paris for many months, it received little critical interest and what it did receive was negative. Le Corbusier wrote that "*Guernica* saw only the backs of visitors for they were repelled by it" (Le Corbusier in Martin, 2004: 121).

Guernica is one of the most important representations of warfare in twentieth-century art, not only because of its arresting size and appearance but also because it captures the effects of military action on a civilian town in a way previously unseen. The extreme violence and chaos attest to the utter destruction of war, while removing any notion of glory or triumph. For Picasso, as illustrated in *Guernica*, war is death, an issue I discuss at length in Chapter 2. Furthermore, as I will show in viewing *Guernica* through the unique lens of comics studies, there are many similarities, both formal and thematic, that can be drawn between this artistic masterpiece and the field of comics.

Initially, it might appear that they have little in common. Comics has long been a part of mass culture, cheaply produced and disposable, and therefore very different from Picasso's works, which are situated in the realm of modernism.[2] Despite this, *Guernica* can be read through the lens of comics for a number of reasons. The first reason pertains to thematic concern. As Peter Childs states, modernisms grew out of "devastation on such a scale that it became absurd to celebrate noble ideas like human dignity in art, or blithely assert a belief in human progress" (2005: 20). Similarly, for Susan Friedman,

> the starting point of modernism is the crisis of belief that pervades twentieth-century culture: loss of faith, experience of fragmentation and disintegration, and shattering of cultural symbols and norms.... Art produced after the First World War recorded the emotional aspect of this crisis: despair, hopelessness, paralysis, angst, and a sense of meaninglessness, chaos, and fragmentation of material reality. (1981: 97)

Both *Guernica* (and modernism more generally) and large swathes of the comics form are preoccupied with devastation; it is not accurate to say that devastation is a concern of all comics, but for a large percentage of comics on the whole—and for almost all mainstream comics—devastation is a prominent theme. I should stress here that I am not saying that comics is a modernist form. Rather, comics is a complex narrative form that, in fact, eschews such narrow classification; while comics has much in common with modernism in terms of thematic concern and representational technique, this reading can only take us so far. Rather, in my reading of *Guernica* and its comics aspects, this relationship with modernism is especially useful when I consider that both forms are concerned with finding ways to give voice to this devastation, which involves developing new and innovative representational strategies. So too, as I will argue, is the comics form, which began to achieve cultural prominence, between the publication of such canonical modernist texts as *The Waste Land* (1921) and *Finnegans Wake* (1939), with the creation of series such as *Les Aventures de Tintin* (1929) and the birth of characters like Superman (1938) and Batman (1939). The forms employed are not only designed to depict devastation but to represent it as accurately and as viscerally as possible.[3]

The second point to make in this reading of *Guernica* is related to form. It is not *just* that Picasso, modernism, and comics are fascinated with devastation.

They are representing it in ways which are comparable. In terms of technical experimentation, comics has the freedom to develop new techniques by the very nature of its form. The number of artistic styles that are employed is constantly increasing.[4] Indeed, the differences of form and technique are, as I demonstrate, crucial to the comics narrative itself. Experimentation is not only employed on a widespread level across the entire comics form, but also within individual comics. A clear example of the extent of artistic experiment in comics is Neil Gaiman's *Sandman* series (1989–2014), which uses a number of different styles within one text, with each separate style's inclusion playing a role within the construction of the narrative and the text as a whole. Charles Hatfield comments that

> the comics form is in flux, becoming more self-conscious in its explorations as creators increasingly recognise the knowledge and sophistication of readers ... Comics has traced an arc of development similar to other cultural forms: away from presentational devices designed to ease audience adjustment and towards a more confident and thorough exploration of the form's peculiar tensions, potentialities and limits. (2005: 66)

In this respect, the relationship between comics and the groundbreaking *Guernica* is complemented by their mutual interest in the exploration of limits and the desire to create works that probe these limits.

Guernica balances on the edge of Cubism: "Guernica is not a Cubist painting, but equally obviously it could not have come into being without Cubism behind it" (Golding, 1968: 186). Cubism is an artistic movement that seeks to observe a subject from different points in space and time simultaneously; the act of moving around an object to seize it from several successive angles fused into a single image, defined by planes and multiple perspectives, is the most recognizable aspect of the Cubist style. This is present in *Guernica* to some extent; the panelized images, planes, and distortions of perspective are central to the structure of the painting. The great difference here is that, in Cubism, the aim is to render one stationary object whereas, in *Guernica*, the central image is not stationary but depicts an active scene. Thus, of all the formal links established between comics and *Guernica*, it is the use of planes, panels, and differing perspectives that provides the clearest relationship. Malcolm Bull discusses multi-aspectival viewing, using the example of Joseph Jastrow's duck/rabbit image. He quotes Stanley Cavell, who writes:

> We may say that the rabbit-aspect is hidden from us when we fail to see it. But what hides it is obviously not the picture (that reveals it), but our (prior) way of

Fig. x.1. *Guernica*, Pablo Picasso, 1937. © Succession Picasso/DACS, London 2015.

taking it, namely its duck-aspect. What hides one aspect is another aspect, something at the same level. (Cavell in Bull, 1999: 22)

The duck and rabbit are not hidden at different levels but at the same level—you cannot see both at once and, according to Bull, seeing both at once is not to see either but to "'recognise the drawing as a duck-rabbit drawing, although we are not then seeing a duck and a rabbit, only a drawing of the particular kind that disguises a duck and a rabbit" (1999: 22). For Bull, multi-aspectival viewing is central to modernism. Although on initial viewing, *Guernica* may appear to be only a massive canvas of chaos, looking closer brings out the panelized images, planes, and distortions of perspective that are central to the structure of the painting. However, if we choose to concentrate solely on the panelization of the image, the overall image is lost. As with comics, the individual panels must be considered within the wider frame and it is within this quadrillage, to use Thierry Groensteen's term, that the panel is given meaning. I would argue that the interest in panelization represents the strongest formal tie between comics and modernism.

Let us look more closely at the panelization of *Guernica*. The work can be divided into four equally sized vertical sections. The two left sections contain one panel. The third and fourth sections contain one panel each. It would be most straightforward to read the painting from left to right, with the figures in the middle panel reacting to the left panel and the right panel occurring last. This logical left-to-right reading suggests movement of time as opposed to one frozen moment. Indeed, despite the lack of chronological movement, *Guernica* contains a complex series of panels. The action appears to be contained within a room, onto which several windows and doors open. The floating head in the third section enters through a window; a door stands ajar at the far right side; a definite corner can be seen at the top right corner. The appearance of a tiled roof in the third section suggests that the action is both inside and outside, framed by walls and windows while not framed at all. The ambiguity created by this complex paneling mirrors the chaos of the painting's content.

Aside from the structural panels created by the walls and frames, the Cubist forms of the human and animal characters within the painting are divided into panels (or "panelized") themselves. The sharp shapes of the figures are spliced by crosshatching lines, making them multi-paneled. Similarly, the bold colors create panels in their harsh contrast. The third section's white shape, juxtaposed to the black background of the horse, puts the two witness characters in a bright white panel, while the gored horse remains in black. Unlike "typical" Cubism, where the panelization is employed to show a shift in time and perspective on a single object, the panels in *Guernica* serve a different purpose. They create different perspectives within one object and create multiple focal points within the painting as a whole. Most paintings have a single focal point that draws the eye before allowing the viewer to take in the rest of the painting; in some cases, there is a definite narrative thread through an image, as is the case in many religious tableaux. The lack of focal point and chaos of multiple panels creates an image that is both distressing to view and representative of the chaos of the event itself.

In January 1937, six months before the bombing of Gernika, Picasso created a series of fourteen etchings, entitled *The Dream and Lie of Franco*. It was his intention to sell them as postcards to raise money for the Spanish Republican aid campaign, though this idea was later abandoned. To the original fourteen he added four more etchings, which are recognizable as preliminary studies for *Guernica*. The original fourteen depict Francisco Franco in a rough narrative. The images display Franco in a series of different guises, including a knight, a tightrope-walking "jackbooted phallus," a courtesan, and a soldier mounted on a pig, riding into battle, having stabbed Pegasus, who lies dead in the tenth scene (O'Brian, 2012: 318). In one particularly odd scene, Franco is depicted as "a grotesque homunculus with a head like a gesticulating and tuberous sweet potato" (Van Hensbergen, 2013: 28). The rough narrative is of Franco's destruction of Spain, its culture, and its people, before he is destroyed by the bull, a symbol of the *Corrida*. John Golding writes that "more than any other work by Picasso *The Dream and Lie of Franco* breaks down, as the Surrealists so passionately longed to, distinctions between writing and visual imagery" (1994: 244). *The Dream and Lie of Franco* can easily be considered sequential art: a series of images in specific sequence to create a narrative flow. The sequence can be seen as a comic strip—and the form of the comic,

I would argue, persists in *Guernica* itself. In line with Golding's comment, the comics form also breaks down the distinction between writing and visual imagery, creating no hierarchy between the two. Furthermore, comics is able to create coherent narratives without the inclusion of words at all.

The central issue of *The Dream and Lie of Franco* is that it precedes *Guernica* and forms the basis of it. The first half is dated four months prior to the bombing of Gernika, showing that it was not initially influenced by the bombing. However, the final four panels are direct studies for *Guernica*, dated late April 1937. The fact that this piece, which influences the creation of *Guernica*, is a comic undoubtedly influenced the comics aspects of the final work. I consider both *Guernica* and *The Dream and Lie of Franco* to be prototypes for the silent comics that I discuss in Chapter 1.

Guernica is demonstrative of a larger issue in representations of conflict and trauma. As I discuss at length over the course of this book, trauma affects representational strategies and insists on new artistic and narrative forms. As I have already shown, *Guernica* breaks with many traditional artistic techniques. Indeed, it is because Picasso rejected what was considered "good art" ("*la belle peinture*") and instead turned to less accepted and less "comfortable" techniques that the painting is effective as a representation of the trauma of conflict. It may be thought that traumatic art of any medium is dependent on a recreation of the traumatic event itself; this is not necessarily true. In the case of *Guernica*, the viewer is faced with a recreation of the event to some extent: the piece is carefully constructed to imitate the terror of the bombing of Gernika and allow those of us who were not present at the event itself to understand some of the trauma of that day. At the basic level, this is the aim of traumatic art. However, it is not enough to simply mimic the symptoms of trauma in order to create "traumatic art," not only because it is reductionist and incorrect to suggest that there is only one goal in the representation of trauma—traumatic art is also about emancipation, relief, revenge, and the need to tell—but also because traumatic events are almost always impossible to recreate with any degree of accuracy due to the nature of traumatic memory and because trauma is so much more than a set of symptoms. It has become shorthand for negative experience, especially experiences of conflict and violence. Jill Bennett writes:

> If the concept of trauma long ago entered the popular vernacular through the discourse of self-help manuals and television talk shows, it was generalised to an unprecedented degree after 9/11. The term "trauma" came to encompass a range of responses, including those that might more accurately be described as anxiety, shock, fear, sympathy, compassion, and so on. But at the same time,

for many "secondary witnesses"—those affected by the tragedy, but not directly involved—the symptomology of trauma offered a means to articulate an affective response—and also to identify as a victim even at some remove from the locus of the attacks. (2005: 20)

Trauma is not necessarily, as Cathy Caruth names it, "unclaimed"; it is an experience owned by someone—though this ownership may be deeply contested—and the recreation of traumatic experience in art of any medium is by its very nature bound up in questions of witnessing and ownership. I discuss this issue in depth in Chapter 1.

In a 2005 article in the *New Yorker*, art critic Peter Schjeldahl writes,

> Over-the-topness is endemic to comics, of course—an industry standard for popular action and horror titles, as well as for manga, and the default setting for [Robert] Crumb's work. But it is ill suited to serious subjects, especially those that incorporate authentic social history. (2005: n.p.)

He is right to suggest that comics is known for "over-the-topness"—bold coloration, stereotyped characters, and story arcs that require suspension of disbelief. This is only an accurate description of one genre within the comics form as a whole. A large number of comics do not fit into this genre and many actively seek to be distanced from it. Comics is a complex artistic medium, which, as I show, is able to represent conflict trauma in new and innovative ways. Schjeldahl's low opinion of comics as an art form (in fact, his opinion seems to be that comics is not an art form at all) is no longer a widely held position within literary, cultural, and art criticism; the academy at large is well aware that there is a large and flourishing body of comics scholarship. The reason that I bring up Schjeldahl's comment at all is his use of the phrase "authentic social history," a central theme of this book. In particular, I am concerned with the representation of conflict. But, like Picasso's mighty painting, rather than tackling this immense subject as a whole, I consider the effects of conflict—and the traumatic aftereffects—on individuals and groups. More specifically, I concentrate on how this conflict trauma is represented in comics. The form does not shy away from representing conflict. In fact, the visual nature of the form makes it ideal for representing trauma and conflict. Both trauma and conflict are intensely visual phenomena. In terms of conflict, this is reflected in the term "theatre of war." This term was first used in about 1580 to describe a geographical area and was used specifically for the location of a conflict in 1914. The Greek root of the word comes from "θεάομαι" ("to see" or "to view"); the concept of theatre is intrinsically bound up in the necessity of viewing. The comics form is not simply visual but aspects of the form can be used to reproduce and mimic the experience of a traumatic rupture, thus acting as a representation of so-called "authentic social history."

Before I move into a discussion of the terms and thematic concerns of this book, I want to outline in brief the history of comics, looking specifically at comics in twentieth-century North America and the question of censorship. This history is a relatively short but tempestuous one. There is no definitive birthday for the form—nor is there a categorical "first text." Certainly, the modern comics form is influenced by more than just its comic predecessors, political cartooning and newspaper daily "funny pages." However, it was not until 1935 that comic strips were combined into what Danny Fingeroth calls "tabloid-sized anthologies, known as 'comic books'" (2008: 13).[5] Such was the popularity of these new "comic books" that the demand for them had to be met with original material not previously printed in the newspapers. One of the most productive publishers at this point was National Allied Publications, now known as DC Comics. It was at this point that superheroes first appeared, starting with Superman in *Action Comics #1* in 1938.

This is a particularly remarkable time for such a character to be created, being the year before the start of World War II. The early superheroes were all, to some extent, symbols of nationalist pride, and Superman is no exception. However, it was the introduction of Captain America in 1941 that opened up the comics form as a medium for conveying nationalist pride and encouraging "homeland morale." Co-creator Joe Simon said Captain America was a "consciously political creation as [Jack Kirby and I] felt war was inevitable: The opponents to the war were all quite well organized. We wanted to have our say too" (Kirby, quoted in Wright, 2003: 26). Living up to his name, the character that was created was shown to be fiercely patriotic, as demonstrated by his costume. In the first issue Captain America deflects a Nazi bullet while punching Hitler.[6]

Fingeroth writes that "by the early 1950s, the superhero comics fad was pretty much dead. DC Comics published Superman, Batman and Wonder Woman, but that was all. The genre that sold in huge numbers was horror" (2008: 14). Unfortunately, at the same time, comics were gaining notoriety among those who feared their children were being corrupted. In 1940, a Chicago journalist, Sterling North, wrote:

> Badly drawn, badly written, and badly printed—a strain on the young eyes and young nervous systems—the effects of these pulp-paper nightmares is that of a violent stimulant. Their crude blacks and reds spoil a child's natural sense of color; their hypodermic injection of sex and murder make the child impatient

with better, though quieter, stories. Unless we want a coming generation even more ferocious than the present one, parents and teachers throughout America must band together to break the "comic" magazine. (North in Duncan and Smith, 2009: 274)

At the time, North's diatribe did very little. However, in 1954 Dr. Fredric Wertham published *Seduction of the Innocent*, the influence of which is still felt in the comics world today. Wertham stated that comics were a major cause of juvenile delinquency. Critics of Wertham's work pointed out that he studied only "juvenile delinquents," without comparing them to "normal" children; Wertham responded that the kids who did not become delinquents may, bizarrely, be worse off (Duncan and Smith, 2009: 275). So far as I know there is no evidence that children who read comics are at risk of delinquency (or, indeed, of mental instability, psychological distress, or any other ill effect). Wertham does not state how the children who avoid delinquency are worse off, nor does he give examples of non-delinquent children suffering from the effects of comics reading. That said, he did argue that comics confused children's knowledge of physics (due to superpowers), implemented homosexual ideas (due to the prevalence of young male sidekicks), and that female superheroes gave children "wrong ideas" about the place of women in society.

The objections of Wertham and his supporters led to a US Senate investigation and to the subsequent creation of the Comic Magazine Association of America (CMAA) and the Comics Code Authority (CCA). Only comics that bore the CCA stamp were allowed to be sold. The harsh regulations killed off the horror genre, leading to the revitalization of the superhero genre into its Silver Age (1956–c. 1970). To a twenty-first-century reader, the regulations of the CCA seem at best strict, at worst hilarious. Perhaps the most amusing to those familiar with the history of female superheroes is the following rule: "Females shall be drawn realistically without exaggeration of any physical qualities" (CCA: CBLDF online, 2012). Although the CCA has not been used since 2011—and no longer has any power over which comics are published and distributed in the US—at the time it brought the comics industry to its knees and was responsible for several companies going out of business.

In the 1920s, '30s, and '40s "Tijuana Bibles," cheaply printed pornographic comics, grew in popularity, mostly due to their ready availability compared to traditional pornography. They usually depicted well-known comics characters engaging in sexual acts. The increased availability of pornographic material in the 1950s meant that this subset died out, but it did act as the predecessor to what became known as "Underground Comix"—the "x" in the word bringing attention to the slightly deviant and "X-rated" potential of their content.

Fingeroth writes that "the underground comix were about as far from the mainstream as it was possible to be . . . that was the whole point" (2008: 17). Underground "comix" intentionally moved away from "house drawing styles," as were common in mainstream comics, and catered to an older readership. Although the movement originally began as a rebellion against the mainstream, it was a huge part of the birth of what may now be called "graphic novels." Perhaps one of the most famous "graphic novelists," Art Spiegelman, began as the founder of *Raw Magazine*—a comix where many artists who became well known started their careers—before achieving international recognition with the 1986 publication of *Maus*. Indeed, Spiegelman has said that "without *Binky Brown* [one of the first underground comix to deal with dark and psychologically rich material] there would be no *Maus*" (Spiegelman in Fingeroth, 2009: 18). The underground movement allowed many up-and-coming artists to hone their skills without being constrained by the requirements and rules of the mainstream comics world and assisted with the move into the popular sphere of a great many artists and, more importantly, a wide range of genres and thematic concerns.

Representing Conflict

> Conflict: c.1500. A war, battle or armed fight, from Latin *conflictus* "strike together," *con* + *fligere*. Competitive or opposing action of incompatibles; antagonistic state or action, The opposition of persons or forces that gives rise to dramatic action. (*Oxford English Dictionary*, 2012)

All of the texts discussed in this book are explicitly about conflict—moreover, conflict that "actually happened" and, as such, are grounded in historical fact. But what is a text of conflict? We may think of films that deal with historical conflicts—for example, Michael Bay's 2001 *Pearl Harbor*, older classics such as *The Great Escape* (1963), and, more recently, the Oscar-winning *The Hurt Locker* (2008).[7] For the most part, the West has turned towards cinema as the primary narrative form of the twentieth and twenty-first centuries. There is a tendency in cinema to glorify conflict, although this is being challenged in recent films. Mark Kermode suggests that this is "Hollywood's attempt to emphasise heroism rather than horror," adding that "they fail in this, only succeeding in erasing all the gore and truth from the battle" (2011: 4). This glorification of conflict is not unique to cinema. A similar trend has long been traced in mainstream comics—in both representations of military conflict and general violence—and has given much ammunition to comics' critics, as

I discuss in more detail in the conclusion to this study. But it is not accurate to say that glorification of conflict is found only in mainstream comics. Frank Miller's comic *300*, and the subsequent film adaptation of the same name, has been widely criticized for its Manichean view of the Spartan-Persian conflict and glamorous yet dubious portrayal of battle as a time of ceaseless glory.

Fredric Jameson writes that "history is what hurts"—in other words, that which is painful and destructive is what creates human history (2002: 102). War and conflict are among the most prevalent of human experiences. In his 1945 work *Mimesis: Dargestellte Wirklichkeit in Der Abendländischen Literatur*, Erich Auerbach discusses literary reality from Homer's *Odyssey* to Virginia Woolf's *To the Lighthouse*.[8] While the study is not specific to the topic of war literature, Auerbach's list of primary texts does include a great number dealing with war, directly or indirectly. This is especially evident in the inclusion of the three earlier texts: Ammianus Marcellinus's descriptions of mob riots and conflicts in Rome; a section of Gregory of Tours's *Historia Francorum*; and *La Chanson de Roland*, a heroic poem of the late eleventh century. It is relevant here to note that the first two are listed as "historical texts." It is not clear how accurate these texts are but their inclusion in Auerbach's study shows the importance of historical battle narrative in the development of literature.

Towards the middle of his survey, Auerbach introduces Farinata degli Uberti and Cavalcante de Cavalcanti, two Florentine aristocrats who are burning together in the tombs of the heretics in Dante's *Inferno* (part one of the *Divina Commedia*). They are from opposite sides of the warring factions in Florence, the Guelphs and the Ghibellines. This conflict tore Florence apart in the thirteenth and fourteenth centuries and was, in part, the cause of Dante's exile from the city in 1301. These two men, though confined to the same tomb for eternity, have no interaction with each other. Their inclusion in the text shows the violent severing of relationships that can—and does—arise in times of conflict. They become a microcosmic representation of the divisions of war. Much of *Inferno* is structured around discourses of political and civil unrest—it has, as Alison Milbank suggests, "war as its framework" (1998: 43).

The final chapter of Auerbach's text concerns Woolf and Proust. Although neither *To the Lighthouse* nor *À la Recherche du Temps Perdu* discuss conflict explicitly, both were written and published around the time of the First World War or shortly thereafter. It is difficult to imagine a text written at this time that was not in some way touched by the effects of the war. Indeed, there is a clear relationship between modernist narrative forms and conflict. The same fragmentation of narrative can be seen in many works of modernist literature as is commonplace in the literature of trauma. The stream-of-consciousness narrative which features in so many modernist works (most notably those by Virginia Woolf and James Joyce) references a similar fragmentation of experience. In this respect, the First World War and its traumatic legacy has affected narrative structure. As Auerbach writes, "If an author wishes to write what is real, he will often have to write what is unpleasant" (1988: 267). Let us return to our initial quotation from Jameson: "History is what hurts." Literature that grows from this history must, then, also hurt.

Auerbach's analyses end with the First World War. As I previously mentioned, the texts from the eighteenth, nineteenth, and early twentieth centuries do not hold conflict as their central concern. There are, of course, many novels of this time period that do discuss war explicitly—for example, Thackeray's *Vanity Fair* (1848), Tolstoy's *War and Peace* (1869), and Crane's *The Red Badge of Courage* (1895)—but it would not be an exaggeration to suggest, as Robert Uphaus does, that the novels of this period are concerned more with scenes of domesticity and the private sphere than with public concerns and war (1988: 17). Although I could suggest that this is not something typically seen in the later twentieth and twenty-first centuries, the truth of the situation is more complicated than that.

There is a healthy corpus of literature of conflict that has been steadily growing since the First World War, much of which has entered the canon. Texts such as Ernest Hemingway's *A Farewell to Arms* (1929), Joseph Heller's *Catch-22* (1961), and Tim O'Brien's *The Things They Carried* (1990) are explicit conflict texts in the tradition of Homer. Looking, for example, at O'Brien's collection of Vietnam short stories *The Things They Carried*, it is not necessarily that there is a clear-cut narrative of conflict as much as an exploration of the complex negotiations between personal relationships and public conflict. O'Brien's stories are concerned with the micronarratives of the war or, more accurately, the soldiers who fight it. In the eponymous story, he writes at great length about each character's personal cargo—everything from photographs to cannabis—which reduces the war further into minutiae than is evident in Heller's *Catch-22*. Heller structures his work around the increasingly bizarre personal relationships of the characters, both professional and romantic, and the now-famous paradoxical statement that inspires the novel's title. Still, "the war" is not discussed as much as the small details of those who are involved in it, regardless of the size of their input or the value of it. "Traditional" Hollywood representations may have lost this, wanting to make war appear a noble act with a victorious conclusion, although recent films such as *The Hurt Locker* (2009) and *Zero Dark Thirty* (2013) are shifting the focus of war narratives onto more nuanced representations of conflict and the individual's relationship to it. War becomes a single, massive event and such representations give no credence to the smaller, more human aspects of conflict. Tim O'Brien writes:

> And in the end, of course, a true war story is never about war. It's about sunlight. It's about the special way that dawn spreads out on a river when you know you must cross the river and march into the mountains and do things you are afraid to do. It's about love and memory. It's about sorrow. It's about sisters who never write back and people who never listen. (1991: 81)

Narratives of conflict, then, are by no means a straightforward genre to analyze; it is far more than accounts of battles and military maneuvers. It is a genre that gives voice to traumatic experiences, the difficulties faced in recovery, and a multitude of small things that combine to create a conflict experienced by the individuals who recreate it in narratives and art. Representations of conflict do not concentrate so much on the overarching conflict as those that exist within it—conflicts within conflicts.

Where do comics fit into this debate? As I mentioned previously, comics has much to add to the academic debate on the representational strategies at play in conflict and trauma. *Comics, Trauma, and the New Art of War* is among the first full-length studies of conflict and trauma in comics and seeks to use existing theoretical frameworks from trauma studies, comics studies, and literary theory to analyze the ways in which American comics create trauma narratives. In his "Homage to Joe Sacco," Edward Said sums up the position of comics as a form that can open new and radical imaginative avenues when he writes,

> comics seemed to say what couldn't otherwise be said, perhaps what wasn't permitted to be said or imagined, defying the ordinary processes of thought, which are policed, shaped and re-shaped by all sorts of pedagogical as well as ideological pressures . . . I felt that comics free me to think and imagine and see differently. (Said in Whitlock, 2006: 967)

For Said, comics moves beyond the "policing" of traditional narrative forms to allow both creator and reader to "think and imagine and see differently."

In her 2016 book *Disaster Drawn: Visual Witness, Comics, and Documentary Form*, Hillary Chute writes that "comics as a medium place pressure on classifiability and provokes questions about the boundaries of received categories of narrative" (2016: 1). Rather than languishing in their history as disposable narratives of little value, the form has developed into one that is both innovative and forward-thinking: the comics form has repeatedly shown that it is capable of representing difficult topics precisely because it dares to "engage the difficulty of spectacle instead of turning away from it" (2016: 17). Chute states that "work that is historical and specifically 'testamentary' or testimonial is the strongest genre of comics" (2016: 6). I am not dealing solely with comics that are "testamentary," but this unique type of historiography does feature in this study. Chute is explicit in her explanation of her corpus: she is working with what she calls "documentary comics"—texts that are representing historical events from the point of view of witnesses, working with Lisa Gitelman's definition of documentary as "an epistemic practice: the kind of knowing that is all wrapped up with showing, and showing wrapped up with knowing" (Gitelman in Chute, 2016: 18). My corpus differs from Chute's; although all of the texts I use in this study are based on historical events, the writers are approaching these events from a variety of different personal viewpoints. I work with autobiographical texts, mainstream series, and fictional one-shots because each one adds something to the conversation of how comics can represent conflict—and specifically conflict trauma—and why these representations are important in the wider scheme of conflict narrative and representational strategy.

When one becomes concerned with conflicts that are grounded in history, it goes without saying that one must also be concerned with the writing and representation of history. This is an area of particular interest throughout the field of comics, especially given that so many of the canonical and groundbreaking comics of the past thirty years deal with historical events. Chute writes:

> The print medium of comics offers a unique spatial grammar of gutters, grids, and panels suggestive of architecture. It presents juxtaposed frames alternating with empty gutters—a logic of arrangement that turns time into space on the page. Through its spatial syntax, comics offer opportunities to place pressure on traditional notions of chronology, linearity, and causality—as well as on the idea that "history" can ever be a closed discourse, or a simply progressive one. (2016: 4)

Chute taps into one of the central facets of comics creation that I talk about in Chapter 5. When considering the comic on the page, time-space relationships emerge as one of the most compelling and intricately crafted elements of the comics form. There are other aspects of historiography that are important to remember when discussing comics. Both Spencer Clark and Ben Lander suggest that it is in the attention to detail that comics are most powerful as historiographical documents. Clark writes that history gets humanized in graphic novels when they show the impact events have on the lives of people and their agency (2013: 498); Lander suggests that "comic histories tend to revel in the minute personal details of everyday life, which receive their due respect because of their personal or symbolic weight within the lives of the characters and the narrative that is being constructed" (2005: 117). As I will show, comics narratives of conflict tend to concentrate on the personal, becoming narratives of individual experience and trauma; rather that giving us the big picture, comics instead present personal stories, bound up in minutiae and nuanced characters—these historical comics are akin to (auto)biography. Given that I am dealing with a large number of these texts that, while not *all* autobiographical, are driven by a great deal of personal input, I now wish to move onto a discussion of the relationship between autobiography and comics.

Trauma and Autobiography

The majority of texts that are discussed here can be categorized as "life writing" or "memoir," slippery terms that blur the line between fiction and non-fiction. There are a number of reasons for my choosing to work primarily with (at least semi-) autobiographical comics texts. First, the most expansive genre of comics is that which is called "the mainstream": works published by DC and Marvel, usually but not always superhero narratives. While some mainstream comics do engage in nuanced representations of conflict and the trauma it engenders (most notably the mainstream publications I discuss in this book), this is not the norm; a more traditional stance veers towards a Manichean glorification narrative. I do not wish to denigrate mainstream comics by this opinion; it is not the desire of the genre to create psychological studies of the effects of violence and conflict on the self, and I do consider some mainstream publications here. I mention it only to explain my reason for choosing to work (for the most part) with non-mainstream comics. The second point relates to the sheer number of available texts. A huge number of comics autobiographies have been published over the past two decades, a great deal of these dealing with traumatic narratives, affording me many choices. And, as I have mentioned above, these biographical texts allow for intensely personal narratives that are deeply involved in individual stories and experiences.

Gillian Whitlock writes that "comics has a distinctive role to play in the work of representing traumatic memory and may be partly adept at finding room to maneuver amid spaces of contradiction and extreme states of violent contestation" (2007: 194). Of course, despite comics' "distinctive role," there are still issues of representation at play. Jane Tolmie suggests that "stories, even in graphic memoir, does not fully capture either the body of the past, though new formats lead us to ask new and perhaps better questions about the nature of the body/text gap" (2009: 84). One of the key ways in which comics can open up new questions about the body/text gap is to make it visual: "Comics locates the reader in space and for this reason is able to spatialize memory... comics is able to map a life, not only figuratively but literally" (Chute, 2011: 108–109). This space-time relationship is discussed in detail in Chapter 5.

The authors are, for the most part, writing their own stories in whatever way they can—these are, as I demonstrate, not stories that lend themselves to clear-cut representational techniques. I could say of these texts that they are representations of, for the most part, autobiographical truth. And yet the term "autobiographical truth" is intensely problematic. Lynda Barry suggests that her work would more accurately be referred to as "autobiofictionalography," a portmanteau that acknowledges the melting together of truth and fiction that is central to the creation of her work, especially *One! Hundred! Demons!* (2002), and speaks to the necessity of using fiction in order to tell one's story in a way that can connect with readers.

I turn to the unusual case study of Binjamin Wilkomirski. In 1998, a controversial article was published in the Swiss periodical *Weltwoche*. Daniel Ganzfried, a Swiss journalist, questioned the veracity of Wilkomirski's highly acclaimed Holocaust memoir *Bruchstück: Aus Einer Kindheit, 1939–1948*, published in 1995.[9] Since its publication, *Bruchstück* had won several awards, including the National Jewish Book Award and *Le Prix Memoire de la Shoah*. The book was widely praised and Wilkomirski enjoyed a great deal of media attention. Ganzfried's investigations proved that the vast majority of the memoir—including his reports of events that happened in both Auschwitz and Majdanek, his date and place of birth and also his name—was fabricated (Ganzfried in Hefti, 2002: 34). Latvian-born Binjamin Wilkomirski was really Bruno Grosjean, born in 1941 in Switzerland. The revelation that this celebrated memoir was completely false was shocking. Many critics and psychologists who were involved in the Wilkomirski affair noted that Wilkomirski appeared to genuinely believe his fabricated past. When challenged by his agent, and confronted with a large amount of evidence of his real identity, Wilkomirski allegedly yelled "I AM BINJAMIN WILKOMIRSKI!" The fact that he appears to actually believe his own lies, and has placed himself in the company of survivors, is of more interest to scholars of traumatic identity than the narrative itself. That this man had a troubled past is proven. In order to overcome his difficult childhood, he takes on the mantle of Holocaust survivor and becomes a victim of the highest order, commanding the respect of millions: "As a child survivor he is the most innocent of all the innocents and the most deserving of pity" (Maechler, 2001: 70). Maechler continues:

> Once the professed interrelationship between the first-person narrator, the death-camp story he narrates, and historical reality are proved palpably false, what was a masterpiece becomes kitsch. (2001: 81)

Although Maechler makes a valid point, the case of Binjamin Wilkomirski brings into question the importance of unvarnished truth in memoir. In reality, there is no such thing. Virginia Woolf likens the writing of biography (and autobiography) to a balancing act, between granite and rainbows. She writes:

> On the one hand there is truth; on the other, there is personality. And if we think of truth as something of granite-like solidity and of personality as something of rainbow-like intangibility and reflect that the aim of biography is to weld these two into one seamless whole, we shall admit that the problem is a stiff one and that we need not wonder if biographers have for the most part failed to solve it. (2008: 95)

Undoubtedly, for a memoir to be a retelling of the experiences of a person's life, basic historical fact must be accurate; there are facts in every narrative that are indisputable. In her comprehensive study of life writing in comics, Elisabeth El Refaie suggests that "it is impossible to draw strict boundaries between factual and fictional accounts of someone's life, since memory is always incomplete and the act of telling one's life story necessarily involves selection and artful construction" (2012: 12). This point is entirely correct; the nature of memory negates the ability to write 100 percent accurate accounts of anything, let alone something as subjective as one's own life story. She goes on to write:

> Some scholars dealing with autobiographical texts have rediscovered Philippe Lejeune's (1989) concept of the "autobiographical pact," a sort of tacit understanding between author and reader by which the former commits him- or herself not to some unattainable historical exactitude but to the sincere effort to be as truthful as possible.... In the cause of autobiography there has to be identity between the author, the narrator, and the protagonist, an identity which can be established by checking the proper name given on the title page... Lejeune's claim of a complete overlap in autobiography between the author, narrator and protagonist can only be upheld if the self is construed as a coherent and unified entity, which remains more or less stable over the course of a lifetime. Such a view of the self is now generally considered to be inaccurate and misleading. (El Refaie, 2012: 53)

If the "standard" biographer struggles to balance the granite-truth and rainbow-personality, the biographer of trauma faces an even bigger challenge. Applying the muddying filter of traumatic experience to the already complex genre of memoir confuses matters further; Wilkomirski's book exemplifies to an extraordinary extent how using the rhetoric of trauma can produce a strong reaction of empathy on the part of the reader. In her discussion of a similar autobiography hoax, Norma Khouri's *Honor Lost* (2003), Gillian Whitlock suggests that, "despite the painfulness of betrayed trust, literary hoaxes are useful: they bring to light the investments elicited by life narrative, and they also remind us of the risks of emotional engagement for readers, publishers, and critics" (2007: 11). She is exactly right; literary hoaxes often upset us mostly because of the amount of emotional investment we have in the story. In other words, to find we have been duped can leave a very real feeling of betrayal. Tim O'Brien suggests autobiography is less about "actual truth" and more about finding ways to communicate the experience to those who were not there:

> By telling stories, you objectify your own experience. You separate it from yourself. You pin down certain truths. You make up others. You start sometimes with an incident that truly happened, like the night in the shit field, and you carry it forward by inventing incidents that did not in fact occur but that nonetheless help to clarify and explain. (1991: 157)

It is O'Brien's opinion—that life writing need not be about the empirical truth of a situation, but instead should focus on finding ways to convey the experience to others—that sits most comfortably with the texts I discuss here. The absolute facts are not what are important. Rather, focus should be placed on what these texts tell us about the author's personal and intensely individual experience, as well as the nature of representation and memory. As Whitlock writes, "Autobiography is a cultural space where relations between the individual and society are thought out intensely and experienced intersubjectively; here the social, political, and cultural underpinnings of thinking about the self come to the surface and are affirmed in images, stories, and legends" (2007: 11–12).

• • •

The corpus of texts that *Comics, Trauma, and the New Art of War* is concerned with has tight national and historical parameters. Every text analyzed herein comes from a North American context; the authors discussed, many of whom are the children of foreign nationals, are residents of North America and have been for much of their life. This distinction allows me to consider the work of Art Spiegelman (born in Sweden to Polish parents) and GB Tran (born in the US but to Vietnamese refugee parents). While these two are not American by blood (i.e., parents' nationality) or, for Spiegelman, by birth, they have adopted American citizenship and live in the US. Furthermore, no primary text discussed in this thesis was written prior to 1975.[10] I specify 1975 because the Fall of Saigon, which signaled the end of the Vietnam War and American military involvement in Southeast Asia, occurred on April 1, 1975. This defeat for the American military shifted the popular opinion of conflict in the American consciousness, though this shift had been ongoing throughout the American occupation of Vietnam, thanks to the growing antiwar movement. Formal demonstrations to the war started small. On May 12, 1964, twelve men in New York City publically burned their draft cards (Gottlieb, 1991: xix). By October 1965, thousands of people were congregating for antiwar protest marches across the world. Such protests as that at Kent State University in May 1970 (this protest was specifically against the invasion of Cambodia and the reigniting of fighting in Vietnam), in which the Ohio National Guard shot and killed four unarmed students in thirteen seconds, injuring a further nine, and the April 1971 march on the Capitol, in which veterans discarded over 700 medals and 500,000 people marched, became public, potent manifestations of the depth of negative feeling regarding the nation's involvement.

Coupled with the thousands of unposed, unedited photographs of the experiences of the front line and the daily televised reports, the Vietnam War was responsible for a shift in the perception of conflict within American society and, furthermore, a shift in the treatment of returning veterans. Vietnam veteran James "Bud" O'Reilly states that "Vietnam vets are among the most fucked up because we had so little training. Twelve weeks, here's your gun, off you go and shoot at the VC. That's no way to prepare a man to kill someone. I don't even think some of the guys realized they were going to get shot at. And we got back to nothing" (O'Reilly, 2012). General David Petraeus notes that "Vietnam cost the military dearly . . . it robbed them of good men and dignity" (Petraeus in Miles, 2011). The Vietnam War caused the American military to seriously reconsider their courses of action, organizations, and personnel strategy. In the wake of the Vietnam War, there has been a shift in conflict literature and, moreover, an increase in the number of combat veterans who have become successful writers, with an emphasis on their writing about their experiences.[11]

In terms of publication development, the founding of Fantagraphics Books in 1976 helped underground comix move into more visible publishing circles, as this was a publishing house willing to print works that were previously of little interest to the more established companies. As a publisher, they were a key force in "[establishing] comics as a medium as eloquent and expressive as the more established popular arts of film, literature, poetry, et al" (Fantagraphics, 2013: online). Spurred on by the increasing popularity and market visibility of comics, Roger Sabin suggests, the biggest year in the forward momentum of this new breed of comics was 1986 (2001: 98). This was the year of publication of three major works, all of which remain popular and influential today: Art Speigelman's *Maus*, an intense retelling of his family's Holocaust experiences and the only comic (to date) to win a Pulitzer Prize; Frank Miller's *Batman: The Dark Knight Returns*, in which the familiar superhero contemplates the threat of a dystopian future; and Alan Moore and Dave Gibbons's *Watchmen*, a work of dense political criticism, set in an alternate America on the brink of nuclear war. Their publication not only opened the American comics world to the prospect of complex plots and "serious" themes, but also gave new possibilities for different and innovative artistic styles.

Before giving an overview of the way in which this book will develop across its six chapters and one excursus, I wish to explain my choice of terms. I avoid using cinematic language, as is so often the case with comics criticism, or suggesting that the two forms are closely connected. Comics is not films. While there is a basic similarity between film storyboards and comics, the vital difference is that storyboards are not a completed narrative and serve only as guidelines for the production team. The finished film is a separate entity again. Film and comics differ most obviously in their amount of reader control over the construction of the narrative itself, as I discuss throughout this thesis. Furthermore, in avoiding filmic terminology, I wish to avoid the suggestion that comics aspires to be films, a comment that occasionally appears in reviews (though this tendency is on the wane). However, some film terminology has been adopted into comics studies, especially when discussing angle and perspective, and is therefore unavoidable.

It is my personal preference to abstain from referring to comics as "graphic novels." This term is most often used to pertain to longer narratives that are contained within one book (the most typical use of the term) or a serialized narrative that is collected into one bound volume (although these may also be referred to as trade paperbacks or TPBs). Art Spiegelman claims that graphic novels are "long comic books that require a bookmark" (Spiegelman, 2011). My quibble with this term is related to both its history and the status that the term has achieved when discussing comics. The history of the term is disputed; it is typically attributed to Will Eisner and his 1978 book *A Contract with God*. This book was almost singlehandedly responsible for the adoption of the term. However, the willingness to credit Eisner with this is likely because of his popularity and seniority within the comics world.[12] In 1976, two years before Eisner's book, three different texts used the term: Richard Corben's *Bloodstar*, George Metzger's *Beyond Time and Again* (previously serialized in an underground comics magazine), and Jim Steranko's *Chandler: Red Tide*, the first self-proclaimed graphic novel to be sold on newsstands. Indeed, from 1976 onwards, the term appeared on comics works of all genres and of varying lengths. There are many issues with the term. On the most basic level, the two words themselves are problematic. "Graphic" can suggest "violent and/or sexually explicit" as much as "image-laden"; "novels" are automatically assumed to be fictional, but a huge number of comics (especially those that are considered canonical) are auto- or semi-autobiographical, reportage, or nonfiction (for this reason, Hillary Chute advocates for the term "graphic narrative"). Furthermore, it is often considered (especially by reviewers) as a compliment but "using it as praise implies that comics as a form aspire to being novels or movies" (Wolk, 2007: 13). Douglas Wolk quotes the example of a reviewer for *The Nation* who, after stating "it has never been a habit of mine to read comics books," notes that she was surprised she enjoyed Marjane Satrapi's *Persepolis* (2000)—and was further surprised to find it to be a beautifully crafted work. As such, this reviewer thought it wrong to call *Persepolis* a "comic book," a term so loaded with snobbish stigma.

Wolk and many other comics creators and theorists are critical of the term "graphic novel." Daniel Raeburn, founder and writer of *The Imp* writes, "I snicker at the neologism first for its insecure pretension—the literary equivalent of calling a garbage man a 'sanitation engineer'—and second because a 'graphic novel' is in fact the very thing it is ashamed to admit: a comic book" (2004: 110). Neil Gaiman makes a similar comment when he claimed that, on being told he wrote graphic novels instead of comics, he "felt like someone who'd been informed that she wasn't actually a hooker; that in fact she was a lady of the evening" (Gaiman, in Bender, 1999: 32). Indeed, the term has faced criticism and ridicule from all manner of voices within the comics world. As a response to this, many comics creators use their own terms to describe their works. Daniel Clowes refers to his 2001 work *Ice Haven* as a "comic strip novel," whereas Craig Thompson prefers "illustrated novel" for his 2003 autobiography *Blankets*.

Several other terms do exist—*bandes-dessinées* for Franco-Belgian comics, *fumetti* for Italian comics, and also photo-comics—but these typically refer to the aforementioned specific subsets within the umbrella of comics.[13] To my mind, the term "graphic novel" serves to give legitimacy to a form that has been unfairly tarnished by its past as a mass-produced medium, or more precisely by high cultural prejudices about the age of mass production. Comics has earned its stripes as a legitimate narrative form. As such, there is no reason why a long comic that deals with "serious" issues and memoir should have any special term, hence my preference for the original term "comic."

• • •

This book finds its theoretical grounding in the two diverse fields of comics and trauma theory. Contemporary trauma theory comprises a complex body of work, drawing on both clinical definitions and cultural understandings of the impact of trauma on both the individual and the wider society, as I explain in Chapter 1, which is divided into two parts. The first part outlines the theoretical framework on which this work hangs: contemporary and Freudian trauma theory. Despite the turn away from a Freudian (or "classic") trauma model, I use Freudian and post-Freudian theory for two reasons: Sigmund Freud's work is still central to contemporary debates surrounding trauma and his massive corpus provides ample material for discussion; a great deal of literary trauma theorists work from a Freudian basis, too, as does psychiatrist Judith Herman. Furthermore, many of Freud's theories are excellent tools for the analysis of comics in particular, as his work often stresses ways of experiencing that emphasize visual and other nonverbal sensations. By using a framework that is rooted in Freud's works, while also opening a dialogue across the field of trauma theory, I hope to provide a theoretical groundwork that gives appropriate space to the wide range of trauma theorists, acknowledges the discursive nature of the field, and also works as an analytical tool in relation to the comics form. In dialogue with Freud, I consider the works of theorists including Jacques Lacan, Dominick LaCapra, Kalí Tal, and Michelle Balaev. To engage with a "pluralistic model of trauma suggests that criticism may explore trauma as a subject that invites the study of the relationship between language, the psyche, and behavior without assuming the classic definition of trauma that asserts an unrepresentable and pathological universalism" (Balaev, 2014: 4).

The second part of Chapter 1 is a detailed analysis of three formal aspects that are of utmost importance in the creation of comics in general and trauma comics in particular. I take each separate aspect and consider it as a typical comics technique and then, in the light of traumatic representation, give a preliminary outline as to how these aspects are used within the comics discussed here. This introductory analysis of the three most visible aspects of the form eliminates the need to repeat myself when considering each aspect. Furthermore, it allows the reader to become aware of and comfortable with some of the more basic comics terminology and analytical techniques.

I begin Chapter 2 with a survey of three key conflict texts: *The Iliad*, *Beowulf*, and *Le Morte d'Arthur*. These important works of Western literature have a single thematic thread in common—that conflict texts are all, to some extent, mourning texts. I do not wish to provide new avenues for analysis in these texts. All of the comics I discuss here are concerned with these themes, although some only to a small degree and others in a tangential manner. These three texts carry a weight of scholarship that is beyond the scope of this study. While I acknowledge some scholars of these texts, my primary aim is to tap into the single thematic thread of mourning in order to give credence to my argument that texts of conflict are oftentimes texts of mourning and traumatic grief, rather than of violence and traumatic experience. The most obvious text discussed in this chapter is Alissa Torres's *American Widow* (2008), which is first and foremost a depiction of the writer's work of mourning.[14] I use Elisabeth Kübler-Ross's famous framework of the "Five Stages of Grief," along with Freud's work on mourning, for my analysis of this text. In a similar vein, there is much to be discussed on mourning and especially shrine-building in the anthologies of short comics published to raise money for September 11th Relief Charities.[15] I compare one of the short 9/11 comics, which uses the framework of the Jewish Yom Kippur celebration with Art Spiegelman's short "Prisoner from the Hell Planet" (1973, reproduced in *Maus*), which takes its cue from his mother's death and funeral. Both comics use religious death rituals to discuss their traumatic experiences, and I compare the depictions, with special emphasis on the use of religion as a comfort.

Chapter 3 tackles the issue of the representations of traumatic dream sequences in five different comics. To strengthen my analysis, I begin this chapter by outlining clinical studies on traumatic dreaming, the Freudian dreamwork and explorations of Freud's work by post-Freudian scholars Lacan and Caruth. The dream sequences I discuss here are divided into two groups—dreams of traumatic experience and dreams of traumatic loss. The first section includes *The 'Nam* and *Maus*. Ed Marks's combat dream is the clearest rendering of a traumatic dream in any comic I talk about. *Maus* is relevant in two ways here. The first is Vladek's dream of his grandfather and the second is not a dream in itself, but a discussion between Art and Françoise regarding Vladek's sleep disturbances. The second section also contains three sequences of interest. Both *American Widow* and "Untitled" depict similar dreams of traumatic loss, both presented as a search for the deceased lover. The last dream is that of a young boy, dreaming of his deceased mother, a distinctly different dream than any other in this chapter. I discuss the dreams within each section individually and then compare them to each other, before then comparing the two separate groups. Although both types of traumatic dreams have similarities, their content and manifestations in comics are markedly different. This chapter considers the reasons for these dreams' use within the wider narrative of each comic and the specific artistic techniques employed in their representation.

Three of the texts in this book (*Maus* [2003], *Vietnamerica* [2011], and the *You'll Never Know* trilogy [2009–2012]) are explicit retellings of family stories, in which the parents of the author were directly involved (and often imprisoned) in major conflicts. A major theme in each of these texts is the author/child working through and coming to terms with the events that their parents survived—events which have unquestionably had an effect on the way the children were raised and their adult selves. The fourth chapter seeks to answer the question of how the trauma of the parents influences the personal identity of their children. I draw on Freud's last book, *Moses and Monotheism* (1939), as well as Abraham and Torok's *The Shell and the Kernel* (1994), and Gabriele Schwab's 2010 book, *Haunting Legacies: Violent Histories and Transgenerational Trauma*. I consider the wider social and cultural implications of these identity crises. In the case of both Spiegelman and Tran, their status as first-generation immigrants is in conflict with the national identity of their parents. In Spiegelman's case, his personal religious identity is at odds with that of his parents; this is compounded when placed in dialogue with the religious identity that sits at the root of his parents' trauma. Finally, I turn to the work of Joe Sacco, a comics journalist whose work is intensely concerned with the question of journalistic distance and how one is meant to maintain objectivity in an artistic form that actively requires personal engagement.

Chapters 5 and 6 move away from questions of content and theme within conflict comics and consider questions of form and genre. In Chapter 5, I open a dialogue between the Bakhtinian concept of the chronotope and the creative process of comics. Despite overlaps between the two, trauma comics break with the conventions of the chronotope, as traumatic representation is wont to do. Much of this chapter deals with challenges to narrative linearity, looking at the use of fractured and framed narratives. *The 'Nam* (1986–1993) uses complex temporal structures and framing devices that are not typical in mainstream publications, helping to mimic the chronological ruptures that a traumatized individual may experience. Similarly, Joe Sacco's *Palestine* (2001) and *Footnotes in Gaza* (2009) work with the materiality of the comics page to create temporal palimpsests that represent the cyclical nature of conflict and memory for the people of a place where conflict is seemingly endless. Lastly, I examine problems of temporal representation created when superheroes become involved, as shown in the 9/11 charity comics, using Umberto Eco's essay "The Myth of Superman" (1997). Eco's critique can also be used in relation to *The 'Nam*, which does involve the characters interacting with actual historical events, though in a different way and to different ends than with superhero involvement.

Chapter 6 attempts to answer the questions of whether both comics and trauma can be seen as postmodernist and, by extension, whether trauma comics are a distinctly postmodern enterprise. In order to answer this, I begin by considering the relationship between modernism and postmodernism. The linking factor between comics, trauma, and postmodernism is time. This chapter is a prolonged discussion of the relationship between temporal ruptures, comics ruptures, and postmodernism's preoccupation with brokenness. I conclude with a discussion of three Holocaust comics and how they sit in relation to the overarching issues created by looking at comics and trauma through a postmodernist lens.

The final section of the study I have chosen to refer to by the grand term "excursus," a term notably used by Jürgen Habermas in his "Philosophical Discourse of Modernity." In this section, I move away from my thread of discussion on representations of trauma and instead turn to an issue that, while by no means a purely contemporary concern, is finally gaining momentum within the comics field: the representation of female characters and the prevalence of women in the industry. The texts I discuss are, for the most part, written by and about men. Where are there female creators? Although I do talk about texts created by women, I will show that these texts are bound up in what may be called "female narratives." And when female characters do appear, they are usually presented, not as agents, but reagents to the male characters. The excursus presents the issue of women and offers a brief explanation and a small sampling of how women are presented in war and trauma comics.

• • •

Each chapter concentrates on a separate issue. As such, each can be read as an individual case study within the fields of trauma and comics. However, collectively this book is a study of the formal and thematic aspects of comics that assist in the artistic representation and recreation of conflict trauma. This is the thread that runs through this book *in toto*—that comics can represent trauma in ways that are unavailable to other narrative and artistic forms.

1

Representing the Traumatic

In *Henry IV, Part I*, William Shakespeare presents an accurate description of the effects of war-induced trauma on an individual. Lady Percy, wife of Henry Percy, questions her husband as to his behavior following frequent military campaigns (Act II, scene iii). She speaks of him refusing his wife's company (line 39–40), losing his appetite (42) and turning very pale (45). She goes on to describe him talking in his sleep and having nightmares (50–56), crying, "Courage! To the field!" (51), and sweating profusely (60). Percy is an able soldier (nicknamed "Hotspur") and so it seems unusual to her that such a man would be given to nightmares and distant behavior; indeed, the notion of the brave soldier as immune to trauma and the traumatized soldier as weak and cowardly was common well into the twentieth century. He does not give in to his wife's questions (though she threatens to break his finger) and so the trauma remains secret and untreated. Lady Percy's appraisal of her husband's condition can be seen as an early record of the symptoms of a traumatic rupture arising from violent military conflict.

Shakespeare artfully presents a character traumatized by the rigors of war but in the 400 years since his death, trauma has become a byword for any distressing or negative experiences in the modern world. This lumping together of emotions and reactions devalues the impact a traumatic experience can truly have on an individual; it also groups all manner of other emotions under one umbrella that may not accurately describe the emotional experience. In this chapter, I navigate the discursive field of trauma studies, considering two models of trauma theory. The first is the "classic" model of trauma that finds its core in the works of Sigmund Freud and many of his ideological descendants, most notably Cathy Caruth and Jacques Lacan. Although this model no longer constitutes the main thrust of trauma theory, it cannot be doubted that the theorists whose work forms its body are key figures in the development of trauma theory *in toto*. The second model, which Michelle Balaev calls the "pluralistic model," "challenges the traditional concept of trauma as unspeakable by starting from a standpoint that concedes trauma's variability in literature and society" (2014: 4). This model "highlights the ranging values and representations of trauma in literature and society . . . Rather than claiming that language fails to represent trauma, pluralistic approaches consider linguistic relationships but not at the expense of forgetting that trauma occurs to actual people, in specific bodies, located within particular time periods and places" (Balaev, 2014: 7).

The aim of this chapter is to lay out a trauma theory framework that will open a dialogue between the classic and pluralistic models. These two models do not necessarily sit comfortably together—indeed, many of the key facets of the latter flatly contradict the former. That said, there are still parts of the Freudian model that can be used as effective analytical tools for comics and there are many persuasive arguments in the pluralistic model for moving beyond the classic Freudian definition of trauma as "unrepresentable." It is my contention that there are two key shifts from the classic to pluralistic model in terms of representation of traumatic experience. The first is the shift from seeing trauma as an "unclaimed experience" that fragments psychic functioning and demands reintegration to a consideration of trauma's "deeply contested ownership" and an understanding of "healthy" mental operations that do not necessarily demand psychic unity; the second moves from a focus on symptomology and a mimicry of medical presentation to a more nuanced focus on affect and personal emotional engagement. Before focusing on these key shifts, I wish to lay out the basic framework of the classic model.

• • •

In her 1992 book *Trauma and Recovery,* Judith Herman writes that "the ordinary response to atrocities is to banish them from consciousness . . . Atrocities, however, refuse to be buried" (1992: 1). Herman's comment stands as a fitting summary of a century of psychological scholarship concerned with the "unknowability" of the traumatic. It is from this central issue—the persistence of atrocity within consciousness—that trauma theory takes its lead. As is commonly observed, the word "trauma" finds its root in the Greek word "τραῦμα" ("wound"). The term was initially a physical one (as one still finds it in much medical literature) but it has become widely adopted in psychological and emotional discourse. The following quotation from Cathy Caruth has become something of a benchmark definition for the classic model of trauma:

> The wound of the mind . . . is not, like the wound of the body, a simple and healable event, but rather an event that . . . is experienced too soon, too unexpectedly to be fully known and is therefore not available to consciousness until it imposes

itself again, repeatedly, in the nightmares and repetitive actions of the survivor. (1996: 19)

Caruth's definition raises many points that are central to discussions of trauma. We are aware of the wound-like nature of psychic trauma; Caruth makes the point that this wound is not "healable," positing that it is not possible fully to be healed of a psychic trauma, though the condition can be ameliorated to some degree. She also writes that trauma is "experienced too soon." This statement is curious in itself but speaks to the shattering of normal temporality that is common in traumatic experience. The event is not experienced as it happens. Rather, the mind works to protect itself and it is only after the event that the individual begins to witness it; hence, "it is not available to consciousness" and the individual may only begin to experience the event retroactively "in nightmares and repetitive actions."

Freud writes at length of the repetition compulsion found in individuals with psychic trauma.[1] The individual is compelled to return to the traumatic event over and over in nightmares and flashbacks, with no control over the recurrence of these phenomena. These "traumatic returns" are not complete; the individual will not experience the whole event nor will any coherent narrative be presented. Flashbacks may be a series of images or feelings with very little context; nightmares will be experienced in a similar fashion. Speaking as a psychiatrist, Herman corroborates much of what Freud says, writing that the symptoms of this traumatic rupture include repetition of the event, flashbacks, nightmares, hypersensitivity, hyperarousal, unprovoked violent outbursts, evasion of certain situations or sensations, irrational anger, emotional and psychological numbing, and a disrupted sense of personal time (Herman, 1992: 35). Coming from a similar medical background, L. S. Brown writes that traumatic events exist "outside the range of human experience" (1995: 35); victims do not have the mental capacity and built-in strategies to process and "cope with" these events—to assimilate them into our understanding of a normal human experience—thus permanently keeping the traumatic experience apart from consciousness.

In her detailed study of Freudian trauma theory, Caruth uses the term "survivor" rather than "victim." The concept of survival creates complex issues for discussions of trauma. The traumatic event has placed the survivor in a situation of serious risk to their life which, possibly by chance, they have overcome. They are then left with the shadow of this "near-death experience" awakening the "peculiar and perplexing experience of surviving" (Caruth, 1996: 61). Survival becomes a part of the trauma because one is left with the knowledge of impending mortality and an intensified apprehension of the fragility of existence. The survivor "[oscillates] between . . . the story of the unbearable nature of an event and the story of the unbearable nature of its survival" (Caruth, 1996: 7). Robert Jay Lifton claims that "any focus on survival puts the death back into the traumatic experience, because survival suggests that there has been death and the survivor therefore has had a death encounter, which is central to their psychological experience" (1995: 128). This phenomenon goes some way in explaining the large numbers of soldiers who commit suicide after returning home.[2] The failure to reintegrate into "normal" life suggests that the basic survival instinct of the individual is irreparably damaged. The heightened "fight or flight" response that is noted in many traumatized individuals would attest to this.

For scholars of the classic model, a traumatic event is one for which the mind has no integrating coping mechanism and thus remains apart from the survivor's psychic functioning, recreating itself within the mind but independently of consciousness. The symptoms of this traumatic rupture relate directly to the individual's inability to understand and find ways mentally to process their experience: "Trauma . . . overwhelms the individual and resists language or representation" (Whitehead, 2004: 3). Here is one of the biggest stumbling blocks in the classic model: the suggestion that trauma resists language. The classic model suggests that this is an axiomatic part of trauma and a part that affects all traumatized individuals equally, a fact that is quite simply not true. While many individuals may face similar experiences of an inability to express their trauma, the degree to which this occurs is unique to the individual. In her 2000 book *Trauma: A Genealogy*, Ruth Leys suggests that trauma theory threatens the ideal of individual autonomy and responsibility (2000: 9). That the subject is considered to be involuntarily mimicking a past traumatic experience suggests a destabilization of the subject's sovereignty. It is pertinent here to note, as Claire Stocks does, that the original testing grounds of trauma have significantly marked all theories that grew from it. Stocks makes the point that one of the central issues regarding the classic model is that it originally derives from work with combat veterans from the late 1970s onwards; this narrow clinical focus can "[obscure] specificity." She adds that "the historical reality is that the war veteran is predominantly male" and so basing all trauma theory on the historically and culturally specific experience of one group of society does not assist in creating a universally applicable approach. A method that is "translatable across traumas tends to erase rather than enforce any specificity" (Stocks, 2007: 75–76).

In fact, in addition to eradicating all traces of difference and personal variance in traumatic experiences, the suggestion that *all* trauma resists interpretation and representation removes the trauma from the individual. As Balaev writes, "One result of trauma's classic conundrum accordingly removes agency from the survivor by disregarding a survivor's knowledge of the experience and the self, which restricts trauma's variability and ignores the diverse values that change over time" (2014: 6). This is not to say that there is not an inherent crisis of representation at the core of trauma, but it does suggest that this crisis is not entirely insurmountable, as the classic trauma model seems to insist. More accurately, the crisis of representation may be said to ask how individuals represent to others an event that affected them in deeply personal and complex ways, a suggestion that is subtly different than the belief that the crisis is of all representation.

The classic model places great emphasis on the "event" as the seat of traumatic memory. For Freud (and also Caruth), it is a prelinguistic event that facilitates dissociation and refuses to be assimilated into typical psychic functioning. According to Laplanche, the event is secondary to the meanings conferred on it "afterwards"; it is these meanings and post-event psychic developments that make a particular memory traumatic (1988: 467–68). In removing the focus from the event itself, Laplanche's theory removes the traumatic experience from the realm of "unclaimed experience" and returns it to the sovereign individual, a key aim of the pluralistic model.

Freud and his Ideological Children

In his 1920 book *Beyond the Pleasure Principle*, Freud describes and interprets a game played by his grandson at the age of eighteen months. Ernst was a "good little boy," manifested no particular symptoms, was of calm disposition, and "never cried when his mother left him for a few hours" (Freud: 2001, 14). However,

> he had an occasional disturbing habit of taking any small objects he could get hold of and throwing them away from him into a corner, under the bed . . . As he did this he gave vent to a loud, long-drawn-out "o-o-o," accompanied by an expression of interest and satisfaction. His mother and [Freud] were agreed in thinking that this was not a mere interjection but represented the German word "*fort*." (Freud, 2001: 14)

Freud interpreted this behavior as a way of obtaining satisfaction by causing things to be "gone." A short time later, he observed the child playing with a reel that had a piece of string tied around it: He would toss the reel away from him to where it could no longer be seen, before pulling it back into view and hailing its reappearance with a gleeful "*Da!*" ("There!"). Freud also noticed that the boy would utter his "o-o-o" sound with reference to himself—notably when, by crouching down below a mirror, he made his image "gone." Freud stresses the fact that the *fort* part of the game was much of the time sufficient unto itself, and was "repeated untiringly" by the child.

These observations led to a number of fundamental questions. Is this a method of mastering a painful experience by reproducing it in an active and playful manner? Or is the child literally taking revenge for the treatment visited upon him (according to Freud, the departure of his mother) by redirecting it onto an object (the reel)? These questions aside, the main issue is the contradiction between the compulsion to repeat and the pleasure principle, the basic human drive to attain pleasure and avoid suffering. How is satisfaction to be derived from repeating actions that have been sources of unpleasant feelings? A child cannot understand death or disappearance but can form an idea of these concepts through a visual relationship to objects, so the child transforms the traumatic departure into a satisfying return, mastering the traumatic experience and regaining pleasure: "*fort*" becomes "*da.*"

Freud postulated that, in a healthy and untraumatized mind, the repetition of loss and return is a positive experience, allowing the development of methods for processing unpleasant and potentially traumatizing events. In a traumatized mind, the repetition compulsion behaves very differently. Unlike Ernst, who is delighted to see his wooden spool return to him, the constant return of the traumatic experience in "the nightmares and repetitive actions of the survivor" neither delights nor comforts (Caruth, 1996: 4). Freud is clear to state that this repetition is truly compulsive, writing that "no lesson has been learnt from the old experience of these activities . . . they are repeated, under pressure of a compulsion" (2003: 290). This "driven, tenacious intrusion of traumatic experience" is one of the most visceral and explosive symptoms of trauma-and so often paired with the nightmares and flashbacks that become its medium (Herman, 1992: 41). For Freud, this repetition sits at the heart of the experience he calls "traumatic neurosis" (2003: 16). Furthermore, as "traumatic memories lack verbal narrative and context . . . they are encoded in the form of vivid sensations and images" (Brett and Ostroff, 1985: 417). This is a particularly compelling theory for this study as these images translate into the world of comics; indeed, it is because of the intensely visual nature of the comics form that it can be used to such good effect in representations of conflict trauma. I give detailed explanations of how Freud's theories—in conjunction with theories of affect—can be used to analyze comics in the latter part of this chapter.

According to a Caruthian reading, central to Freud's theories of traumatic neurosis is the innate unknowability of the experience. In part, this stems from the underlying concept of the "Pleasure Principle";—namely, that "the course taken by mental events is automatically regulated by the pleasure principle" but that this is "the most obscure and inaccessible region of the mind" (2003: 7). If the psychological concept that underpins the entire basis of Freud's work on trauma is largely inaccessible, then all works arising from this principle must be similarly compromised. This leads us to a key issue in the creation of trauma texts. If the trauma that is central to the text is "unknowable," then how can the artist recreate it in a way that will be intelligible to the reader?

For Freud, the symptomatic picture of a traumatic neurosis can be reduced to two key factors. First, he discusses "fright, the factor of surprise" and makes it clear that this is to be kept separate from fear and anxiety:

> "Fright" ... is the name we give to the states a person gets into when he has run into danger without being prepared for it. I do not believe that anxiety can produce a traumatic neurosis. There is something about anxiety that protects its subject against frights and so against fright-neuroses. (Freud, 2003: 7)

The unexpectedness of the traumatic event, then, is key to the creation of the traumatic neurosis. It is the fact that the individual is struck as if out of nowhere by the trauma that creates the initial traumatic rupture. Secondly, Freud suggests that the presence of a physical wound "works as a rule *against* the development of a neurosis" (2003: 8). In *Moses and Monotheism*, he writes:

> It may happen that a man who has experienced some frightful accident—a railway collision, for instance—leaves the scene of the event apparently uninjured. In the course of the next few weeks, however, he develops a number of severe psychical and motor symptoms which can only be traced to his shock. He now has a "traumatic neurosis." It is a quite unintelligible—that is to say, a new—fact. (2001: 309)

It is the apparent survival—and the accompanying incomprehensibility of that survival—that breeds the traumatic neurosis. Furthermore, it is this unquenchable need for psychic healing that leads to the symptoms of traumatic rupture that are noted by Herman and Caruth. Many years previous to this, in *Studies in Hysteria* (1896), Freud had written of *Nachträglichkeit*, "deferred action":

> There is in principle no difference between the symptom's appearing in a temporary way after its first provoking cause and its being latent from the first. Indeed in the great majority of instances we find that a first trauma has left no symptom behind, while a later trauma of the same kind produces a symptom, and yet the latter could not have come into existence without the co-operation of the earlier provoking cause; nor can it be cleared up without taking all the provoking causes into account. (2000: 30)

According to Freud, it could be that a person is seemingly unaffected by, for example, a mugging but the traumatic response becomes apparent after the person experiences some other relatively insignificant event, such as colliding with someone in the street. This deferred action is something that is commonly reported by combat veterans. It is similar to the more common response of psycho-physical numbing that many individuals experience after a particularly distressing event. However, rather than seeming to be emotionally "dulled" and devoid of desire or sensation, those whose response is delayed will not appear to be affected at all and will carry on as usual.

Jacques Lacan takes his primary lead from Freud's work on trauma in relation to the pleasure principle:

> In effect, the trauma is conceived as having necessarily been marked by the subjectifying homeostasis that orientates the whole functioning defined by the pleasure principle. Our experience then presents us with a problem, which derives from the fact that, at the very heart of the primary processes, we see preserved the insistence of the trauma in making us aware of its existence. The trauma reappears, in effect, frequently unveiled . . . emerging repeatedly—if not its face, at least the screen that shows us that is it still there behind? (1977: 55)

There are some marked distinctions between notions of trauma for Freud and for Lacan. For Freud, a trauma is retroactively induced when excess psychic excitations penetrate the ego defenses without warning and in a potentially life-threatening situation. For Lacan, a trauma occurs when there is an encounter with the "real," that which denies signification. He writes:

> There is an anxiety-provoking apparition of an image which summarises what we can call the revelation of that which is least penetrable in the real, of the real lacking any possible mediation, of the ultimate real, of the essential object which is not an object any longer, but this something faced with which all words cease and all categories fail, the object of anxiety *par excellence*. (1988: 164)

These encounters with the Real are traumatic experiences where the "link between two thoughts have succumbed to repression and must be restored" (Lacan, 1988: 170).

While Lacan makes reference to the encounter with the Real as traumatic, he further suggests that this encounter is a secondary experience and that the actual trauma occurs belatedly and through repetition. This repetition of the event can "activate symbolic meaning where the scene was traumatized, elevated into a traumatic real, only retroactively, in order to help [the individual] to cope with the impasse of his symbolic universe" (Žižek, 2006: 73–74). In Lacan's theory, trauma is at the origin of the subject. It is something that marks the subject irreparably, but also something that the subject doesn't experience. As such, the experiences are not mastered by the subject; instead, they produce the subject. In this regard, one's whole life can be considered as repetition compulsion. Here there is tension: trauma is the universal element of psychoanalytical theory of the subject. However, specific traumata that threaten normal functioning of the psyche, and which result in more drastic symptoms, often outshine their less dramatic counterparts and become the focus of psychoanalytical attention. This awkwardness of hierarchy is seen repeatedly within theories of trauma. Like Freud, Lacan discusses trauma in relation to *Hamlet*, showing the suitability of psychoanalytical theories of trauma for literary analysis. I return to Lacan and his discussion of trauma in relation to the dream state and Freud's "dream of the burning boy" in Chapter 3.

· · ·

This is the classic model in brief: trauma is an event that exists outside of typical psychic processes and thus cannot be fully known, but returns in repeated, compulsive images and sensations. At a basic level this is not inaccurate. The pluralistic model does not dispute that "trauma causes a disruption and reorientation of consciousness, but the values attached to this experience are influenced by a variety of individual and cultural factors that change over time" (Balaev, 2014: 4). Given that the pluralistic model emphasizes that traumatic experience is, at the core, a personal experience unique to the individual, there is much debate around Caruth's famous contention that trauma is "unclaimed." Bennett reminds us that this position on the part of Caruth is tantamount to "usurping the position of trauma victim—of appropriating testimony and treating trauma as an available or 'unclaimed' experience when, in fact, its ownership is deeply contested" (2005: 6). It is precisely the desire to see trauma both as a universal experience and one that is inherently unowned that forms the largest stumbling blocks of the classic method for contemporary trauma theorists. The experience of (and recovery from) a traumatic experience is highly culturally charged and regulated by socially and historically determined sets of signs and psychological markers that assist the individual in their narrativization of the experience. When one brings narrative into the equation, a whole new set of questions arise. How much of oneself should the individual expose in order for the traumatic experience—itself intensely bound up in personal circumstance and history—to be comprehended by the reader (or viewer)? Do representations of trauma attempt to lay claim to the lived experiences of others?

A further issue that arises in any examination of trauma theory is the question of the medicalization of trauma. Traumatic experience entered the clinical sphere via the *DSM* (*Diagnostic and Statistical Manual of Mental Disorders*) in 1980 under the name "Post-Traumatic Stress Disorder." In his review of DSM's fifth edition, Ian Hacking questions the efficacy of such a guide, which is based on rules of Linnaean taxonomy; he writes: "Perhaps in the end the DSM will be regarded as a *reductio ad absurdum* of the botanical project in the field of insanity" (2013: 7–8). Taking a similar view, Christine Ross argues that "diagnostic criteria decontextualize the illness and its symptoms, separating them from the subject's life history and his or her social and cultural background" (Ross in Price, 2013: 147). The classic model is rooted in clinical application and, as such, faces similar issues of decontextualization and universalization of personal experience.

Moving Away from Freud

In the previous section, I laid out the groundwork for trauma theory in the briefest terms, using the works of Freud, Caruth, and Lacan. As I have indicated, it is no longer enough to use these works alone in any well-rounded discussion of trauma theory. To understand trauma in a more holistic sense makes it necessary to move beyond the Freudian model of universal unknowability and unrepresentability. I should reiterate here than neither I nor any of the contemporary trauma theorists herein discussed wish to suggest that trauma is *not* a life-changing experience that disrupts "normal" functioning in a very real sense. Nor do I wish to suggest that the representation of traumatic experience is a simple endeavor; it is more accurate to consider it a monumental endeavor that can be both intensely cathartic and also incredibly difficult. What I do wish to claim is that traumatic experience is not universal nor is it a simple matter of rupture and healing. Stocks calls on the work of Malcolm Bull, who "suggests that the complexities of the modern world create a self which is not only fragmented, but that is only really fully acknowledged when its multiplicity is recognised" (2007: 72–73). She adds that "the shared emphasis on the reintegration of a consciousness fragmented by an unassimilable event assumes the pre-existence of a state of perceived psychic unity that 'healing' aims to restore" (2007: 74). I wish to progress from this point: the understanding that the human brain is not, as a matter of fact, a unified psychic entity, and therefore a return to such a state is not possible. Furthermore, trauma *does* create fissures and fragmentations within an individual's psychic functioning, as Freud et al. suggest, but simple healing (as of a physical wound) is not the solution because it is not possible. Rather, as Caroline Garland writes:

> Whatever the nature of the event . . . eventually [the traumatized individual] comes to make sense of it in terms of the most troubled and troubling of the relationships between the objects that are felt to inhabit his internal world. That way the survivor is at least making something recognisable and familiar out of the extraordinary, giving it meaning. (1998: 12)

Both Dominick LaCapra and Kalí Tal wish to maintain the focus of traumatic representation on the experience of the individual. In his landmark text on the subject, *Writing History, Writing Trauma* (2001), LaCapra writes that "the notion of trauma [should not] be rashly generalized or the difference between trauma victim and historian or secondary witness—or, for that matter, between traumatization and victimhood—be elided" (2001: 97). For LaCapra, trauma is a singular experience that belongs primarily to the individual. His main focus is on how traumatic experiences—he refers to these as "limit experiences"—relate to historical writing. Unlike Lacan and Caruth, whose work is based on a Freudian framework and influenced by semiotic theory, LaCapra integrates concepts from psychoanalysis, literary and critical theory, and philosophy, as well as ideas of historiography, in order to explain two historical methodologies: "documentary or a self-sufficient research model" and "radical constructivism" (2001: 1). In the former, "priority is often given to research based on primary (preferably archival) documents that enable one to derive authenticated facts about the past which may be recounted in a narrative (the more 'artistic' approach) or employed in a mode of analysis which puts forth testable hypotheses (the more 'social-scientific' approach)" (3002: 2). This method aims to describe what happened and how, with an emphasis on facts, dates, and places.[3] Radical constructivism, on the other hand, argues that history is one mode of writing among many, holding no superior position above other writing forms; it is inaccurate to believe that historical writings are in any way more objective or "real" than a literary or philosophical text. LaCapra calls for a "middle voice," which acknowledges the strengths and weaknesses of both methodologies and creates a dialogue between the two, allowing for objective facts, but also giving credence to "the performative, figurative, aesthetic, rhetorical, political, and ideological factors that 'construct' structures" (2001: 1).

In what has become his most famous and compelling argument, LaCapra explores two distinct concepts: "acting out" and "working through." In "acting out," "tenses implode and it is as if one were back there in the past, reliving the traumatic scene. Any duality (or double inscription) of time (past and present or future) is experientially collapsed or productive only of aporia and double binds" (2001: 21). This is a compulsive behavior—similar to Freud's "repetition compulsion"—which negates the individual's capacity for recovery. In contrast, LaCapra uses the term "working through" to describe "an articulatory process ... one is able to distinguish between past and present and to recall in memory that something happened to one (or one's people) back then while realizing that one is living here and now with openings to the future" (2001: 22). He is careful to suggest that "those traumatised by extreme events, as well as those empathizing with them, may resist working through because of what might almost be termed a fidelity to trauma, a feeling that one must somehow keep faith with it" (2001: 22). In the crudest terms, this "fidelity" is related to survivor guilt. Here is a problem similar to that of the more explicitly Freudian model—the issue of universalism. The suggestion is that the traumatic experience will return to the individual in a manner similar to Freud's repetition compulsion and, furthermore, to be restored to full mental health, one must engage with the process of "working through" in order to recall and reunify memory.

Although LaCapra is not explicitly Freudian, he does use a Freudian term—"transferential implication"—to refer to historians' need to recognize that history is not separate from us. By writing history, we implicate ourselves in it, a fact that positivism and the "self-sufficient research model" fail to realize. This ignorance, coupled with the lack of empathy for victims and awareness of the wide range of narrative forms, accounts for the failure of these methodologies individually. It is only in finding a middle ground between them that LaCapra claims these two methodologies can be utilized in discussions of trauma and historiography. In this sense, LaCapra and I are on similar paths—to find a way of creating dialogue between two methodologies, albeit different ones and to different ends.

In a move that was, for its time, decidedly groundbreaking, Kalí Tal's 1996 book *Worlds of Hurt: Reading the Literature of Trauma* moves away from theoretical considerations and instead places emphasis on personal experiences of traumatic events. She describes three strategies of "cultural coping":

> Mythologisation works by reducing a traumatic event to a set of standardised narratives ... turning it from a frightening and uncontrollable event into a contained and predictable narrative. Medicalisation focuses our gaze upon the victims of trauma, positing that they suffer from an "illness" that can be "cured" within existing or slightly modified structures of institutionalised medicine and psychiatry. Disappearance—a refusal to admit to the existence of a particular kind of trauma—is usually accomplished by undermining the credibility of the victim. (Tal, 1996: 6)

Tal uses examples of Holocaust, Vietnam War, and incest-victim narratives throughout her analysis, critiquing any attempt to conflate the literature of conflict and all other genre classifications. Instead, she calls for interrogative cultural, sociological, and historical approaches to trauma literature that avoid the postmodernist tendency to dismiss personal testimony and accept that "the specific effects of trauma on the process of narration" must be acknowledged (1996: 117).

What makes Tal's book unusual is the attention paid by the final chapter to the narratives of rape and incest survivors. Such narratives had, at the time of Tal's writing, received little consideration from the academic world. She argues that traditional conceptions of literature are extraneous when attempting to understand and analyze these narratives:

> Literature of trauma is written from the need to tell and retell the story of the traumatic experience, to make it real both to the victim and to the community. Such writing serves both as validation and cathartic vehicle for the traumatized writer. (Tal, 1996: 137)

While clearly wishing to argue that victims of what I shall euphemistically dub "personal trauma" deserve to be given a voice within trauma studies on an equal footing to all other victims, Tal does not probe the "obscuring of specificity" that I mentioned earlier; she is careful to use gender-neutral pronouns throughout the text but does not question whether or not the traumatic experience at the center of trauma studies is, in fact, fitting to her argument. I reiterate my earlier point that it is neither accurate nor fair to suggest that trauma is a universal experience, especially given that the benchmark is that of white male experience.

Tal's work is skeptical of the importance of theoretical understandings of trauma. She is quick to argue that theory can cloud that which is important when considering representations of trauma. Her insistence on the importance of the individual is compelling; an overemphasis on theory tends to ignore the massive personal impact of the traumatic. I wish to find a balance, using both the heavily theoretical and psychoanalytical works of the classic trauma model and the more victim/survivor-focused pluralistic model that favors a sociocultural, non-universal view to create a framework for analyzing representations of traumatic experience in the comics form. In order to do this, I turn to the concept of affect.

From Symptomologies to Affect

If trauma theory had not moved beyond the classic method, it would be very easy to use the list of symptoms and ways that trauma typically presents in an individual as an analytical framework for any artistic representation. Indeed, to an extent, it is not an ineffective method. However, when placing the classic method in dialogue with the pluralistic method, this technique loses much of its efficacy. Considering traumatic representation in relation to affect provides a method for analysis that circumvents the rigid symptomology of the classic method and acknowledges the sociocultural, historical, and personal aspects of trauma and its representation.

Affect is at once both delightfully simple and notoriously complex; definitions are multitudinous and theorists have long thrashed out the most effective way to explain it. Aristotle contends that affect is "that which leads one's condition to become so transformed that his judgment is affected, and which is accompanied by pleasure and pain" (1991: 6). In *Poetics*, he argued that a tragedy "should . . . imitate actions which excite pity and fear" (1984: 1). Affect's direct relationship to mimesis can clearly be seen here—the aim of art is to imitate actions to excite reactions. Clement Greenberg criticizes this concept in his essay "Avant-Garde and Kitsch," insisting that art which exists to produce affect is "kitsch." He compares paintings by Illya Repin and Pablo Picasso to illustrate his point: "Where Picasso paints cause, Repin paints effect. Repin predigests art for the spectator and spares him the effort, provides him with a shortcut to the pleasure of art that detours what is necessarily difficult in genuine art. Repin, or kitsch, is synthetic art" (1961: 15). Kitsch produces affect for a passive viewer who need do no work to create it. To my mind, Greenberg's comments are not only unfair, but they miss the point of art that produces affect. In this book, I deal with (narrative) art that uses affect and affective mimesis to allow the reader to comprehend (at least part of) something that is largely incomprehensible. To suggest that such works are kitsch denies them their proper credit.

A large number of scholars link affect and cognition; one of particular note is William James, whose model of emotion unifies affect and cognition. In "What is an Emotion," James writes:

> Common sense says, we lose our fortune, are sorry and weep; we meet a bear, are frightened and run; we are insulted by a rival, are angry and strike. The hypothesis here to be defended says that this order of sequence is incorrect, that the one mental state is not immediately induced by the other, that the bodily manifestations must be first interposed between, and that the more rational statement is that we feel sorry because we cry, angry because we strike, afraid because we tremble. (1922: 13)

For James, then, perception produces immediate affect, which is later transformed into an emotion. James's work forms the basis of affect theory that is later discussed in great detail in the works of Félix Guattari and Gilles Deleuze. In their groundbreaking essay "What Is Philosophy," they argue that art is "a bloc of sensations, that is to say, a compound of percepts and affects" (1994, 163). Although this quotation directly references "art," this term can be taken to mean all artistic representation and not just the visual arts. Acknowledging the writing of Guattari and Deleuze, O'Sullivan states that "you cannot read affects, you can only experience them" (2001: 126). It is from this point that I derive my use of affect in relation to traumatic representation—as a feature of a text that demands to be felt rather than read in order to convey something beyond the purely factual.

In this study, I argue that comics uses its arsenal of formal representational techniques to produce affect in the reader and, in doing so, mimics (some part of) the feelings and experience of trauma. I do not claim that these texts fully represent the experience of trauma; it would be nearly impossible for them to do that. Nor do I claim that these texts aim to traumatize the readers. Trauma is a firsthand experience that reconfigures the self and (usually) arises from a situation in which the individual's life was in serious danger; such experiences do not occur when reading a book. Rather, I wish to show how, through careful formal and representational techniques, the comics herein discussed create affects within the reader than can assist in comprehension of the events and experiences discussed.

At this juncture, I turn to Derek Attridge's excellent article on affect and literature, "Once More With Feeling: Art, Affect and Performance." Using a passage from Cormac McCarthy's *Blood Meridian* (in which a character is decapitated in front of a witness), Attridge describes the response of the reader:

> Anyone reading or hearing [the passage from McCarthy] is bound to have a strong response, a response that one could not call simply cognitive. At the same time as apprehending the meanings of these sentences, the reader or hearer will clearly feel something. It's not easy to fix on an appropriate name for this feeling—repulsion? Disgust? Repugnance? Horror? . . . the fact that we can't name the feeling—or perhaps "complex of feelings" would be a better expression—is significant: it reflects not only the paucity of our vocabulary in dealing with affective emotion, itself a reflection of the poverty of our understanding of this domain of our lives, but also the capacity of literature to engage powerfully and subtly with the extraordinary complexity of emotional responses, in which the psychic and the somatic are so inextricably entwined. (2011: 329–30)

Attridge is entirely correct to say that we are not necessarily engaged with our own emotions and the way in which we process affective emotion. What is more important in this passage, however, is his claim that literature can engage "powerfully and subtly" with human emotional response. This is not a matter of theme but of form. An account of a decapitation (or, indeed, any gruesome and affecting event) may not necessarily produce a response in the viewer (or listener or reader) if it is not crafted in such a way to do so. It is in the presentation—the form of the account—that its true affective power is found. It should be noted, of course, that responses are both different than the response of a firsthand witness and also unique to the individual:

> Even the effort to conjure up a real event of this nature is enough, I think, to show that although there is a clear connection between the feelings aroused by the passage and the feelings that might be aroused if we were actually sitting by that campfire, there is a crucial difference. A viewer of the scene who was not already hardened by similar sights would be likely to be psychically damaged for life: it would be a traumatic experience to which the body would react violently and by which the mind would probably be overwhelmed. (2011: 334)

The readings I produce in this study are presented from the viewpoint of someone who has not experienced tremendous traumata personally, nor been "hardened" by repeated exposure to graphic violence. Although I try to create readings that demonstrate the point of view of a "standard" reader, I am aware that my readings are unavoidably touched by my own experience as a white Western woman and thus *cannot* speak for everyone but sit as one opinion among many.

At the close of his essay, Attridge is careful to remind us that "the emotions experienced by the reader of a work of literature are real; of this there can surely be no doubt" (2011: 340). He further adds "that [the reader's emotions] are not identical with the emotions that would be felt as a result of direct exposure to the people and events portrayed is also unquestionable" (2011: 340). This is exactly the sentiment I wish to reiterate in this book. The consumption (by any method) of traumatic narrative art is not equal to the experience of a traumatic event; to suggest this is both patently untrue and insulting to those who have experienced true trauma. This is the issue that riles Kalí Tal in her book on the subject, as I have mentioned, and an issue that the classic model fails to address. To use LaCapra's terms, the elision of trauma witness (or, in this case, trauma art consumer) and trauma victim is wrong. Through my multi-pronged trauma studies framework and sustained argument for the comics form as a method of creating affect, I hope to avoid this unnecessary elision and analyze traumatic representation in a nuanced and fair manner. To this end, I now move onto three distinct formal techniques and demonstrate how each can be used to produce affect in trauma comics.

The Gutter, the Bleed, and the Bubble

The purpose of the artist of trauma in any form is to instill in the reader some suggestion of the traumatic experience, to bring them as close to the experience of the traumatized party as the form will allow through the use of carefully crafted affects. Michael Rothberg uses the term "traumatic realism" to categorize the variety of formal techniques that the artist of trauma uses to bring the reader into the experience of the text (2000). In text-based literature, this effect is achieved at the most basic level by words, through the careful choice of word and phrase, syntax and grammar, as well as deliberate placement of the words in relation to the page. A notable example of this literal placement of words is found in Jonathan Safran Foer's 9/11 novel *Extremely Loud and Incredibly Close* (2005), in which the words of the protagonist's grandfather become increasingly crowded until the page is a solid block of black ink. Moreover, the often clipped and linguistically economical description in such texts—especially in relation to a traumatic event—is a recurrent feature of conflict literature. Physical descriptions of place and person are often, but not always, limited; words are used sparingly and description, where offered, does not present a clear image, but a distorted one.

Moving away from the basic units of the text, trauma writers introduce atypical narrative techniques, especially in relation to time and disrupted narrative linearity; not only is this disrupted sense of personal chronology an important trope in the representation of a traumatic rupture, as I have previously mentioned, but it is also something that the author can manipulate to great dramatic effect (and affect). In *Slaughterhouse-Five* (1969), Kurt Vonnegut's hero, Billy Pilgrim, is a time-traveler. His experience of World War II, and specifically the firebombing of Dresden, traumatizes him in such a way as to force a disconnection between Billy and the normal temporal workings of the universe. Vonnegut is an extreme example; he is not the only writer to play with time in dramatic ways for the purposes of mimesis in a conflict trauma narrative. When boiled down to the very basic level, this is the aim of a trauma text: to use every available linguistic, syntactical, grammatical, and typographical tool available to bombard the reader and stir up emotions that will, in some small part, mimetically evoke the feelings related to trauma, be it shock, fear, horror, or a sense of psychic numbing, while at the same time allowing the reader to appreciate that what they are experiencing is *not* trauma itself.

The aim of the trauma comics creator is the same as that of his text-based cousin, although a different tool kit is used. In comics of conflict and trauma, the affects of traumatic experience are created in the formal techniques of the comic. The comics creator has a range of devices that the traditional writer does not. In order to demonstrate the interplay between the comics form and trauma theory, there is a need to analyze different formal aspects and consider how the transformative nature of a traumatic rupture (for all models of trauma theory agree that trauma is a transformative experience) affects the creation of the narrative. To this end, I discuss three of the most striking elements of the form: transitions across the gutter, page bleeds, and the bubble. I should note that further discussion of all three elements occurs throughout this study as a whole, but I mention them specifically here in order to give the reader an opportunity to acquaint themselves with them and how I will use form and theory in my close readings in due course.

Comics theorist Scott McCloud discusses the importance of the "gutter," the space between each panel of a comic. He argues that what goes on between the individual panels—"closure"—is essential to effective comics writing and reading: "comics panels fracture both time and space . . . but closure allows us to connect these moments and mentally construct a continuous, unified reality" (1994: 45). Closure, he claims, is the grammar of the form, and the entirety of the form hinges on the arrangement of elements, a point that Thierry Groensteen readily agrees with in his concept of arthrology: "the true magic of comics operates between the images, the tension that binds them" (2007: 23).

The process of closure is one that most readers adapt to without thinking; most readers have no issue constructing a coherent narrative from a comic and, furthermore, do so without thinking about the reading process involved. The amount of mental movement required to jump across the gutter depends on which transition is employed. McCloud asserts that there are six types of transitions, each requiring a different level and type of reader engagement (1994: 72). Each type of transition will alter the way the text is read and the way the reader reacts to the text. This is a key technique by which comics creators work when piecing together the narrative elements of a story. Indeed, I would go so far as to say that the gutter is the most important aspect of the comics form. However, all this changes when the variables shift slightly and introduce a dimension that by its very nature disrupts and resists representation—trauma. In order to discuss the use of transitions in trauma comics, I will look at a pair of two-page comics excerpts, both of which use the physical nature of the book to assist in the act of closure, emphasizing the effects of the transition, thus creating an "extreme transition" of sorts.

• • •

In February 2002, DC Comics published an anthology of short comics by a wide range of creators to raise money for 9/11 charities. The first comic of the anthology, which set the tone for the entire book, is presented recto-verso, meaning that the page must be turned half way through reading in order to complete the narrative. In "Unreal," the first page shows Superman using his powers to stop a space shuttle from crashing into a satellite (2002: 15). However, on the second page, according to Smith and Goodrum, "we see that the first page is metadiagetic; it is a Superman comic held by a child being carried from the burning WTC by a fireman" (2002: 16). The comic is presented in a typical mainstream artistic style, using bold colors and clear lines, as one would expect from a Superman comic. Page one shows us only a superhero comic; this page on its own is unremarkable. Page two zooms out from the pages of the boy's comic, making the panel transitions jarring and uncomfortable. The final panel breaks down the barriers between a comics universe and the real universe as the page-bound Superman salutes the fireman as he runs back into the breach with an American flag. It is presented in such a way as to necessitate the reader to turn the page in order to complete the narrative;

it is in this movement from page to page that the biggest and most difficult leap of closure occurs. Put crudely, in this context the page turn creates the "punch line." While transitions exist between all contiguous panels in comics, as well as between pages, the necessity of the page turn—and the fact that the next part of the narrative is hidden until this point—intensifies the transition between pages. The fact that the action has shifted so quickly from the fantastical world of Superman to the events at the World Trade Center mimics the sudden and unannounced experience of a traumatic rupture, for which the reader, like the traumatized individual, is wholly unprepared. The punch line of the second page destabilizes our reading and momentarily overwhelms us with information we may struggle to process in line with what has come before.

Page one of "Unreal" uses what McCloud labels action-to-action transitions (the type which is most widely used in Western mainstream comics), following a single subject in distinct progression of action. However, the subsequent pages do not follow this, using moment-to-moment transitions which, while requiring less closure, are not typically used in Western comics and so will not be as easy to read as the reader must change their reading method. It zooms out slowly from the comic page to the crying little boy, then to the fireman, and finally to the image of the flag and the burning building. This takes six panels and moves with agonizing slowness compared to the usually fast pace of superhero stories. Although this comic uses the artistic style and basic techniques of mainstream comics art, the difference in transitional elements serves to disquiet the reader and assist in the creation of traumatic affect.

Alissa Torres and Sungyoon Choi's 2009 comic *American Widow* opens with a two-page spread that, like "Unreal," asks the reader to abandon their typical comics reading methods. However, unlike "Unreal," there is no sense of false security, but a sudden and violent leap. The two full-page images are placed next to each other. There is a huge demand of closure needed for the reader to fill the gap between these two images. By McCloud's classification, this looks like a "non sequitur"—two contiguous images that appear to have no relationship beyond the spatial one (1994: 72). However, the jump from a clear, blue sky with birds to a screaming television with the now-famous image of the towers imitates the mental jump that many people around the world experienced on that day as witnesses, not trauma survivors. This huge leap of closure has several uses. First, it mirrors the shock and suddenness of the event. Secondly, it unsettles the reader from the beginning, creating an air of insecurity and setting up the text as both unsettling and potentially shocking. Thirdly, Torres is using readers, who are made complicit in creating the text's disquieting tone by the huge amount of closure they are forced to do.

These two short examples are indicative of two of the main ways in which comics transitions serve to recreate the traumatic rupture. In "Unreal," the comic begins in an unremarkable fashion but makes a dramatic twist, which disrupts the narrative mid-flow, forcing the reader to change reading method very quickly, while also creating a traumatic rupture within the text's diegetic flow. In *American Widow*, this does not happen, and the reader faces the trauma, mimicked in the unusually vast transitional leap, from the first page. Thus, these two examples show the manipulation of panel transitions that is so commonly used to mimic a traumatic chronology and can occur at many points throughout the narrative. Indeed, ruptures such as these occur so frequently that the narrative is held together, in places, by the reader's self-created chronology alone.

• • •

Not every page employs gutters or borders. When a single image fills an entire page to the edge, it is called a "bleed." Bleeds have a relatively short history in Western comics art and are far more common in manga and manhwa (Japanese and Korean comics, respectively). The rarity of the bleed in American comics—especially mainstream publications, in which they are even rarer than usual—makes it something of a novelty and, moreover, very powerful when employed. Referring to bleeds, McCloud writes that "time is no longer contained by the familiar lines of the closed panel, but instead haemorrhages and escapes into timeless space" (1994: 1030). Bleeds are, by their nature, violent. The image's domination of the page is striking and demands the reader's complete attention. The absence of frames on the page edges removes any sense of constriction or confinement—the image has total control of the page. It is for this reason that Frank Miller drew *300* (1998), which depicts the violent battles at Thermopylae, entirely in two-page bleeds. If the bleed page follows a series of ordered panels, its presence breaks the flow of visual uniformity and shakes the reader's sense of security.

Although influenced heavily by the Franco-Belgian tradition, GB Tran uses bleeds frequently in *Vietnamerica* (2011). In one section, Tran recounts the serious wounding of his uncle, Vinh, in a firefight during his time in the army (2011: 178). The bleed is on the left-hand page and so accosts the reader as they turn the page. It is not only the violence of the subject matter that confronts the reader, but also the violent use of color. Although Tran is not shy about using bold color throughout the comic, he uses relatively subdued coloration for the background of this image to create a dramatic contrast with the red of the blood. The use of a bleed in this instance not only mirrors the violence of Vinh's situation with a violent confrontation of the reader, but also suggests a sense of continuing action. Were this page to be framed, as is typical, this incident would be seen as "closed." However, the lack of a frame lends the image a sense of timelessness; the blood continues to flow. The fact that the blood flows off the page attests to this—the severity of the injury is shown in the careful use of the bleed.

At another point in the narrative, Tran uses a two-page bleed to depict Saigon Airport, just before the Fall of Saigon on April 30, 1975 (2011: 162–63). Thousands of people descended on the airport in the hope of escaping the country. As with the previous example, Tran uses a vivid and ominous shade of red for the sky but keeps the rest of the image muted in color. This draws the eye, unnaturally, to the top of the page, then to the exclamation mark in a jagged bubble, before allowing the more natural movement of the eye across the page. In this example, the bleed gives the artist space to force this unnatural eye movement. Again, as with the previous example, the removal of frames adds to the chaos of the scene. It seems as if the confusion and pandemonium is bursting out of the page, especially as the crowded nature of the page makes it uncomfortable to look at.[4] The bleed, then, is a violent device, removing constraints and encouraging chaos.

. . .

In order to function as a narrative form, comics is required to make visible many intangible things, most notably speech and thought. This is where the use of bubbles enters the form. On the most basic level, bubbles are containers for speech or thoughts. They usually involve a directional pointer that links the bubble to the source of the information contained therein. Traditionally, speech bubbles have smooth lines, connected directional pointers, and a roughly oval shape, while thought bubbles have a cloud-shaped outline with a directional pointer typically not connected to the bubble itself. Will Eisner calls the bubble a "desperation device [which] attempts to capture and make visible an ethereal element: sound" (2008: 45).

Despite this criticism, the bubble is present in almost all comics, though it has been developed over time so that the shape of the bubble has become a narrative device in its own right. To give two examples, jagged-edged bubbles can denote shouting or show the reader that the sound is emanating from an electronic device, as in the Torres panels mentioned previously, while wobbly edged bubbles suggest a dreamlike tone or possibly inebriation. The contents of the bubble, too, can be used to illustrate features of the speaker. In Goscinny and Uderzo's famous Astérix series (1959–2010), for example, fonts that can be recognized as stereotypes of certain tongues are used to show that characters are speaking in different languages, including Gothic and Norse. In some cases, images are used to represent words within bubbles. For example, a bubble may contain an image of a cup of coffee, rather than a character speaking the words "a cup of coffee, please." The use of an image in the bubble changes the relationship that the reader has to the comic but gives them far more power in the creation of the narrative than they have when the bubble contains words. It is not clear if the image represents a demand, a request, a question, or any other type of statement; it is for the reader to decide. Similarly, does the cup represent coffee, tea, or soup? Again, the reader decides. Furthermore, the use of an image removes any linguistic barrier that may exist. The image-as-speech introduces a universality that is not available to comics that include words. By this reckoning, the bubble is a wonderfully flexible device.

Why, then, does Eisner consider its use to be a sign of desperation? In many of Eisner's comics, the dialogue is an integral part of the image, artistically woven into the fabric of the panel. To encase dialogue within a bubble is to relegate it to encapsulation within blank space, segregating it from the rest of the panel. This changes the position of the dialogue; it can serve to create distance between the dialogue and the rest of the panel. Similarly, McCloud discusses the distancing implications of thought bubbles:

> A thought caption—with or without borders—embodies each thought in a way that encourages us to assume ownership of it as we read. The thought balloon, just by virtue of its pointer, brings a third party into the relationship: the author, gently putting his hand on our shoulder and pointing to the face of the thinker with the words "he thought." (2010: n.p.)

By keeping thoughts constrained by thought clouds, rather than in, for example, a voiceover-style caption, the creator places another boundary between himself and the reader. His thoughts do not become ours, as McCloud suggests a caption would allow, but the cloud reminds us starkly of the distance between the creator's experience and our own. The implications for representations of trauma are crucial here. There is a clear link to the idea of trauma as an individual, owned experience. Keeping speech encased within a bubble maintains this individualism. It also links back to the debate as to whether trauma is prelinguistic or not. Explicitly containing traumatic utterances within bubbles makes them a visual reality within the comic. This is not to suggest that, just because a character speaks, they have not experienced trauma; what it does suggest is that the classic model's insistence on the prelinguistic nature of traumatic experiences and the unspeakability of trauma is not, in fact, an absolute. As I show throughout this study, the representation of trauma is by no means a straightforward mimicry of the classic model but speaks to a wide range of personal, social, and cultural experiences that differ person-to-person. That most of the texts discussed in this study include conversations in which traumatized individuals discuss their experience in some way speaks to the spectrum of unspeakability in survivors of (and representations of) traumatic experience. Not only is the bubble a central formal device, but its presence in narratives of trauma speaks to trauma as a collection of non-universal symptoms and presentations that exist on a spectrum.

The written aspects of the comic, encased usually in bubbles but also sometimes in caption or voiceover boxes, are the part that most people read and, subsequently, what people think of when they think of reading comics. However, to read any comic relies on the reader adopting a new way of reading, which I propose should be considered in terms of levels. The first level is the typical act of reading text—the basic comprehension of words. To this I would add the recognition of objects and people in drawn form. In comics, this level allows us the basic skill of reading dialogue and captions. The second level—that which is required for the reading of comics—is, for most people, an unconscious skill. This level involves an understanding of the demands of closure and the creation of a system of time. Although most seasoned comics readers will probably not be aware that they employ any special skills in reading, this does not mean they are absent. To this level I also add the recognition of comics-specific symbols, such as emanata and grawlixes, as well as an awareness of conventions of the form.[5]

This way of reading is undermined entirely when considering "silent" comics—comics in which there are no bubbles at all and often few captions. In silent comics, the first level is removed as there is little or no text to read. The reader, then, is reliant entirely on their second-level skills and, in order to construct a coherent narrative, must work especially hard. Silent comics disrupt the standard methods of reading comics. By this definition, silent comics is particularly relevant for traumatic representation. The removal of first-level reading skills is disorienting and has a destabilizing effect on the reader. This omission in itself can make the experience of reading the comic mimic the traumatic experience, the reader being to all intents and purposes diegetically stranded. Silent comics are relatively rare in Western mainstream publishing, which is still very much driven by the influence of the "house style," standardizing artistic technique. However, in trauma comics, silence is much more common, often for the simple reason that there is nothing to say or no way of saying it. Silent comics allow the events to be presented without comment, involving the reader to a much higher degree. Not only does this increase reader engagement but it also allows a traumatic experience to exist without words. Returning to Herman's suggestion of trauma as intensely visual, it is extremely difficult to give words to trauma, though images may provide an outlet. The removal of words, then, can assist the author in the creation of the text, while simultaneously creating a disturbing textual experience that unnerves the reader.

Keith Giffen and Bill Wray's short comic "Dust" is an excellent example of a silent comic that uses a linking motif to create narrative movement (2002: 111–13). It is not unusual for comics artists to use linking motifs—images or symbols that exist throughout a text to maintain continuity—but these are not usually present in all panels. Each panel of "Dust" contains an image of discarded papers fluttering in the breeze. This persistence of images speaks more of a traumatic repetition than a stylistic linking motif. Despite this, "Dust" contains no discernible storyline. By the end of the comic, the reader has not completed a storyline as much as witnessed a small snapshot of a situation but with no commentary to explain the scenario or guide the reader in any way. The reader gains no information from the comic, remaining instead in a state of confusion and distress.

• • •

Although this discussion is by no means an exhaustive investigation of the comics form—or even of the three aspects examined—it gives an introduction to the form itself, as well as the demands that traumatic representation has on the development of such formal devices. The reason for a more sustained look at these three aspects in particular is because of their importance. As I previously mentioned, the gutter is the most important part of the comics form; it provides the grammar of the form and does more than any other aspect to involve the reader in the flow of the narrative. The gutter and the six types of transitions form a very large part of my close readings of comics and, as such, it is essential that the reader understands how they work. The bubble and the bleed are two aspects that are distinctive to the comics form and are the most likely to be harnessed and manipulated by the artist of trauma, as the reader will become aware throughout this study.

2

Rituals, Mourning, and Grief

What separates us from the animals, what separates us from the chaos, is our ability to mourn people we've never met.
—**David Levithan,** *Love is the Higher Law* (2009)

There is no satisfactory way to look at any text of conflict without also looking at the effect that such widespread violence and devastation has on the self. However, it would be unwise to suggest that the traumatic experience ends with the psychological and psycho-physiological effect on the individual. Rather, the experience of trauma has another layer: the culturally defined and performative expression of mourning. The comics I discuss are testament to the "persistence of the trauma's desire to exist" and attempt to recreate it both visually and linguistically (Kopf, 2005: 10). The need to recreate trauma is inextricably bound up in the need to memorialize and to mourn. For many, the huge sociopolitical changes that arise from conflicts are seen as the death of an ideal and a way of life, a notion that speaks to Freud's definition of mourning when he writes that "mourning is regularly the reaction to the loss of a loved person, or to the loss of some abstraction which has taken the place of one, such as one's country, liberty, an ideal, and so on" (2002: 248). Many people find it difficult to engage with those who are mourning, but for Freud the process of mourning is necessary and healthy: "We look upon any interference with it as useless or even harmful" (2002: 244).

As I argued in the introduction, texts of conflict are rarely overblown and glorious epics. Rather, as O'Brien declares, war stories are stories of "love and memory" (1991: 81). In order to provide a basis for this chapter, I begin with a discussion of three classic texts and the importance that each places on mourning and grief following conflicts. From this analysis, I demonstrate the roots of the concentration on mourning in conflict literature. I should make it clear that the following analyses barely scratch the surface of the depth of scholarship on these three texts. My engagement with these texts is slight and this is entirely deliberate; it is not my intention to provide new readings of classic literary texts and I will not delve into the massive amounts of scholarship on each text. That said, I insist that these texts are incredibly useful signposts to this particular trend in the literature of conflict and so present these short analyses here in order to provide a loose historical and cultural framework for this chapter. I am invoking these three texts as influential cultural models—as important texts in the development of Western literature that help to create a certain type of focus in the literatures of conflict.

Three Case Studies in Conflict and Mourning

Homer's epic poem *The Iliad*, generally accepted as being written around 1190 BC, is a landmark work in both Classical poetry and conflict literature.[1] James Tatum argues that part of the enduring nature of *The Iliad* is its internal dichotomy: "Read as history, *The Iliad* seems only a fragment of war; at the same time it says everything there is to say about war" (2004: xii). He is right to note this odd split within the text, but more unusual is the literal locational and thematic split that permeates the whole poem. Homer does not limit his text only to the theatre of war. Throughout the text there are frequent returns to domestic settings, usually as male characters return to their homes to visit family. The interweaving of familial and military duty, of "hearth and battlefield," creates a space in which the poem's most predominant theme can be cultivated. It is its focus on mourning and grief that lends the poem much of its power.[2] Homer builds his narrative not around a glamorous image of handsome and aesthetically pleasing warriors, but of devastation and extreme loss. Our preconceived ideas of heroism and valour are crushed. Homer writes of Hector:

> all around, the black hair [of Hector]
> was spread, and the whole head lay in the dust,
> just before so charming; now Zeus has granted
> to his enemies to debase [the corpse] on native land. (2003: 401)

Formerly the Hope of Troy and a figure of great military prowess, Hector is reduced to a corpse—desecrated and lying in the dust. The poem closes with no great celebration, but a funeral and the elegies of three women. Tatum writes:

> Our lasting memory of *The Iliad* is not only of the imminent fall of Troy, or of the victory of Agamemnon, or even of Achilles and his approaching death, but of

the burial and tomb of Hector, and of the final speeches of his wife and mother ... *The Iliad* stops when the devastations of war are plain ... [but] the whys and wherefores of war itself are as unanswered at the end of the poem as they were at its beginning. (2004: xiv)

The lack of "closure" and reluctance to offer opinions or solutions are familiar issues in modern conflict literature. It is comforting to know that the inability to give reasons for war is nothing new, and more comforting still to recognize Homer's honest admission of this. *The Iliad*, therefore, provides a mile-marker from which it is possible to trace a history of conflict literature. The tropes that Homer employs—the epic form, the duality of the domestic and the military, the emphasis on relationships between individuals—are central to countless texts of conflict that have been written since.

What the Greeks enjoyed and perfected in the epic genre is something seen in literatures around the world. Of the Old English epic poems, the most famous is probably *Beowulf*. However, J. R. R. Tolkien takes exception to the characterization of this work as "epic"; he writes:

> *Beowulf* is not an "epic," not even a magnified "lay." No terms borrowed from Greek or other literatures exactly fit: there is no reason why they should. Though if we must have a term, we should choose rather "elegy." It is a heroic-elegiac poem; and in a sense all its first 3136 lines are the prelude to a dirge. (1937: 3)

Whatever its generic classification, this text is something of an enigma as there is no known (or supposed) author and its date of writing is vague indeed—between the eighth and early eleventh centuries. Despite this, the narrative is remarkably consistent in all of the early printed versions. Tolkien suggests that the text's "weakness lies in placing the unimportant things at the centre and the important things on the outer edges" (1937: 33). To an extent, this repeats what can be seen in *The Iliad*. That which, in a conflict text, seems to be unimportant—the daily interactions of a family, the experience of the individual—is given heightened status. Furthermore, as we noted in *The Iliad* and will see in *Le Morte D'Arthur*, *Beowulf* questions the "might is right" ideal. Beowulf's might is undeniable as he slays the monster, Grendel, and restores peace to Heorot. However, as with many of the Greek heroes and also many of Malory's knights, Beowulf's might is corrupted by other personality traits. In this case, it is Beowulf's pride, overconfidence in his own abilities, and desire for individual glory that cause his downfall.

As with Homer's poem, *Beowulf* is shaped by mourning and loss. However, *Beowulf* is structured around death in a far more literal way than *The*

Iliad. The poem is clearly arranged around three funerals, which are paired with three battles; each battle and each funeral has a different focus (Abrams and Greenblatt, 2000: 29). Regardless of the differences, it is the emphasis on death and mourning that resonates. Gale Owen-Crocker (2000) contends that the poem is structured around four funerals (rather than three, as previous scholarship has held). In her study of the poem she writes, "the placing of funerals at the beginning and end of the narrative is a deliberate act of structuring, which completes a circle of grief" (2002: 2). Tolkien concurs that defeat is the theme of the poem. Triumph over the foes of man's precarious fortress is over, and we approach slowly and reluctantly the inevitable victory of death (1937: 32).

Sir Thomas Malory's compilation of Arthurian legends *Le Morte D'Arthur* includes bloody battle scenes, discussions of political and civil unrest, and, most interestingly, the individual conflicts between characters. *Le Morte D'Arthur* was probably written during Malory's time in prison in the late 1400s, during the War of the Roses. Unlike Homer, Malory is generally nonchalant in his depictions of war's violence, offering the gruesome scene with little additional comment. However, there are many similarities within the three texts. All three show situations in which violence is not the only option but is considered with no suggestion of any other method of reconciliation. In *Le Morte*, this leads to much of the tragedy—especially when characters engage in mortal combat with a supposedly unknown assailant, only to realize that they were fighting their close friend or relation. In these interchanges, the pointlessness of violence and its bitter aftertaste become evident. Indeed, there are many instances within the text of two knights engaging in hand-to-hand combat without knowing each other's true identities and then regretting the action. Sir Tristan is horrified to find that he has fought for hours with Sir Launcelot. Sir Launcelot is distraught to find he has slain Sir Gareth and Sir Gaheris—more so when this "accident" is escalated to war by Sir Gawain's desire for revenge for the murder of his brothers. T. J. Lustig notes dryly: "Smite first and ask questions later: it is the standard operating procedure. But the potential for making mistakes in these circumstances is so great that one wonders why nobody modifies the rules of engagement" (2013: 12–13).

All three texts end with death and rituals of mortality. In *The Iliad*, the deaths of Hector and Patroclus unite the warring two factions in mutual grief and mourning. In order to allow Priam to conduct Hector's funeral without disruption, Achilles declares a ceasefire. The experience of grief for a loved one violently lost reminds the men of their common humanity and the text closes, leaving the reader in no doubt that Homer sees grief and loss as the

Rituals, Mourning, and Grief

outcome of conflict. Beowulf's funeral is dealt with differently. While it is evident that Beowulf's death is a great blow to the Geats, it is also a time of celebration for his life as the "most gracious and fair-minded warrior king, kindest to his people and keenest to win fame" (Heaney, 1999: 121). However, despite the hint of a festival atmosphere around his funeral, there is still an overwhelming attitude of grief at the end of the poem. *Le Morte* finds its ending in funereal grief. Arthur is slain in battle by his son Mordred, despite a papal bull demanding a cessation of the conflict, and is taken away on a barge—not unlike the sea funeral of Scyld Scefing in *Beowulf*:

> And when they were at the water side, even fast by the bank hoved a little barge with many fair ladies in it, and among them all was a queen, and all they had black hoods, and all they wept and shrieked when they saw King Arthur. Now put me into the barge, said the king. And so he did softly; and there received him three queens with great mourning; and so they set them down, and in one of their laps King Arthur laid his head. (Malory, 1889: 480)

With Arthur's death and "funeral"—as with Hector, Patroclus, and Beowulf's— "the ladies wept and shrieked that it was a pity to hear" (1889: 481). At the end of battle, there is no jubilation, nor glory. These three texts unite in their conclusion of violence and conflict as a destructive force that results in death and grief, often with very little achieved as a result.

The "work of mourning" (to use Freud's phrase) forms a huge part of comics of conflict. In this chapter, I take the concept of "conflict text as text of mourning" and apply it to representations of mourning and funeral rites in *American Widow* and *Maus*. I also consider the inclusion of these themes to a lesser extent in a selection of other texts. I show how the "work of mourning" acts in conjunction with traumatic representation within the text. Prior to this, however, I discuss the relationship between mourning, shrines, and the necessary physicality of the comic.

Mourning, Manipulation, and Materiality

The creation of shrines is a normal and healthy part of mourning; a way to honor the deceased and to offer them a final token of love or respect. Of course, it is possible for shrine-building to become decidedly unhealthy, as John Hewitt contends: "This drive towards creating a 'museum to the deceased' is one way to ensure a lifetime of grief, our method of refusing to let go" (1980: 44). For Freud, this unhealthy reaction speaks more of melancholia than mourning. In his book *On Mourning*, William Watkin agrees, stating that the attempt to keep someone alive by means of words

> suggests to us the beginning stages of a melancholia or a refusal to see mourning as a ritualised process of self-healing, but rather conceiving of mourning as a magical process of linguistic reanimation. (2004: 5)

Words are one aspect of memorialization; memorialization in a physical sense is generally conflated with shrine-building and memorials. However, the creation of an artistic work is just as much an act of physical memorialization and mourning as the building of a shrine. Indeed, in a medium such as comics, where the materiality of the work is of great importance to the narrative, this idea can be developed. Watkin writes: "All memorialists strive to create a physical location for remembrance from the manipulation of the material world" (2004: 7). The first part of the statement is relatively straightforward—the creation of a physical location for remembrance. However, it is not as simple as saying that this refers purely to memorial masonry and the like. As I discuss in Chapter 5, the physical existence of the comic book is an important factor in the creation and development of both the plot development and, more specifically, the representation of traumatic experience contained therein. The creation of works of art as physical memorials to the dead is by no means a new phenomenon, but comics take this further by adding an extra layer of meaning and necessity: In order to be comics, they must exist in a specific, physical sense. Unlike many forms in which representation does not affect the message of the work, comics must be presented in their originally created format in order for the message to remain as intended.[3] In this respect, then, the comic item itself becomes a memorial. The 9/11 charity comics attest to this most readily in their being created for the dual purpose of praising emergency responders and raising money to support their families too.

Let us consider the second part of Watkin's quotation. The concept of manipulation and the material world raises a number of issues. The word "manipulation" has an intriguing etymology:

> Manipulation: c.1730, a method of digging ore, from Latin Manipulus "handful," from manus "hand" + root plere "to fill." Sense of "skilful handling of objects" is first recorded 1826. (*Oxford English Dictionary*, 2012)

The earliest definition of "digging" holds some relevance to the process of unearthing the core of a traumatic experience, in which one is often forced to find the root of their emotions and experience "rock bottom" before beginning the work of mourning and recovery. The latter sense of the word refers us back to the concept of the careful presentation and handling of the physical object of the text. Although Watkin is not discussing comics in this quotation, his point is salient; the comics form relies on careful handling and manipulation of the physical object of the book to a far greater extent than other artistic forms. When the comic involves a discussion of mourning, and, more specifically, the rituals and tangible manifestations thereof, it is reasonable to consider that the relationship between the physical object and the content is intensified by the culturally charged importance of material remembrance. It is important to remember that traumatic grief is a different experience from that of being directly affected by a traumatic event. Bennett defines traumatic grief against a more sudden and incisive type of trauma: "Unlike the sensation of a cut, grief is not something that can be understood as occurring within the moment; it is a more diffuse and extended process" (2005: 61). For this reason, these texts need to take into consideration the differences in this type of trauma and any potential limits of representation that arise.

Structured Grief in *American Widow*

Alissa Torres, in collaboration with Sungyoon Choi, makes no attempt to understand the magnitude of the events of September 11, 2001, in which her husband, Luis Eduardo "Eddie" Torres, died. In *American Widow*, Torres tells only her own story, aware of her lack of full understanding, which is not technically possible, given the basic nature of trauma. Despite the intensely personal nature of the text, this does not alienate the reader. Unlike many of my primary texts, *American Widow* is unusual because the conflict event has not begun at the start of the text. In other words, the narrative shows the beginning of the conflict and "witnesses" the very early stages of trauma and shock instead of entering the narrative at a later date. Furthermore, Torres does not retell the story of what happened. Indeed, the wider sociopolitical aspects of the event are not covered in great detail at all; the only engagements with this within the text are the many instances of Torres's visits to the Red Cross. Instead, the text is a carefully constructed comics representation of her work of mourning.

It becomes apparent that Torres is acutely aware of her own mourning. It is possible to track a shifting, although clear, demarcation of different stages of the mourning process.[4] In Kübler-Ross's "Five Stage Model," grief involves denial, anger, bargaining, depression, and acceptance. In her book *On Death and Dying*, Kübler-Ross writes that "the stages are responses to loss that many people have, but there is not a typical response to loss as there is no typical loss. Our grief is as individual as our lives" (Kübler-Ross, 1997: 4). All of the five stages can be seen in *American Widow*, and the Kübler-Ross model is a useful tool for analyzing the way that grief is represented in the text.

The first stage, denial, is evident in the chapter of the text set on September 11—which I discuss presently. In this stage, Kübler-Ross writes that "the world becomes meaningless and overwhelming . . . we refuse to believe in the loss" (1997: 24). Torres writes of her efforts to track down Eddie in New York hospitals. She writes:

> You didn't come home so I searched for you in the hospitals . . . there was a Doris Torres. I knew she was a woman; I knew she wasn't you. I checked anyway . . . On day four, I accepted the truth. (2008: 47–50)

Although Torres accepts that Eddie is dead, she has not reached the "acceptance stage." I should note at this juncture that one criticism of Kübler-Ross's model is the cleanly delineated process of mourning that she lays out; this is not an accurate portrayal of the way that many people experience grief. Instead of working through each stage in clear sequence, the process is messy and intensely personal. In the text, the next three stages (anger, bargaining, and depression) appear all at once. The use of the black page bleeds features prominently, especially in depictions of a depressive mood. Similarly, the image of Torres surrounded by speech bubbles is repeated over and over (2008: 43, 106–109). Although there is no malice in the words, the effect of them is stifling. The pointers of the speech bubbles begin to encircle Torres and grab hold of her. The use of bleeds and stark contrast on the page, together with the ghostly and nightmarish images, illustrate Torres's mental state. The images seem as if Torres is suspended in air—or falling. Either way, she is not on solid ground. This lack of solidity is both disconcerting and effective in giving the reader a sense of her state. These images represent the constant barrage of well-meaning friends and relatives that wanted to help Alissa. This speaks to the concept of collective grief and the need of many to feel something in the aftermath of 9/11, as I discuss in due course with reference to the work of David Holloway.

In the middle of the text, Torres gives birth to her son. The birth itself is discussed in an indirect manner and is, unusually, not presented in a comics style. Rather, the episode is recounted as continuous prose, accompanied by small, childlike images, making this chapter less of a comic and more of a children's illustrated story. This shift in presentation technique creates a break in the text, moving from comic to "straight" prose text, which disorients the reader. The jolt created by the shift in presentation also forces the reader to consider what exactly is being said here. This is a narrative of birth, a joyous event for most families and one that should be greeted with positive emotions. Torres's description does not read like a typical birth narrative. She likens the experience of the pain of contractions and trauma to the body to sex, describing each part of labor as though it were a part of a sexual encounter. The passage is written as though she is talking directly to Eddie, giving the text an overwhelmingly personal feel, as though the reader is intruding on their private correspondence. Torres links the experience of birth and sex with her grief as she writes, "I welcomed the grief in the screams of my hard-earned labor. I invited you into each one, mourning you each time as I had not done previously" (2008: 83). In this respect, her grief has permeated every aspect of her life, including the beginning of the life of her son. This is one of the few points in the text where the reader is given insight into the Torres's physical relationship; the difference in representational style highlights the omission of this theme from the rest of the text.

Torres's depiction of her postnatal depression is honest and harrowing (2008: 89). The view jumps uncomfortably around the room but without any movement. The reader is presented with four views of the same scene. Again, there are constrained thought bubbles. The most unusual features of this page are the intense black gutters. They give the impression of a blink. We see the image of the light, and then blink. We see Torres and the nurse, and then blink again. In each black gutter, time in slowed down. This manipulation of time is central to the reconstruction of trauma and I discuss it at length in Chapter 5. The blink-gutters in this section of *American Widow* allow us to be party to Torres's grief and depression, while still remaining separate from it. Kübler-Ross writes: "In the depressive stage empty feelings present themselves and feel as though they will last forever" (1997: 67). The heavy black coloring on these pages emphasizes this. The black page bleed is used to excellent effect here. This is an intense depiction of the seemingly never-ending depression of mourning.

The page bleed is used beautifully in the section of the text on Eddie's funeral. The vast emptiness of the church mirrors the vast emptiness of Torres and the mourners. There is nothing cozy about this church; it seems more like a barn in this image. The immeasurable loneliness of Torres is made manifest in this image—a cave-like church that should be a place of great comfort but only represents sorrow. This sits in contrast to the image of the cemetery presented later in the text (2008: 173). One would typically expect the church to be the place of comfort, and the cemetery to be the place of sorrow, but

Torres inverts this. The cemetery, though bleak, is more reminiscent of the book's first image of a calm blue sky. The three panels are uniform in size and shape but show very different images. The top panel shows rose petals in the air. These petals then float into the middle panel, a winter view of the cemetery. The bottom panel shows the same scene again, but this time in summer. Again, there is a huge jump to make between the images—this time spanning seasons to achieve closure. And again the image of the rose appears, this time as petal confetti. As with the analysis of "Dust" in Chapter 1, the use of a linking image connects panels that may otherwise seem too disconnected to contain a discernible narrative. Not only does the petal motif link three panels across a lengthy timespan, it also connects these images of death and the passage of time to the repeated images of roses that are seen throughout the text.

· · ·

Kübler-Ross's second stage is anger. Of this she writes:

> At first grief feels like being lost at sea: no connection to anything. Then you get angry at someone . . . Suddenly you have a structure—your anger toward them. The anger becomes a connection from you to them. It is something to hold onto; and a connection made from the strength of anger feels better than nothing. (1997: 40)

There are many instances in the text of Torres's anger and they are presented to us in such a way as to make us both complicit in and accepting of her rage. At the start of the text, Alissa and Eddie have had an argument. Alissa is still angry at Eddie near the end of the text, almost a year later, as she writes, "You told me, 'I want to turn 90 beside you,' but you didn't. So that's how I got here. I am still so mad at you" (2008: 200).

Kübler-Ross suggests that bargaining is the most irrational stage of grief: "We become lost in a maze of 'If only . . .' or 'What if . . .' statements. We want life returned to what it was; we want our loved one restored. We want to go back in time . . . if only, if only, if only" (1997: 51). Torres spends three pages on a wide range of "what ifs," but receives no answers and does not attempt to answer them herself. The unavailability of an answer is represented in an intensely disturbing Genie and lamp image. The lamp is emitting a multi-faced ghoul that taunts with guilt and jibes to remind Torres—and the reader—that, no matter how hard she wishes, hopes, and bargains, Eddie will not come back. This is the opposite side to Torres's pleas. Rather than show the asking of the questions and the begging itself, she has chosen to show the frightening replies instead. In order to move on, she must address these questions and accept that there are no answers, only more questions.

As I previously mentioned, Torres's emotions are a fraught jumble; she does not move through the emotions of grief sequentially. Her work of mourning is both a disorderly journey through the unknotting of the traumatic aporia; Torres must learn to confront her trauma before she can move on from it. Acceptance—the fifth stage—is dependent on the mourner's ability to face the truth of the situation. As Kübler-Ross writes, "Learning to live with it—it is the new norm with which we must learn to live, though we wish it were otherwise (1997: 66). It is not possible to say that Torres reaches this point within the text. The issues of her grief are entangled with the national and international nature of the events and her own entry into motherhood. Torres poses the unanswerable question: "What would motherhood be like without widowhood?"

American Widow begins prior to the event itself. Not only does this mean that the text shows the collapse of the World Trade Center "as it happens" within the text but that the reader is also party to Torres's moments of realization. Torres is still reeling from a marital dispute and the aftermath of the argument still hangs over her as the news of the first plane hitting the World Trade Center reaches her by telephone. In four panels, she shows her reaction (2008: 35). Here the reader is presented with a reading challenge. The panels are of uniform size. There is no indication of the amount of time that passes. Readers are left to insert the timespan of these panels with no assistance from Torres; this train of thought can last for ten seconds or ten minutes. The heavy white-on-black contrast makes these images stark and uncomfortable to view. Within four panels is more information than could be covered in a text novel in as much space, though there is little information to suggest how much time passes. However, the reader can extrapolate a sense of timing as the times at which the first tower was initially hit and then collapsed is common knowledge—and as the second tower's collapse is shown in the text. It is at this point in the text that the work of mourning begins, so to speak, and Torres's four-panel reaction captures the mental development of shock.

Later in the same chapter comes a second moment of realization. The final page spread is an image of smoke billowing from the World Trade Center as a tower collapses (2008: 41). Torres's stricken and tear-stained face hovers above this image as she asks after her husband. The most striking feature of this page is the shiver lines that surround the image of the collapsed (or collapsing) tower. It is as if the page itself is shaking with the impact of the collapse as well as representing the trembling reaction to shock. The representation itself is traumatizing. The top-right panel shows a silhouetted image of people on shaking stairs. The implication in the text is that these two events are occurring at the same time: the tower collapses as people rush to escape. This is the last page that records the event "live." The text follows Torres's mourning from the moment of initial realization. The reader's implicit involvement with the construction of the narrative places us in a privileged position, as close as is possible, although not able to breach the void of knowledge that exists between Torres and the reader. The reader cannot be fully party to Torres's experience, but her honest and bold rendering of her experience of mourning can reproduce some part of the experience. The affect this produces is not grief, nor is it trauma, but is instead sadness and sympathy. In these emotions, the reader feels something of what Torres felt, recognizing a measure of our own experiences in hers while also allowing the true emotions of the experience to remain with her and not become a collective emotion.

• • •

The public nature of 9/11 leads *American Widow* to bring up the troublesome issue of "trauma and grief by proxy." David Holloway writes:

> Media coverage of 9/11 . . . helped construct the attacks as trauma by collapsing the distinctions between those who experienced the attacks at first hand and those traumatised by images of them, and between those traumatised in real time and those traumatised after the fact in media replay time. (2008: 64–65)

The intensity of the image—and the repetition of it—resulted in a heightened emotional response in huge numbers of people who were not party to the initial traumatic event—a trauma by proxy, if you will. Leon Wieseltier writes that this was "an event that we never saw, which is precisely the character of collective memory: knowledge made so immediate that it feels like experience" (2002: 38). In line with what Holloway says, the barriers between victims of "actual trauma" and "trauma by proxy" became blurred to the point that very little distinction could be made.[5] The "collectivization" of trauma is evident in many of the 9/11 charity comics, a term I am using to collect together the four anthologies released by Marvel, DC, and Dark Horse to raise money for 9/11 aid charities. These stories are not written by those who were involved in the event itself. Instead, they are the recollections of artists and writers who felt compelled to "write out" their own experiences as Americans and human beings on that day. It would be incorrect to suggest that these artists are latching onto the grief of others. Rather, these artists are telling their own story of what became a hugely important event worldwide. They refer us back to Holloway's words regarding the collective memory of grief: without personal grief, but feeling the need to feel something after such a tragedy, we attach ourselves to the grief of others.

In an article for *Salon*, Torres writes: "As a widow of 9/11 with a new baby, I am on America's patriotic payroll" (2002: online). Her experience is not *just* hers. Her situation makes her a unique but "reluctant" media figure. She is not alone in this. There are many issues with the use of victims of traumatic experience as "poster people" for a certain event because, as Balaev reminds us, "trauma is a lived experience" (2014: 7). Bennett quotes Yazier Henri, who

> has argued that the use of the image of a "victim" as a trigger for an affective response is a violation of the individual depicted. Such a strategy is presumptuous—even if well intentioned—because it fails to respect the dignity and autonomy of the subject, reducing him or her to a cipher of victimhood. (2005: 64)

Torres is a reluctant media icon—to become a media icon is to become a cipher and thus to lose one's own experience to the realm of "collective experience." She fights against this loss of personal experiences within the text, and two episodes discuss it explicitly. In the first, a woman tells Torres that she televised her child's birth (the woman was presumably, like Torres, pregnant and lost her husband on 9/11). In the second, Torres talks on the phone to a man who insists that, since she did one interview, she is needed for more.

In both conversations, Torres's reluctance to be involved in the media is palpable. This leads us, logically, to ask why she decided to write (and publish) a book on the topic that would surely push her further into the spotlight. However, one gets the sense throughout the text that Torres is not "against the media" at all; instead, she is against the media's way of doing media. On her own terms, she is happier and better able to face the camera. Writing *American Widow* gave her the opportunity to speak out on her own terms. There is a second layer to this. The drawings throughout the text are very plain; the faces could be the faces of any number of people, allowing us to impose ourselves on the narrative much more easily. This is a common technique in comics—the simpler the faces, the easier it is for readers to implant themselves into the story. In *American Widow*, the simplicity of drawing is asking us how we would feel about giving birth on television: "Would I want to be interviewed as a '9/11 widow'?" This question remains throughout the entire text.

The events within the text are things that are unexceptional—buying a dress, answering the phone on the bus, sitting in bed—but they are all tainted by the event that came before (2008: 66). Torres is placing us into ordinary situations with extraordinary knowledge and asking us: How would you deal with this situation? What would you do or say differently? In her use of the comics form to ask these questions, Torres is able to illustrate the context in which she exists. This does not necessarily make it any easier for us to empathize with her position. It serves to both help and to hinder our understanding: to help, by showing us her experiences of grief in stark visual manner, but to hinder, by the unavoidable distance between reader and text that does not let us fully enter into the experience of the author.

American Widow contains both Torres's mourning and healing. This is most clearly illustrated by two parts of the book. First, the book's cover shows a picture of Eddie and Alissa that occurs in the body of the text in a flashback to their first date. The fact that the picture shows them from behind suggests that they are looking into the text; Eddie's arm supporting Alissa in it and through it. When reading the text itself, the image becomes all the more poignant and the film noir effect created by the limited use of color makes the image of Eddie appear both ghostlike and enduring. The second illustration comes at the book's conclusion. At the end of the narrative—which falls on September 10, 2002—Torres and her son travel to Hawaii. The final few pages show a boat in the ocean and the view zooms out over a number of panels to reveal the islands and the sea in a similar way to that which one might see in a film. The last two-page spread shows two separate images. On one side, a photograph of Torres and her son snorkeling; on the other, a plain blue sky—a repetition of the book's first page (2008: 210).

The inclusion of the photograph needs little explanation—it is an image to measure "how far we have come," reminding the reader of the autobiographical nature of what has gone before and of the complex nature of autobiographical writing, as I outline in the introduction to this book. That the photograph is not drawn in the same style as the rest of the images but is reproduced "as a photograph" creates what Groensteen calls "a semiotic break" (2013: 100). It causes the reader to pause and to be reminded of the graphic nature of what they have been reading; this technique is used to similar effect in Spiegelman's *Maus* and Tran's *Vietnamerica*. In *American Widow*, Torres depicts the cyclical nature of human history and experience. At the end of the text, with the return to the pale blue sky, coupled with the suddenness of the TV screens at the beginning, the reader is asked to be aware that tragedy does not give a warning. This suggestion of cyclicity makes the ending ambiguous. However, when paired with the text's epigraph, an alternative interpretation arises. The epigraph is taken from a report in the *New York Times*:

Everything the people of Beslan thought they knew about living, his aunt said, had changed. She rubbed bits of the filament of eggshell onto the boy's blisters and burns, and said the lesson was indelible: "We never knew how happy we were." (Chivers in Torres, 2008: n.p.)

This quotation is attested to repeatedly in the text. Alissa is angry at Eddie and so they part on poor terms. It is only after he has died that she realizes just how much she has lost. This quotation contains an invisible "if only" that receives no answer. It speaks of the regret and lonely bargaining seen in Kübler-Ross's third stage. But more than that, placing this quotation in relation to the cycle of history and the traumatic text creates a call to live in the moment. Torres writes throughout the text that she was living "one day at a time"; this quotation asks us why people live like this after a tragedy. It is only at the end of the text—and Torres's closing words—that there is some sort of resolution of this issue. Torres writes: "Although I was so confused by who I was and how I was supposed to be, I knew so fiercely that I was alive, together with my son, and that it was a beautiful day" (2008: 210). In this single sentence, Torres accepts her situation and her own state of grief. Many of the conflicts within the text are unresolved—and will always remain so; there is still much healing to do. This is as much "closure" as one will receive but, for Torres, it is sufficient.

Collective Mourning and Communal Grief

The depiction of mourning ritual and shrines has much precedent in the literature of conflict, as already seen in *The Iliad*, *Le Morte D'Arthur*, and *Beowulf*. In these texts, the result of conflict is death and destruction and, as such, the depictions of mourning are outpourings of grief and anguish, rather than an attempt to reconcile the ego and restore psychic balance—the harrowing conclusion to a destructive text. The 9/11 charity comics do not handle mourning in this fashion. For them, it is not the end of the story, but rather another period within it. The images of shrines suggest that there is somewhere to move onto—an acceptance that the work of mourning is neither irrelevant nor complete. This gives the texts an aura of hope that is missing in many other conflict comics, in which the overwhelming horror of the traumatic experience keeps the text and its characters locked in traumatic limbo.

The presence of shrines and mourning rituals is not only indicative of communal grief and healthy emotional regeneration; it also serves as a way to "bear witness" to the event. Cooper and Atkinson write that 9/11 was "distinguished [from] other human atrocities . . . by the lack of actual images of human carnage" (Cooper and Atkinson, 2008: 69). Rather than producing (as has been the case in many previous situations) large numbers of photographs of the human casualties of the event, photographic representation of 9/11 concentrated more on the heroism of emergency responders, "people grieving at the site of the attack without depiction of the site itself [or] people viewing depictions of the site of the attack" (Zelizer, 2003: 51). In the charity comics, it is superheroes who are seen bearing witness and presiding over shrines:

> The act of witnessing is the only form of action because the superheroes could not intervene in an event that has already occurred. Mourning and witnessing become heroic acts where the anguished expressions and muscular stances of the exceptional figures serve as indexical signs marking out the event in history. (Cooper and Atkinson, 2008: 70)

Joe Kubert's single-page comic in *Heroes* shows a shrine constructed amongst rubble and posters of missing people (2001: 4). Captain America's shield forms part of the shrine; it appears to have been placed as an offering. Its presence here can be read in two different ways. First, the shield is an image of strength and power to defend the nation, an image compounded by its physical qualities and indestructibility. Its presence at the shrine is a desire to imbue those represented here with these same qualities. Cap is unable to help, but wishes to share his superhuman ability with those who can. An alternative reading of this image sees Cap's shield not as being offered but being discarded. Just as superheroes are rendered powerless, so their brand of macho vigilantism has no place in the shrines and rituals of the 9/11 aftermath. Kubert's image makes no comment on how the placement of the shield is supposed to be read. However, the central part of the image shows a fireman's helmet and jacket, both more visibly presented and physically larger than the shield, lessening its status as a tool of heroism. The courage and strength that has defined Cap as a superhero pales in comparison to the qualities of the first responders on 9/11. In Kubert's splash page, their heroism far outshines that of the superheroes because they have no magical abilities to help them. They are ordinary people, working in extraordinary ways.

• • •

Many of the 9/11 charity comics use images of religious ritual in relation to mourning and funeral ritual. In "Ayekah," the liturgy of Rosh Hashanah (Jewish New Year) is combined with a narrative of post-9/11 mourning (Boyd,

2002: 168–69). Although the comic mostly uses captioning, the first page's captions are split into two categories: a retelling of the story of Abraham and Isaac, part of the traditional Rosh Hashanah liturgy, and a series of short quotations which the reader is led to assume are from the depicted fireman's wife, stating their intent to travel from Boston—presumably on one of the planes that crashed into the World Trade Center. The second page uses captions of the biblical passage only, ending with a single tier-length panel in which the fireman is calling "Here I am!" This is the same line that Abraham calls out when God is testing him. The biblical narrative of Abraham is generally read as being a test of faith—will Abraham's love and devotion to God be strong enough that he will follow all commands, even when they involve the death of his son? His cry of "Hineini!" ("Here I am!") is his ascent to duty. Thus, the fireman is a modern-day Abraham, facing his test of faith with courage and conviction. The juxtaposition of the biblical story of Abraham's test and the fireman's call to duty allows the fireman to be seen as one who is doing work that is in accordance with a call from God.

"Ayekah" is presented in high-contrast format, a style made famous by Frank Miller in *Sin City*. This style uses only black and white, playing with the effects of light and shadow to create highly effective images. However, the starkness of these images—and the discomfort one experiences while viewing them—mirrors the bleakness and lack of comfort within the narrative. The two pages are presented verso-recto, requiring no page turn. The first page is presented with consistently sized and evenly spaced panels. This becomes disjointed on the second page, where, although the tiers remain evenly sized, the panels are not uniform. The panel transitions employed are atypical. The vast majority of transitions in American (and, more generally, Western) comics fit McCloud's second category definition of action-to-action transitions: "a single subject in distinct progression" (1994: 70–74). While there are some action-to-action transitions here, the majority are aspect-to-aspect transitions, as shown in the analysis of "Dust" in Chapter 1. This particular type of transition is not often used in Western comics, meaning that a Western comics reader will not be familiar with it. This unfamiliarity alone will create an air of unease in the text.

The depiction of religious ritual in "Ayekah" introduces a major theme in the depictions of mourning and ritual in the charity comics. In "Ayekah," the fireman lights the traditional pair of candles and recites the *Shehecheyanu* blessing. The candles are present throughout the comic. Candles occur frequently throughout the charity comics as a symbol of mourning and the lighting of them becomes a key part of the ritual. The use of candles in mourning rituals has roots that can be traced back thousands of years and is prevalent in the vast majority of religions and secular belief systems. Indeed, candles are presented as symbols of mourning and memorialization without comment in most of the comics. In "Untitled," a mother Dalmatian tucks her children into bed, while her son asks her about the whereabouts of his father (Fields, 2002: 59).[6] The dialogue begins mid-sentence, with the mother explaining the job of firemen. The dialogue would suggest that their father is working a night shift. However, in the background there is a large framed picture of him, surrounded by lit candles and next to his fireman's helmet. While the children are placated by the mother's answers, the reader is aware, simply by the presence of the shrine, that the father is dead. In this comic, the candles are part of a shrine, a trope that is repeated throughout the charity comics. However, in "Ayekah" there is one further aspect of ritual and mourning. By going through the ritual of the Rosh Hashanah prayers and rites, the fireman gains strength. It is the words of the Torah that give him the strength to answer his call to duty (Boyd, 2002: 169).

Boyd structures his comic around the framework of Jewish funeral rites. In a similar style, Art Spiegelman's short comic "Prisoner on the Hell Planet" (reproduced within the body of the text of *Maus*) is built around the suicide and funeral of Spiegelman's mother, Anja. Unlike "Ayekah," in which the protagonist draws strength from ritual and faith, Spiegelman suggests that rite and ritual have provided no comfort at all. He describes the rituals of shiva, the period of mourning traditional in Judaism, as being a dreadful and discomforting experience: "That first night was bad . . . my father insisted we sleep on the floor—an old Jewish custom. He held me and moaned to himself all night. I was uncomfortable. We were scared!" (Spiegelman, 2003: 104). Spiegelman wishes to make it very clear that his experience of mourning rituals has done little to alleviate his disquietude. A bandeau panel of his mother's funeral makes this abundantly clear, as his father throws himself, screaming, onto the coffin and Art looks on in startled shock.

In contrast to the clean lines and the high ratio of white to black in the artwork in "Ayekah," "Prisoner on the Hell Planet" is visually distressing, the artistic style being representative of the extreme mental anguish Art is experiencing. The images themselves are reminiscent of German Expressionist woodcuts of the early twentieth century. There is also little stylistic commonality between this comic and the rest of *Maus*, in which the facial expressions of his characters are minimal and very little facial detail is given at all. Instead, Spiegelman produces figures with grotesquely distorted faces and misshapen bodies.

"Prisoner on the Hell Planet" gives us a very different picture of mourning from that which has been presented in other conflict comics; the text's relationship to conflict (in this instance, the Holocaust) may appear tenuous on first reading but in truth the Holocaust permeates the entire narrative. The text ends with a three-panel tier as the viewer moves away from Spiegelman locked in a stereotypical prison cell, berating his mother for her suicide and its effect on him (2003: 105). Rather than a vigorous call to action, here is a prisoner of grief. Spiegelman's imprisonment within his own emotions is clearly represented by the fact he draws himself in the uniform of an Auschwitz prisoner. The inclusion of "Prisoner on the Hell Planet" is the only discussion of mourning that arises in *Maus*. At no point in the rest of the text is this issue discussed; it is conspicuous by its absence. Indeed, this embargo on the subject makes the inclusion of this short comic all the more powerful. Its strong contrast to the rest of the text is instantly unnerving, as is the shift in perspective from Art's father, Vladek's, unemotional testimony of the Holocaust to Art's intensely personal rendering. In both *American Widow* and the 9/11 charity comics, the work of mourning is healthy and constructive, aiming to allow the participants to heal themselves, while still accepting and recognizing the magnitude of what has occurred. For Spiegelman, the silent trauma of the effect of his parents' experiences on him, which I discuss in Chapter 4, and the guilt that has arisen from this together create a complex traumatic wound that reaches a bursting point when his mother commits suicide. The complexity of the experience—the amount of personal guilt and instability that is bound up in it—means that Art's grief becomes melancholia. Freud defines melancholia as being the result of an unhealthy work of mourning: "The patient allows the loss to absorb him entirely.... He vilifies himself and expects to be cast out and punished" (2002: 245). This type of mourning is demonstrated in the final tier, depicted previously, in which Art declares, "You murdered me, Mommy, and you left me here to take the rap!!!"

"Ayekah" is explicit in its declaration of strength through faith, but that is not to say that strength and comfort is to be found solely in religious rites. The use of candles in mourning is also found in secular memorialization. Ritual can be intensely comforting, even when not imbued with religious significance. Indeed, it is a common idea that funerals are held for the benefit of the living and not the deceased, to bring succor and closure. For Torres, the funeral of Eddie does not offer closure; she must continue her battle with various organizations for aid and also the return of his personal effects. However, the inclusion of rituals of mourning in both *American Widow* and the 9/11 charity comics emphasizes their importance in the completion of a healthy work of mourning and healing of the psychic rift caused by the traumatic event itself. While none of these comics comment on the hope of a positive future, they are not devoid of hope entirely. The emphasis on both individual heroism and the communal courage of New York's first responders works to counteract some of the intense trauma that is felt in these comics. *American Widow* ends with an overall feeling of hope for Alissa and her son, while "Ayekah" is a demonstration of strength and hope through faith. Although these texts have a generally positive ending, both deny the reader total closure. Can there be closure for the reader when there is no closure for the traumatized individual?

3

Trauma Invading Sleep

Long have they pass'd, faces and trenches and fields,
Where through the carnage I moved with a callous composure, or away from the fallen,
Onward I sped at the time—but now of their forms at night,
I dream, I dream, I dream.
—**Walt Whitman**, "Old War Dreams" (1855)

On returning from his second tour with the US Army in Vietnam, Adam Blaine began a long cycle of psychotherapy, medication, and intermittent hospitalization that continues to this day.[1] He describes in detail the nightmares that became the defining feature of his trauma. The nightmares that Blaine described were vivid re-enactments of the events at My Lai; they recount with horrible accuracy his movements on that day. Such nightmares have been an enduring part of Blaine's life since the early 1970s, beginning shortly after the My Lai tribunal. The disruptions they have caused to his daily life have meant that he has never held down a job and has been divorced three times. Blaine blames the repetitive nightmares for his broken life; he is not unusual in this respect. According to the clinical picture alone, an estimated 78 percent of Vietnam veterans reported nightmares following their return to the US (Davis et al, 2007: 190)—this figure increases to 96 percent in individuals with a diagnosis of PTSD and another condition, such as Panic Disorder, Generalized Anxiety Disorder, or Episodic Paroxysmal Anxiety (Davis et al., 2007: 201). When considering the nature and effects of traumatic dreaming, it is difficult to navigate through the various clinical and psychoanalytical standpoints while also ensuring that the trauma remains with the individual and does not become diluted into a mere metaphor. The problem is further compounded when it becomes apparent how little is understood about dreaming, its reasons, and developments.

The aim of this chapter is to discuss the basic nature of traumatic dreaming and its relationship to trauma comics. I begin with an outline of the psychological and psychoanalytical theories of dreams, using both clinical research and Freud's *The Interpretation of Dreams*, specifically his four-part description of the dreamwork. Following this, I consider the relationship between the comics form and the creation of the dream using a Freudian analytical framework. As is the case throughout this text, I use Freud's works as a tool to assist in breaking down a complex and deeply personal manifestation of trauma. I am not claiming that Freud's dream theory is the only way that one can analyze dreams in any context, let alone trauma, but given his interest in the intensely visual nature of the dream, I find his work to be fitting. I construct a close analysis of dream sequences in comics, discussing their formal construction and their purpose within both the narrative and the overall representation of trauma within each comic.

Neuropsychology, Psychoanalysis, and Traumatic Dreaming

Dreams are a recurring issue throughout psychological and clinical studies in trauma.[2] Harry Wilmer states that "war nightmares are a unique form of dreams—there are no other dreams like them" (1996: 85). Caruth makes the point that it is in the nightmares of the sufferer that the traumatic neurosis makes itself known. Similarly, for Herman, disturbance of dreams and a tendency towards nightmares are two of the most common—and often most terrifying—symptoms of a traumatic experience. The relationship of the dream state to consciousness becomes a factor here. Traumatic neuroses exist outside of consciousness and it is because of this location within the psychic self that they are incomprehensible. Dreams, too, occupy a space that exists in an awkward relationship to consciousness because they occur during sleep. However, as with all aspects of traumatic experience, traumatic dreaming is not universal. Balaev reminds us that "psychological research indicates that amnesia, dissociation, or repression *may* be responses to trauma but they are not exclusive responses" (2014: 6, emphasis in original). To this I add dreaming—it may be that the individual has nightmares but such is not always the case. The focus on traumatic dreaming in representations of trauma may suggest that they are among the most common experiences of traumatized individuals; it is likely that the heavy emphasis is based on the visual nature of the dream, which translates well to screen or page.

There is another factor pertaining to trauma and traumatic dreams that is of special relevance to the study of comics. Herman contends that "trauma is encoded in vivid sensations and images"; there is an immediate relationship between the comics form and the nature of trauma (1992: 38). Comics is a visual medium and trauma is typically seen to be encoded in image and sensation more than in word. Therefore, comics tends to hold a privileged relationship to the representation of traumatic experience because form and content can be paired so effectively; in relation to traumatic dreams, this relationship is particularly clear, as I show in this chapter.

• • •

At this juncture, I wish to give a brief explanation of neuropsychological studies into traumatic dreaming that have assisted in shaping both definitions of nightmares and wider definitions of trauma and PTSD. I should make the point that nightmares in the form of bad dreams are not as uncommon as one may expect in the adult civilian population: 5 percent report having nightmares regularly (Hamblen, 2011: online). As Ernest Hartmann explains, the content of nightmares can be anything but "almost always involves the dreamer being chased, threatened, or wounded by some sort of attacker . . . there is almost always danger of some kind to the dreamer" (1996: 102). These types of nightmares typically do not recreate a specific event and are not usually treatable with medication. In contrast, "the characteristic terrifying nightmare of the actual [traumatic] event is as if it were recorded by *cinema verité*. The dream portrays a single event in recurrent replays" (Wilmer, 1996: 88). For the purposes of clarity, I will use the terms "nightmare" and "traumatic dream" to refer to the dreams that arise from a traumatic rupture, but with the awareness that what I am discussing differs from the clinical understanding of these terms and I make this distinction where necessary.

Given that nightmares are a common symptom of a traumatic rupture, it naturally follows that they would be the subject of considerable academic research and clinical interest.[3] One of the key proponents of traumatic dream research is Bessel van der Kolk, who coordinated the first (and, to date, largest) study of nightmares in veterans at a Veterans Affairs outpatient clinic, in which 410 individuals completed detailed questionnaires. Of this initial group, thirty were selected for further interviews (van der Kolk et al., 1984: 187). The study showed that "the chronic traumatic nightmares of men who had been in combat (PTSD) were found to differ from the lifelong nightmares of veterans with no combat experience (LL)" (1984: 187). In his paper on the same study, Hartmann discusses the two main groups: the study contained a further "control" group of men who had "severe combat experience but had no history of nightmares" (1984: 187). The study sought to investigate whether

Table 1 – "Who Develops PTSD Nightmares and Who Doesn't," Ernest Hartmann, 1997: 107.		Group 1 PTSD (N=15)	Group 2 LL (N=10)
When nightmare occurs in sleep cycle			
Beginning (2300 to 0200)		4	1
Middle (0200 to 0430)		11	3
End		0	4
Nightmare replicates an actual event	Yes	11	0
	No	4	10
Nightmare is repetitive in content	Yes	15	3
	No	0	6
Body movements concurrent with nightmare	Yes	15	0
	No	0	8
Positive effect of medication on nightmares	Yes	8	2
	No	4	7
Positive effect of psychotherapy on nightmares	Yes	6	2
	No	2	5

there are any differences between "regular" nightmares and traumatic nightmares. The features of nightmares that were identified went beyond the narrative content of the dream itself and also considered treatment options, sleep movement, and the time of the nightmare within the sleep cycle. The findings from the two groups are shown in the following table:

• • •

The differences shown in this table are clear. Hartmann states that "repetitive post-traumatic nightmares are not nightmares" in the traditional sense and "could be induced by a slight 'nudge' or mini-arousal" (1996: 105–106). Traumatic nightmares have a closer relationship to waking flashbacks than to non-traumatic nightmares: "the same post-traumatic nightmare sequence involving the same content can occur not only during various stages of sleep but during waking" (Hartmann, 1996: 108). I do offer the disclaimer that, as with much trauma studies clinical research (and as previously mentioned), this study is again focused on male veteran experience. However, as I am analyzing representations of these very subjects, there is no major disjunction between comics representation and clinical research groups. I have discussed clinical literature in order to confirm that traumatized patients suffer from nightmares that are of a different nature from those experienced by non-traumatized patients.

To complement my study representations of traumatic dreams in comics, I use Freud's *The Interpretation of Dreams* (1899) in considering the nature and structure of the dream. Freud's dreamwork provides a useful tool for the analysis of the formal features of dreaming. For Freud, the nightmare of the survivor of trauma is connected to a conscious mental block:

> I am not aware . . . that patients suffering from traumatic neurosis are much occupied in their waking lives with memories of their accident. Perhaps they are more concerned with *not* thinking about it. (2003: 13)

By this reckoning, it appears logical that that which is consciously avoided during waking hours is unable to be contained during sleep. However, Freud challenges this idea:

> Anyone who accepts it as something self-evident that their dreams should put them back into the situation that caused them to fall ill has misunderstood the nature of dreams. It would be more in harmony with their nature if they showed the patient pictures from his healthy past or of the cure for which he hopes. . . . We may argue that the function of dreaming, like so much else, is upset in this condition and diverted from its purposes. (2003: 13)

Rather than dreams being the place in which the traumatic neurosis is presented to the individual, it is another case of the trauma's intrusion into the mind: "Freud stated that dreams in war neuroses were better viewed as fear enactments" (Barrett, 1991: 412). The traumatic rupture is one that effects all aspects of the individual's mind. However, the basic nature of the dream—the method of construction and stages of representation that latent content goes through to become manifest—sets it apart from waking recollections; the fact that dreams exist in tenuous relationship to consciousness and are created through the dreamwork makes them different from flashbacks and other waking recollections.

In order to discuss Freud's theories of dreaming more fully, I turn to a self-proclaimed Freudian, Jacques Lacan, who claims that the dream holds a different meaning in relation to trauma. I should add here that I am very much aware of the issues of using these psychoanalysts. Balaev writes that the traditional Lacanian approach only works if the psychological definition of trauma conforms to a particular theoretical recipe that draws from Freud to portray traumatic experience as a prelinguistic event that universally causes dissociation. (2014: 2)

There are obvious issues with using Freud's and Lacan's work on dreams and trauma, but I intend to do so for two reasons. First, as so little is known about the nature of dreams, I use their work to provide a framework for my analysis. I am not seeking to create clinical analyses of the texts at hand but am providing a literary analysis; the scientific accuracy of the framework is secondary to its usefulness as a literary tool. Secondly, I am not necessarily agreeing with the view of Freud and Lacan that dissociation is universal; indeed, I am aware that it is not, as I have previously mentioned, but in comics representations of traumatic dreams, this dissociation *does* appear as a common feature.

Lacan writes that "awakening [from dreams] is itself the site of a trauma" (1977: 25). This comment is made in relation to one of the shortest and most famous of Freud's dream analyses, commonly known as "the dream of the burning boy":

A father had been watching day and night beside the sick-bed of his child. After the child died, he retired to rest in an adjoining room, but left the door ajar so that he could look from his room into the next, where the child's body lay surrounded by tall candles. An old man, who had been installed as a watcher, sat beside the body, murmuring prayers. After sleeping for a few hours the father dreamed that the child was standing by his bed, clasping his arm and crying reproachfully: "Father, don't you see that I am burning?" The father woke up and noticed a bright light coming from the adjoining room. Rushing in, he found that the old man had fallen asleep, and the sheets and one arm of the beloved boy were burnt by a fallen candle. (Freud, 1991: 652)

For Lacan, it is the act of waking that is the key to this dream. While in the dream, the father remains with the child in an ideal state—he sees his child as alive. As Caruth writes, the act of awakening represents

the inevitability of responding . . . awakening to the survival of the child that is now only a corpse . . . the father, who would have stayed inside the dream to see his child alive once more, is commanded by the same child to leave the dream and awaken. . . . To awaken is thus to bear the imperative to survive. (Caruth, 1996: 105)

Awakening, then, repeats the trauma. The father sees his son alive in a dream but must awaken to the traumatic realization that his son is dead. The action of waking—of opening one's eyes—is a reopening of the traumatic wound. Furthermore, it re-emphasizes for the traumatized individual the absurdity of one's own survival, thus returning us to this key facet of trauma once more.

• • •

In *The Interpretation of Dreams* (1899), Freud divides the "dreamwork"—that is, the processes behind the creation of dreams—into four stages: condensation, distortion, representation, and secondary revision. Each manifest image within a dream does not necessarily equal one item of latent content; one manifest image may represent a multitude of latent images. Freud gives the example of a dream regarding one of his patients, Irma, in which the figure of Irma stands for many of the women in his life; one image is a condensation of many. Freud states that although this can be seen as a form of translation, there are many substantial differences:

> a translation usually strives to respect the discriminations expressed in the text, and to differentiate similar things. The dream-work, on the contrary, tries to fuse two different thoughts by looking ... for an ambiguous word which shall act as a connecting link between the two thoughts. (Freud, 2001b: 171)

Although two or more items of latent content may condense into one manifest image, the relationship between them may be convoluted.

The convolution of the dream image is echoed in the second part of the dreamwork, distortion, a term which draws our attention to the fact that the latent content of the dream is distorted by a variety of techniques. In *Studies in Hysteria*, Freud uses the term "überdeterminierung" ("over-determination") to describe that multiple causation for a single symptom or manifest image (Freud and Breuer, 2001: 43). That is to say, a single image or event within the dream may have roots traceable to several different causes and it is likely that there is no "right answer" as to which, if any, is the singular cause. Thus, the repetition of images in the dream may be the same item of latent content repeated in varying forms—*over*-determined. This links the process of the dream with the process of the traumatic neurosis, the unconscious repetition of images and sensation.

The next stage of the dreamwork—the stage that is most pertinent when considering traumatic representation in comics—is the "consideration of representability [consisting] of transforming thoughts into visual images" (Freud, 2001b: 207). This stage questions why each item of latent content is included in a dream and why the latent content is translated into each item of manifest content. However, Freud is quick to point out that these questions are unanswerable due to the very nature of the dreamwork. The selection of images that combine to create a dream is an unconscious process and thus resists analysis. The mission of dream analysis is to trace the manifest content of the dream to its latent roots. The images that persist in the dreams, flashbacks, and repetitions of a traumatic neurosis are similarly constructed, being separated from consciousness and often being a smaller part of the overarching traumatic event.

If the visual and sensational output of the traumatic neurosis can be likened to the manifest content of the dream, the latent content can be likened to the original traumatic event. Just as the analyst of dreams must work through the manifest content to understand the reasons for the dream's creation and the meaning, if any, contained within, so too must the analyst of trauma be able to work through the symptoms of a traumatic neurosis to uncover the (latent) event that sits at its root. What the trauma artist must then do is to take the latent content and translate it, along with the manifest content, into a piece of art—be it literature, comics, film, or another form—that can help the reader to understand some aspect of the traumatic experience. It is here that the artist of trauma faces the enormous task of representing their trauma in a way that will show others (some part of) its horror, especially when the subject fully understands the full horror or importance of the traumatic event.

The final stage of the dreamwork concerns what Freud terms "secondary revision." The first two stages of the dreamwork are a disguise; they hide the latent content of the dream in convoluted images and distortions. Secondary revision is a second-order disguise. It hides the disguise. It is this stage that conceals the contradictory and improbable material of the manifest content within a seemingly normal narrative. If, for example, a dream has a particularly filmic nature, this is attributed to the influence of secondary revision on the other parts of the dream work. The seeming normality of the situation within the dream will conceal all traces of abnormality of image or subject matter.

The Freudian dreamwork and the construction of traumatic dreams are very different. While Freud's dreamwork is concerned with the construction of the dream narrative itself—and specifically the interplay of latent and manifest content—traumatic dreams and nightmares do not undergo the same process because they are direct renderings of a specific event. There is no relationship between the latent and the manifest because the latent level does not exist as it does in the dreams of a healthy mind; while there is a latent level in traumatic dreams, the manifestation of the dream does not necessarily conceal deeper meanings. Despite these differences, both theories are relevant to the representation of traumatic dreaming in comics. Comics creators use their own experiences of dreaming, as well as expectations of what a traumatic dream should be like, in conjunction with comics-specific techniques in the construction of the representative dream sequences. For the purposes of this chapter, I have divided the dreams analyzed into two sections: dreams of traumatic experience and dreams of traumatic loss, while recognizing that there will inevitably be overlaps.

• • •

Dreams exist on a separate level of consciousness than waking life, as does trauma; the individual does not experience the dream in the same way as other memories (or waking life). Within the text, the dream occupies a separate narrative level to the overarching narrative. In his 1972 work *Narrative Discourse*, Gérard Genette proposes that narrative occurs in levels. The main plot of the story occurs at the extradiegetic level; the events within the story are intradiegetic. An embedded narrative—for example, a character telling a story within the body of the main narrative—sits at the metadiegetic level. Dreams exist in the text at the metadiegetic level. The inclusion of a dream sequence, while not necessarily crucial to the narrative flow, assists in the development of the character and the mood of the scene; while a dream may not add anything to the movement of the storyline, it will heighten the sense of the traumatic within the text, as well as create affect.

The inclusion of a dream introduces another dimension to the text. According to Genette, metalepsis is a method of playing with variations in narrative level in order to create an effect of illusion or disquietude. A metaleptical move within a text can occur between any narrative level, but in the case of dream sequences, the shift is from metadiegetic to intradiegetic. The narrative has moved from an embedded narrative (the dream) to the events within the story itself. As Genette suggests, this can create unease within the narrative, not simply because the reader must reposition themselves within the text and re-assimilate the events of the dream into the text at the correct narrative level, but also because the shift in itself is unsettling. To make sense of our own dreams can be difficult enough, but the added traumatic dimension—the fact the dream may make little coherent sense or includes manifest content that is distressing to consider—often makes this impossible; this difficulty to codify one's dreams is key to the understanding of traumatic dreaming as a whole. The visual nature of the dream lends itself well to representation in

Fig. 3.1. "Three Day Pass" in *The 'Nam Volume 1*, Murray and Golden, 2009. p 12. © Marvel Entertainment.

comics form; the near-impossibility of mentally collating traumatic dreams when awake—as well as the trauma of waking—is made manifest in the metaleptical leaps that can be seen in these comics renderings. Comics, then, can represent traumatic dreams effectively not only because it is a visual medium, but because the physical space of the comic itself is suitable for creating visually effective narrative shifts.

Dreams of Traumatic Experience

As I have previously stated, dreams that recreate a specific event are generally considered to be a common experience of a traumatized individual. Many comics of conflict use dreams to assist in their representations of trauma but they are not necessarily constructed in line with how clinical research claims that traumatic dreams work. These dreams are narrative devices within the wider comics story arc and, as such, are not meant to be clinically accurate representations of traumatic dreams. Moreover, the need for comics (or any medium) to be artistically striking requires the artist to look beyond the literal representation and create something that is both representative of the traumatic event at hand, visually arresting, and able to create affect.

According to van de Kolk's research, the majority of traumatic nightmares begin after the individual is in a safe environment. For example, most Vietnam veterans did not begin to experience nightmares until at least three months after returning home; some do not experience nightmares until several years later (van der Kolk et al., 1984: 188). It is rare for the nightmares to begin while the individual is still in the midst of the traumatic event or series of events; however, as with all aspects of trauma, this is dependent on the individual. Despite this, one of the most vivid and dramatic renderings of a traumatic dream is found in *The 'Nam* issue "Three Day Pass."

• • •

The story follows Ed, Mike, and Lonnie on a three-day R & R pass in Saigon. In the early hours of their second day, a group of Vietcong soldiers blow up the hotel in which they are staying, resulting in Lonnie being injured. The hotel explosion rouses Ed in the middle of a graphic and terrifying nightmare. The nightmare image acts as an encapsulation of the events that Ed has experienced during his time in Vietnam. The wedge-shaped panel shows Ed's sleeping face at the very bottom, cast in a blue light to suggest darkness in his bedroom. His face is slightly contorted in a worried expression, with a knitted brow and open lips. In terms of Genette's narrative levels, Ed sits at the intradiegetic level. Behind him, as if radiating out from him, is the action of the dream, the intrusion of the metadiegetic on the intradiegetic—metalepsis. As suggested by Genette, the metaleptical effect of this panel creates a sense of illusion and disquiet. The reader's eye is immediately drawn to the repeated image of a Vietnamese woman in *ao dai* who appears to walk from the top of the image to the bottom, getting bigger as she moves. In the smaller, full-length images she appears to be holding out her hand, but in the final image—a close-up of her face—she is holding a gun. This is a reference to an incident earlier in the same issue where the naïve Ed leaves a Saigon nightclub with a young woman (it is implied that she is a prostitute) and is then nearly robbed and shot in an alley. Around the girl are realistic images of Ed's colleagues in the heat of battle; cartridge cases pepper the panel. No figure is shown completely; they are shown only by close-ups of their faces (and several pairs of legs). In the background at the top of the image is a Vietnamese village, with a host of traditionally dressed civilians in shadow.

Throughout the series, *The 'Nam* uses bold, high-contrast colors; violent scenes are often rendered in bright greens, purples, and pinks to create a vivid visual effect. However, the coloration is *either* vibrant and clashing *or* "typical" (*id est* items are depicted in the colors they naturally are). In the nightmare panel, these two color styles combine; the bold atypical coloring of Ed and the girl clashes with the typical coloring of the rest of the panel. This contrast confirms for the reader that this is a dream sequence and adds to the visual chaos within the frame. The dream can be read in the light of both Freudian dreamwork and clinical understandings of dreaming. In line with van der Kolk's study, Ed's nightmare retells actual events. But a Freudian analysis can also be performed. The condensation stage can be read as represented in the repeated figure of the woman; her presence and the addition of the gun is the attempted mugging incident neatly condensed into one image. Similarly, distortion is present in the recurrent images of Ed's colleagues' faces and discharging weapons. The event that is being represented here is not evident—it could be many events in one image, making this an excellent example of overdetermination. The same could be suggested of the repeated image of the woman. The third stage, consideration of representability, is more difficult to recognize in comics because it is an unanswerable question to begin with.

In relation to comics, let us consider why the artist chose each item within the dream sequence. This dream is relatively straightforward. Ed's colleagues are important to him and so images of them in peril are likely to traumatize him. Their presence in the dream—most of them screaming and shooting—can be read as a substitute for his own image in the dream. The inclusion of the woman has two potential reasons, both of which may be relevant. First, the events in the alley had only just happened and were still fresh in Ed's mind. More serious, however, is the implication of a prostitute with a gun. To Ed, who has little experience of women in general, the human act of sex (and the notion of physical closeness) has become bound up with violence and death, heightening the traumatic experience of an attempted mugging. That this dream has no discernible coherent narrative strand heightens the traumatic chaos of the dream itself; the abundance of visual material—manifest content—intensifies the visual chaos.

The dream is presented in one panel that takes up roughly half the page. That it is confined within a frame immediately contains the event in time, removing the timelessness that would occur if it was presented as a bleed. However, the gutters that separate this panel from the adjacent two are not uniform. Rather, the panels appear to overlap at the bottom corners and then are separated by a gradually widening gutter that divides them lengthways. This atypical guttering has two effects on the page and the narrative. First, it is unusual enough to create a destabilizing effect on the reading of the page; the page lacks a comfortable, uniform layout and instead mimics the chaos of the dream. Secondly, the fact that the panels gradually separate suggests a distancing from reality, while the overlapping suggests that the two events of the panels (Ed sleeping and dreaming and the explosion in the hotel) influence each other. The layout of the two panels, then, suggests both a cognitive separation of dream and reality and also an implication that the violence that surrounds him in sleep is, in part, responsible for the content of Ed's dream. Here there are echoes of Freud's "dream of the burning boy" in that it is the action directly outside of the sleeper while they sleep which influences the construction for the dream.

Despite being contained in one panel, this dream's inclusion in the narrative assists in the development of the wider story arc. This dream makes the reader aware of the impact of combat on Ed's emotional and mental health. The fact that this traumatic sequence occurs so early in the overall comic series emphasizes the seriousness of combat trauma, as well as the high probability that Ed (and, by extension, most conscripted soldiers) will suffer from symptoms of a traumatic rupture and that these symptoms will have a profound effect on their daily living for a long period of time. This dream also underscores the relative *naiveté* and immaturity of Ed and many other conscripted soldiers.[4] Clinical research suggests that such an extreme traumatic dream after a relatively short exposure to combat would be unlikely in soldiers with no previous combat experience. This dream foreshadows the traumatic aftermath that Ed and his colleagues are likely to experience on return from the theatre of war, as well as introduces the concept of combat trauma to the reader in a visceral, easily comprehensible way.

● ● ●

As with *The 'Nam*, *Maus* also contains discussion of traumatic dreams. Whereas in *The 'Nam* Ed's dream serves to summarize the trauma of his situation and represent the prevalence of trauma among soldiers, dreams in *Maus* are used to discuss the potentially supernatural aspect of dreaming and also the ways in which one person's traumatic dreams can impact those around them. There are two mentions of traumatic dreams in *Maus*: a dream itself and a discussion of dreams in a more abstract manner. In the first sequence, Vladek recounts an episode that occurred while he was a prisoner of war in a work camp near Nürnberg in 1939. He says that he dreamed of his grandfather, a rabbi, speaking to him and telling him he would be saved from the camp on "the day of *Parshas Truma*" (Spiegelman, 2003: 57), some three months from the night of Vladek's dream.[5] The dream comes true, so to speak, as it is in the week of *Parshas Truma* that Vladek and his fellow prisoners are taken from the work camp back into (now-occupied) Poland. Vladek adds that this same *parsha* has become very special to him, as it was in the week of this *parsha* that he married Anja, that Art was born, and that Art had his *bar mitzvah*. That this dream happened is not necessarily unusual—dreams in which people receive "premonitions" are not unheard of—but that it came true is definitely not common. Vladek includes this dream in his narrative because, as he explains, the *parsha* has become so important to his life and the life of his family. Moreover, the dream gave him hope. It was something for him to focus on during his time in the work camp and became a target to work towards.

Formally, this dream has many aspects in common with other comics renderings of dream sequences and is presented in the same artistic style as the rest of *Maus*. As with Ed's dream in *The 'Nam*, the sleeper is at the intradiegetic level and the dream at the metadiegetic; there is a metaleptical shift within one panel. In the main panel of the dream, Vladek is presented as a basic line drawing with no crosshatching, making him appear brighter on the page. His grandfather, depicted with traditional Jewish *tallit* and *tefillah*, is drawn with much crosshatching to make him appear very mouselike (and hairy) and also physically substantial.[6] As with the rest of the text, the dream sequence combines Vladek's retrospective narrative, presented in either caption boxes or outside of the frame itself. The words of the dream are presented within the frame, which keeps the words of the dream and the image of the grandfather closely linked. The fact that the dream is not presented in a different style than the rest of Vladek's narrative suggests that it has been assimilated into his memory in the same way as the rest of his life.

When analyzed in isolation from the rest of the text, this dream sequence appears to be a straightforward declaration of the basic human need for hope. However, placing it within the overall narrative gives this section renewed importance. The significance of this section is wider than the dream itself. This passage can be seen as "the key to the deep religious significance of *Maus*, as well as to Vladek's character" (Tabachnick, 2004: 2). *Parshas Truma* (the "offering passage") is Exodus 25–27, which begins, "The Lord said to Moses: Tell the Israelites to take for me an offering; from all whose hearts prompt them to give you shall receive the offering from me." Tabachnick states that this passage holds special relevance in *Maus*, not only because it is repeated throughout Vladek's life, but by donating a portion of his wealth to others [Anja, Mandelbaum and Felix] of his own free will and at considerable risk, Vladek is fulfilling the injunction in the first two verses of *Parshas Truma* to make offerings in God (2004: 5).

Spiegelman has stated that his Jewish heritage is not something he actively engages with; his Jewishness is a secular part of himself.[7] However, the passage of *Parshas Truma* suggests that Spiegelman is very aware of his Jewish identity and how this identity framed his parents' existence. Alan Berger writes:

> That Vladek feels compelled to tell [the story of the *Parshas Truma* dream and its outcome] to his son indicates some belief that divine providence played a role in his rescue and survival. . . . This would tend to undermine Vladek's assertion that God was not in Auschwitz. (1998: 202)[8]

This dream sequence, then, is less a representation of traumatic dreaming and more a statement on the importance of religion for the survival of Vladek during the Holocaust and also for the text as a whole. It is also the only mention of Jewish ritual and praxis made by Vladek in the entire text, emphasizing the importance of this episode for him.

The second instance of dreams in *Maus* is not a direct rendering of a dream sequence, but a conversation that occurs between Art and Françoise. After a tense day at Vladek's holiday home in the Catskills, Art and Françoise sit on the porch. In the background, Vladek is wailing in his sleep. Art is unsurprised by the noises and explains that they were a common occurrence throughout his childhood, though it is not mentioned whether or not his mother had similar sleep issues. The conversation, presented in uniform panels, gives a very brief snapshot into Vladek's thirty-year sleep issues. Although Art describes the noise as "moaning," the size of the "moan," which is not contained within a bubble, seems too large to represent a mere moan. Rather, it seems that Vladek is wailing loudly and dramatically. The disjunction between Art's comment and the apparent reality makes it clear that Art has become used to Vladek's sleep disturbances; he himself states that he assumed it was normal adult sleep behavior. That this behavior has been a part of Vladek's daily life for so long—even affecting the way his son sees the world around him—shows that the disturbances of sleep that traumatic ruptures can cause have an effect on both the traumatized individual and those around the individual. The inclusion of this vignette shows the depth of Vladek's trauma and also shows the wider issue of sleep disturbance in Holocaust survivors.[9] Unlike with *The 'Nam*, the inclusion of dreams in *Maus* serves a varied purpose and does not use the concept of traumatic dreaming as a straightforward depiction of a symptom of the traumatic rupture. Rather, Spiegelman uses the dreams to raise wider issues—in this case, the necessity of hope and the prevalence of sleep disturbance for Holocaust survivors.

The inclusion of Vladek's dream is also a clear illustration of a specific issue of representation that is unique to comics. As with Ed's dream in *The 'Nam*, Vladek's dream is a clear, visual, single-panel representation of metalepsis. This is something that comics can do particularly well and in ways unavailable to other media. Vladek sits at the intradiegetic level, with his grandfather at the metadiegetic. The two are seamlessly connected in the single panel, and it is only on reading the caption that the fact that this panel contains a metaleptical shift is made clear to us. This would not be achievable in text-based literature, nor would it be achievable in the same way in film, due to the spatial differences. When the narrative moves out of Vladek's dreamscape, it is still possible to view the metaleptical dream panel alongside the intradiegetic narration. This is not possible in film, as all images inhabit the same space.

Dreams of Traumatic Loss

Trauma is often represented not only as that which happens directly to an individual, but also through that which is witnessed by others, especially the relatives and companions of those directly involved. In the introduction, I referenced Bennett's contention that trauma offers a way for "secondary witnesses to articulate an affective response . . . and also to identify as a victim even at some remove from the locus of the attacks" (2005: 20). The nature of witnessing and the suggestion of "trauma by proxy" is hotly contended, with many writers suggesting that claiming that witnesses can be traumatized in a similar way to those who are directly involved negates the experience of "actual" trauma victims. In the comics I am working with, individuals who are traumatized by proxy experience traumatic dreams in a similar way to those directly affected.[10] Because there is so little clinical research in this area, it is difficult to determine what form the traumatic dreams of witnesses may take. In comics, the dreams of witnesses and those close to the direct victims are most often represented as what I categorize as "dreams of traumatic loss." Instead of concentrating on the event itself, these dreams consider the trauma of loss for those who remain.

In *American Widow*, Alissa Torres dedicates a chapter of the text to a dream in which she is reunited with her late husband. Torres writes that "high-voltage traces of our lust and love flowed through our mattress nightly . . . until one night when the power surged and overflowed" (2008: 121–22). She describes an intense dream in which she and Eddie "tumbled slowly around the universe" (2008: 123). There is little narrative content to the dream and it is described more as a collection of sensations and vague images; this is not to say there is little material to analyze. The atypical color scheme of the entire text—using pale green-blue as a highlight color alongside stark black and white images—is used to emphasize specific images within each frame and to accentuate the supernatural aura of the chapter. Torres's dream begins when she wakes to the aforementioned "overflowing of power" and her bed is caught in a whirlwind.

Later in the dream, Torres describes the initial sensation as "[perching] on [her] lips like a determined sparrow" (2008: 124). The page presents three equally sized bandeau panels, each containing a single image (a sparrow, Torres's upturned face, her wrist). There are no bubbles, only words in caption boxes, separated from the images. The images seemingly have no relationship to each other—in McCloud's terms, the transitions would be classed as "non sequiturs"—and without the captions would be impossible to understand. That these images are presented so simply is emphasized by the pale blue highlighting on each image. Furthermore, the simplicity of the image works in a similar way to masking,[11] allowing the reader to place the image itself into whatever narrative of the dream sequence has been constructed from the limited information available. Torres's dream, though unusual, is not particularly traumatic. The trauma in dreams of loss is shown to be found in the waking, in line with Lacan's and Caruth's readings of the "dream of the burning boy." As with the bereaved father, it is on waking that Torres most acutely experiences the trauma of the dream; asleep, she is with Eddie but on waking, she is alone again.

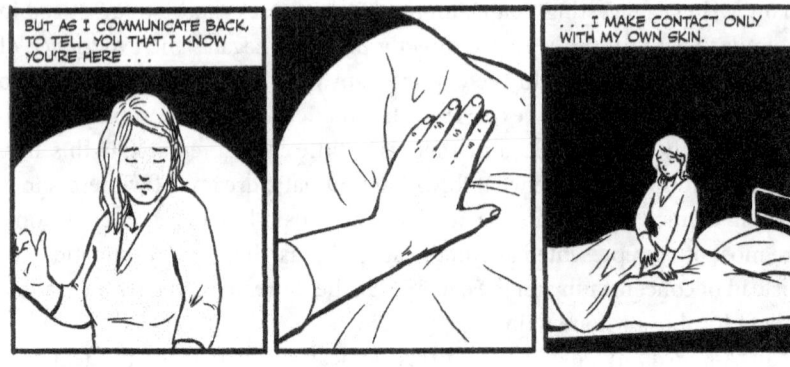

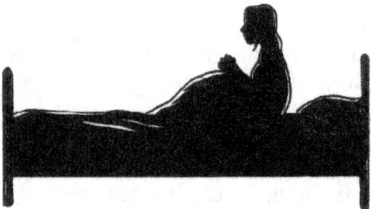

Fig. 3.2. *American Widow*, Alissa Torres and Sungyoon Choi, 2011. p 125. © Penguin Random House.

Torres presents the moment of waking in a single image on a white page. The starkness of the image—high contrast white on black in a silhouette with blue highlights—mimics the shock of the awakening and the lonely return to her traumatic existence. In a previous panel, Torres states that, when she tries to reach out to Eddie, she "[makes] contact only with [her] own skin" (2008: 125). It is this touch that wakes her. Again, there is a parallel with "the burning boy"—the activity within the dream waking the dreamer. Torres's waking is presented as a bleed and, as with most bleeds, appears timeless because of its uncontained nature. The large expanse of white page is a striking sight and the eye is immediately drawn to the image of Torres sitting in her bed at the bottom of the page. The loneliness of the image can be read in her blacked-out face, staring forward, while her hands rest, clasped, on her knees. The bed appears to be enclosed within a bright white empty space, heightening the effect of loneliness and loss. Compared to the unusual and visually busy dream sequence, the bold emptiness of this final page gives traumatic emphasis to the act of waking.

The trauma of waking is a common theme in post-9/11 trauma comics. *American Widow* presents one example but two more are found in the 9/11 charity comics "Untitled" and "Wake Up." In "Untitled," an anonymous dreamer floats around the shell of a half-built skyscraper and then sees her deceased lover moving towards her across the sea, before disappearing, ending the dream. The comic has no bubbles or caption boxes, and the few words that are used are written in the gutters; they are short statements, presented without punctuation or capitalization. As the gutter is the place where the shift between panels occurs, the fact that this shift is interrupted by words disrupts the flow of panels. The disruption of the visual and linguistic relationship in this comic attests to the changing operations of language in traumatic situations. The words are not complete sentences, but fragments that do not appear to have a connection to the images, further intensifying an atmosphere of disconnection and disorder. The dreamer within the images is searching for a connection but is unable to find one and, on locating what she believes to be her deceased partner, realizes that there is still no connection and the attempt to find one is futile. The artwork in "Untitled" is heavily shaded and crosshatched, accentuated by the borderless panels and the broad white gutters. The final panel is plain white, bordered with a broken black line and accompanied by the words "only in dreams" (2002: 143). "Untitled" shares many formal features with the dream in *American Widow*. The most obvious similarity at first glance is the austere color palette (exclusively monochromatic in this case). The starkness of the final panel is very similar to the starkness of the final bleed in *American Widow*. Furthermore, the panel transitions are similar to those used by Torres, creating a sense of confusion and mimicking the fantastical aspects of the dream itself.

The dreams in both *American Widow* and "Untitled" recreate the trauma of waking to one's own solitude and loss. Unlike Ed's dream in *The 'Nam*, these representations of dreams of traumatic loss do not place the emphasis on the content and presentation of the dream itself but on the act of waking and the dreamer's return to their traumatic situation. In dreams of traumatic loss, the content of the dream itself is not a replay of an event that happened but an eerie return of the lost one who remains out of reach; the inability to reach their lover causes the dreamer to awake. In contrast, the dream sequence in "Wake Up" shows a positive dream that does not end in a return to traumatic loss. "Wake Up" begins with a young boy, Jimmy, sitting up in bed in the early hours of the morning. His mother comes in and comforts him, mollifying his fears of "bad guys" who commit crimes and act to hurt others. The mother is revealed to be a NYPD officer—Jimmy's interaction with her was a dream and she was, in fact, killed in the 9/11 attacks. The comic ends with son and father remembering the mother and Jimmy "standing tall [because his] heart is unbreakable" (Kelly et al., 2002: 23). "Wake Up" has less in common with the other two dreams of traumatic loss and more in common with Vladek's dream of his grandfather in *Maus*. Although the dream is born out of a traumatic situation, the underlying message of the dream is one of hope. The dream of *Parshas Truma* gives Vladek a goal toward which he could aim during his time in a Nazi labor camp; Jimmy's dream reminds him of his mother's unconditional love for him and the strength that he can derive from this. The innocence of a child attempting to come to terms with a terrible traumatic event—and one that the child cannot possibly understand—is encapsulated in the simple message of the comic.

Artistically, "Wake Up" is drawn in a typically mainstream style, realistically colored and with action-to-action transitions. However, towards the end of the comic there are aspects of the artistic style that are not typical in mainstream comics and, in this instance, assist in the development of the narrative. As Jimmy decides to get some sleep, his mother stands at his bedroom door. In the previous panel, she was wearing a dressing gown and T-shirt, but now she is dressed in full police uniform. Her legs appear to be fading away, making her appear ghostly and creating the final "punch line"—Jimmy's mum has only appeared in a dream. She has, in fact, passed away; he is asleep and wakes to the realization that she is still not with him. A single bandeau panel marks the brief period between dreaming and waking. This is the most atypical panel in the comic; it is also the simplest. Gradational color on either side of the words "I love you, sweetheart" makes the words appear as if a bright white light is radiating out around them. These are the last words Jimmy's mother speaks within the dream, and the white light makes them appear supernatural. This is not a typical mainstream technique; it clashes with the rest of the comic and reminds the reader of the fact that what they just read was only a dream. "Wake Up" ends with Jimmy celebrating his mother's life rather than mourning her death. It is strongly implied that he is able to take the dream to bring about positive forward movement in his work of mourning and in his relationship with his father. This dream sequence is very different than the two other examples of dreams of loss, both in terms of artistic style and treatment of the subject matter. Like Vladek's dream in *Maus*, "Wake Up" shows that trauma-induced dreams are not necessarily nightmares.

The divide that I have created between two sets of traumatic dreams hinges on the ways in which the individual experiences the trauma. In terms of the dreams discussed here, the first set of dream sequences is prompted by a direct traumatic experience, and the second set is the result of trauma by proxy. It is not necessarily accurate to suggest that trauma by proxy is less serious than a direct traumatic experience; the dreams of traumatic loss presented here, though very different in content and context to the dreams of traumatic experience, are born out of a trauma that is in no way inferior to direct experience. However, it is important to recognize the difference between these two phenomena and not fall into the trap of conflating them, an error which negates both experiences and creates false beliefs about the nature of both direct traumatic experience and witnessing.

Despite the differences I have discussed between these dreams, there is one key similarity across the two collections: In all the dreams presented here, the dreamer is a visible character, either within the dream or sleeping outside the dream action. Thus, there is still some attempt on the part of the artist to make sure that the distinction between dreaming and waking is maintained. However, within the dream itself, this distinction becomes blurred. Dreams are a useful narrative device for conveying large amounts of visual information in a single panel, as with *The 'Nam*, or for emphasizing the importance of a certain theme within the narrative as a whole, as with the dream of *Parshas Truma* in *Maus*. The inclusion of Art and Françoise's discussion of Vladek's sleep disturbances shows that one's nightmares are not necessarily a personal problem and can affect those around them to a great degree. The dreams of individuals who are not the victims of direct traumatic experiences are no less relevant as representations of that trauma, though they operate in a different way and, in these cases, the trauma of the dream is often to be found in the act of waking, rather than the dream itself.

4

The Search for Identity

It is the identity of the story that makes the identity of the character.
—**Paul Ricœur,** *Oneself as Another* (1994)

In the late eighteenth century, Rip Van Winkle falls asleep on a grassy knoll and wakes to a world completely altered by conflict, seemingly in the blink of an eye. When he falls asleep, the village pub sign depicts King George III; on waking, he finds it changed to a portrait of George Washington. Once a citizen under the king, Rip is now a citizen of a new republic, without even knowing it. His identity has been changed by the conflict that has caused major shifts in the overarching structures by which he previously aligned himself. Washington Irving's short story attests to the suddenness with which conflict can transform one's identity and understanding of the world, as the waking Rip exclaims, "I'm not myself—I'm somebody else— . . . I'm changed, and I can't tell what's my name, or who I am!" (Irving, 1998: 43). The irony of Irving's story is that the day-to-day existence of Rip and his neighbors has not changed dramatically. In many ways, life goes on as it always did in Rip's village. Nevertheless, the constancy of everyday life that Rip experiences jars with the differences brought about by the shift from Crown colony to republic. Similarly, although there are many massive changes in the life of an individual by conflict, there is also much constancy. After a traumatic event, the individual returns to a world that has not intrinsically changed, though their experience of it has. Their identity, too, has shifted; they have become a victim or survivor, or both.

Although many factors affect our identity, in this chapter I specifically consider the environment in which an individual exists. When this environment is shaken by conflict and traumatic experiences, our sense of self is likely to be shaken, too. Herman writes that "traumatic events call into question basic human relationships. [They have] primary effects on the systems of attachment and meaning that link individual and community" (1992: 51). Thus, the relationship between a traumatized individual and those around him will be changed—if not damaged—by the traumatic event. In this chapter, I discuss the effects of a traumatic rupture on the construction of identity, not just for the individual, but the whole family. For many comics artists, the experience of being raised by parents who have witnessed conflicts forms the basis of their work. This chapter concentrates on comics artists who use the form to discuss events that did not directly happen to them but that they witness through close relationships with directly affected individuals. Of the four artists I discuss here, three are talking about their family histories and how the experiences of their families affect them and their own identities and histories. Three artists I consider in this chapter are writing from different backgrounds, spanning two conflicts—the Second World War (including the Holocaust) and the Vietnam War. Art Spiegelman's *Maus* centers on the experiences of the artist's parents during the Holocaust. *Vietnamerica* follows both parents but there is an emphasis on the experience of Tri, Tran's father; C. Tyler's *You'll Never Know* excludes her mother to give the narrative limelight wholly to her father. The shift in focus affects both the narrative and the artist, as I discuss in due course. The other artist I will consider in this chapter comes from a slightly different angle; Joe Sacco's comics journalism has been roundly praised for taking a form that by its very nature relies on personal interaction with the subject matter and using it for reportage. Sacco's work demands distance, by its journalistic nature, and insists upon closeness, by its comics form. This issue forms the concluding discussion of this chapter.

There are three main thematic strands running through these texts. The first aspect is the relationship between parent and child. The father is usually the narrator and the focus of the text, but I also consider the mother-child relationship and its seemingly diminished importance to both text and artist. I give equal consideration to the influence of both parents. The next issue is that of nationality and cultural identity. The fact that the children/artists were, with the exception of Tyler, born and raised in a different country than their parents has an impact on the children's personal identity. Furthermore, the parents' first language is not always the same as the child's, and this impacts communication between child and parent, as well as on the narrative itself. Finally, I look at the possibility of authorial distance and how this, too, influences identity construction.

As I have already stated, trauma will have an effect on the individual's conception of identity, albeit not in universally definable ways. When the traumatized individual is a parent, the issue becomes far more complex. Not only is it highly likely that the individual will face difficulty in the construction of basic relationships, but they face further difficulty in adapting to the role of parent. For a child, their parents form the first and arguably most important relationship they will establish; if those parents struggle to form relationships of any kind, the child will invariably suffer. As I discussed in Chapter 1, traumatic ruptures are intrinsically bound up with the incomprehensibility of one's survival. The individual's "fundamental assumptions about the safety of the world" are destroyed (Herman, 1992: 51). If an individual is unable to feel safe and protect him- or herself, then it logically follows that they will be ill-equipped to protect and care for a child. The child is the embodiment of the incomprehensible survival and is therefore incomprehensible.

Nicolas Abraham and Maria Torok's concept of the "transgenerational phantom" takes its lead from Freud. They argue that the phantom is not "the dead, but the gaps left within us by the secrets of others" (1994: 171). They claim that the phantom exists in the same psychical dimension as a firsthand traumatic rupture; it "is a formation of the unconscious that has never been conscious.... It passes from the parent's unconscious into the child's" (1994: 173). Although the child may know what the parent experienced, this can only be a superficial knowledge (something as basic as "my father survived a terrible incident"), removing the capacity for a deeper understanding of the experience which may have assisted the child in their comprehension of the experience of secondary trauma within themselves.

There is a wealth of research on the transmission of trauma across generations, the majority of which concentrates on Holocaust survivors and their descendants.[1] This is understandable, given the magnitude of what happened (as well as its international repercussions). These research findings are invaluable for my analysis of *Maus* but raise concerns when looking at the transmission of non-Holocaust traumata. Is it appropriate to use this research in the context of a different traumatic conflict situation and to use this as a case study that is indicative of other situations? Given what is known about trauma and transgenerational trauma on a basic level, the findings of Holocaust research appear to be applicable to other situations. That said, it is essential to bear in mind the (often huge) social and cultural differences between each event and not take Holocaust research findings as absolute truth for every traumatic event. Furthermore, as I have stated repeatedly throughout the previous chapters, we must be careful to remember the primacy of trauma as an individual experience and avoid using individual's testimonies as benchmarks for certain types of traumatic experience.

Dan Bar-On and Ğûlyā Čaytîn's 2001 book *Parenthood and the Holocaust* analyzes survivor testimonies alongside testimonies from their descendants, while keeping them within their socio-historical context. Their research is not strictly a psychological exercise but aims to create a "historically contextualised psychodynamic approach" to the subject (Bar-On and Čayṭîn, 2001: 4). As I intentionally avoid using sources that seek to emphasize neurological or chemical determinants of trauma, this text works well; it sees the traumatic experience in a social, cultural, and historical light. Bar-On and Čayṭîn note several key themes that arise in research into transgenerational traumata. First, that survivors "remained married even though they lacked the emotional resources necessary for the development of intimacy" (2001: 5); second, that many survivor parents "were found to be emotionally unavailable to their children's needs"; and finally, that "survivor parents either excessively exposed their children to their horror stories, or alternatively, were uncannily silent ... creating a 'conspiracy of silence'" (2001: 5, 7). Although this research concentrates on a specific event—and a specific cultural group—these three phenomena are noted in parent-child relationships of many different traumatic experiences.[2]

There is a squeamishness inherent in discussions of the Holocaust, especially when placed in dialogue with other traumatic experiences. The Holocaust has become a benchmark for indescribable trauma. Wolfram Schueffel suggests that the "Holocaust is the ultimate measure of traumatic stress, surpassing every catastrophe" (Schueffel et al., in Dasberg, 2003: 315). To discuss any other incident in the same breath seems disrespectful, as if it belittles the experience of the millions who were affected. I do not wish to disparage the experiences of Holocaust survivors at all, but I do contend that it is neither fair nor accurate to create an *absolute* scale of "traumatic severity." Although some events, by their magnitude, are considered "worse," there is no way to suggest that the experience of a Holocaust survivor is necessarily more traumatic than that of, say, a Vietnam veteran. They are very different and cannot be compared. Although the basic symptoms of a traumatic rupture are comparable across a wide range of individuals, the exact presentation of the rupture is unique to the individual. There is no way to suggest that a specific person's representations of traumata are more (or less) accurate, and the trauma itself more severe, than another's. By this reckoning, then, the work of Bar-On and Čayṭîn can be used to understand parenthood in traumatic situations in general, with the Holocaust as a key case study.

As I mentioned previously, our environment has a major influence on our personal identity. When an individual grows up surrounded by adults who have lived through traumatic experiences, it is highly likely that the child will be affected. The "clubbing together" of survivors of traumatic situations differs greatly. It has been noted that Holocaust survivors tend to form communities that isolate them from non-survivors (Bar-On and Čayṭîn, 2001: 42).

However, veterans of the Vietnam War do not appear to engage in the same social behavior. While there are several Vietnam veterans organizations, such as Vietnam Veterans of America (VVA), these do not operate in the same way as Holocaust survivor communities; they are organizations that may have regular meetings for discussion and socializing, but they do not usually move beyond this. If anything, Vietnam veterans are more likely to be isolated within their community.

Whereas Holocaust survivors are able to maintain these tight-knit communities due to family ties and the displaced persons camps that were set up internationally after 1945, Vietnam veterans usually returned to their original homes, scattered across America. Although several veterans may live close to each other, they may not have served together and may not have had the same combat experiences. Furthermore, as Wayne Scott writes in his book on PTSD and Vietnam, "isolation may be either physical, psychological or both. Many veterans elect to live in isolation, feeling secure on their own piece of land often in geographically isolated regions" (2001: 23). However, in his comprehensive history of the Vietnam War, Stanley Karnow notes that the lack of communal experience among Vietnam veterans began as soon as the soldier was in theatre (2008: 122). Because most of the low-ranking soldiers were draftees and volunteers (many men volunteered to avoid the infantry), it was not feasible to send soldiers into Vietnam in regiments. Rather, soldiers were placed individually in combat units with spaces left by men returning home at the end of the 366-day draft. This meant that combat units were in constant flux as men left and joined; this was not a solid group which remained stable and was therefore able to build strong bonds. That these soldiers did not have a community with which to share their experiences is in itself isolating.

The Sins of the Parent

The relationship between parent and child sits at the center of the texts discussed in this chapter. Although each relationship is different and rendered in a different style and format, there are marked parallels between them. Moreover, although the parent-child relationship in general poses questions about the transgenerational nature of traumatic experience, it is in the specific father-child and mother-child relationships that this "traumatic transmission" is encapsulated. Thus, I separate the parents and consider their impact on the child individually. In *Maus*, *You'll Never Know*, and *Vietnamerica*, the father-child relationships show similar marks of the influence of trauma on the parent and, by proxy, the child. In all three of these texts, this is the relationship that drives the narrative; although *Vietnamerica* does not concentrate solely on the father, it is the narrative of his early life that is awarded the most space within the book. This is not to say that the mother's story does not feature at all in these texts. Indeed, it is Tran's mother who acts as narrator in *Vietnamerica*. That said, the role of the mother within these texts differs in many ways to that of the father. The reasons for this are not the same in all texts. In *You'll Never Know*, the lack of maternal input largely occurs because Tyler is concerned with her father's war memories—something that her mother, Hannah, was not part of, nor has ever been party to. Similarly, while *Vietnamerica* does give space to Dzung's story, it is Tri, the father, who is the focus. He is the one who worked to support the family during the invasion and escape from Saigon, as well as the one who was imprisoned by the army. Although Dzung went through traumatic events, too, the burden on her is different simply because of her role as wife and mother, as I discuss in due course.

Maus opens with a vignette of Spiegelman's childhood; he is skating with some friends and, after his skate breaks, his friends disappear without him. It is a silly and childish game, the sort that most children engage in at some point, and Art cries to his father. Rather than a consoling hug and some kind words, Vladek replies with, "Your friends? If you lock them together in a room with no food for a week . . . THEN you see what it is, friends!" (Spiegelman, 2003: 6). Art is unable to reply to this; the experiences of a ten-year-old boy in 1950s New York are very far removed from those of a Holocaust survivor. Hamida Bosmajian writes that "survivor parents often cannot connect with their children because of unresolved mourning, survivor guilt, or psychic numbing" (1998: 3). Although these symptoms are seen in Vladek, the most striking feature of his survivor trauma is his complete inability to bond with his son because he is unable to see outside of his own experience; the short and succinct introductory vignette is a microcosm of the father-son relationship that is written out more fully in the body of the text. For Art, his father's inability to recognize his son's personal experiences and understand their differences belittles his own life experiences because there is no way they can ever be equal to what his father went through. Art must construct his self-image in the light of memories that are not his own (Hirsch, 12: 1993). Freud writes that civilized society "[makes] every effort to limit man's aggressive drives" (44: 2002) but, being unable to do so, must instead contend with the destruction of the civilized ideals that violence and conflict bring to humanity. To Vladek, the notion of civilization crumbles in the light of his Holocaust memories and all human experience is viewed through the lens of his survivor identity, regardless of whether or not that experience is analogous to his own.

Similarly, the first page of *Vietnamerica* sets up a distinction between the experiences of father and son. The first page shows a blood-red sky above Saigon, with a small plane ascending. The caption, part of Dzung's narration, reads: "You know what your father was doing at your age . . . He . . . WE left Vietnam" (2011: 2). Although she corrects herself, Dzung's initial comment sets up an immediate distinction between Tri and GB. As with Art and Vladek, the division between the two created in this comment negates the son's experiences in the light of the father's. Dzung's correction to her statement ("he" to "we") does not fully remove this barrier between the two, but broadens the scope of it. GB is disconnected not only from his father's experiences but the experiences of his whole family. In the cases of both Tran and Spiegelman, this initial statement of opposition is reiterated in several forms throughout the duration of the text and poses several questions. Can the child live up to the parent's experiences and, furthermore, should he have to? These questions are compounded further by the fact that the parent disrupts civilizational ideals; they are unable to fulfil the basic role of parent adequately and, as such, cannot assist the child in healthy development.

For Spiegelman, the character of his father poses a problem of representation. Vladek is a difficult man, miserly and permanently anxious. Spiegelman grapples with this image of his father, saying that "it's something that worries [him] about the book . . . in some ways he's just like the racist caricature of the miserly old Jew" (2003: 133). It is understandable that Spiegelman would want to avoid his father being seen as a stereotypically negative portrayal of a Jew. However, the testimonies of Vladek's wife, Mala, and neighbors—as well as Spiegelman's wife, Françoise—suggest that Vladek does display many facets of the stereotype. Regardless of this, Art seeks to justify his father's character by suggesting that "Auschwitz made him like that" (2003: 182) but Mala refutes this—she survived the camps and is not like him at all. It is through his discussions of the neuroses of his father that Art becomes aware that "lots of people are survivors [and] if they're whacked up it's in a different way from Vladek" (2003: 182). In this statement, Spiegelman makes reference to the individualism of a traumatic rupture. The traumatic experiences of Vladek emphasize his survival instincts to an extreme extent. His "can-do" attitude and skill with materials and communication—the qualities that enabled him to survive the Holocaust and relocate to the US—become extreme. Vladek is still able to fix things, to manipulate those around him, and to maintain a good quality of life for his family but he does so with a mindset of preservation and preparation. His actions suggest a fear "that Hitler might come back" (2003: 238) and, while this fear is unfounded, it is difficult to criticize a man who survived such horrors for wanting to protect himself and his family from a recurrence.

Although Vladek's behavior is not entirely condemnable, it is shown to be damaging to all his relationships, especially the relationship with his son. Vladek's self-image is entirely bound up in his identity as a Holocaust survivor; he is unable to view himself as anything else. As everything in his life is mediated by this view of himself, Vladek imposes this view on his son. Art has nightmares of the camps and "Zyklon B coming out of the shower" (2003: 176). As Victoria Elmwood writes:

> despite Art's denial of any obsession with Holocaust culture, it seems that he has been profoundly affected by his parents' past. His nightmares and morbid fantasies, while not necessarily symptoms of trauma *per se*, certainly reveal a child whose everyday imagination is haunted by events to which he has no direct connection. This lack of connection is compounded by Vladek's fragmentary processing of his own traumatic experiences. (2004: 697)

Thus, Spiegelman faces the double-layered issue of trying to comprehend not only a traumatic experience (which is in itself almost impossible to understand) but a traumatic experience that is not his own. This is only exacerbated by the "conspiracy of silence" that exists within many survivor communities, preventing parents from speaking about their experiences in any coherent way while simultaneously expecting their children constantly to remember the past (Bar-On and Čaytîn, 2001: 6). Elmwood describes this as the "gaps and absences created by extreme events [bleeding] into the next generation" (2004: 692). Not only is a gap formed by the parents' inability to speak but also by the children's inability to understand.

This same parental silence is discussed at length in *You'll Never Know*. Carol Tyler describes her father Chuck's memories as being "buried under tons of mental concrete" (Tyler, 2009: Vol. 1, n.p.). Although she knows her father served in the European theatre in the Second World War, he has never discussed this with her or, it seems, anyone else. This silence, as with the Holocaust "conspiracy of silence," pervades the whole of Chuck's generation. Tyler writes that "six million men . . . are tight-lipped about the biggest, baddest thing in their lives. Did they make a pact of secrecy? Guess I'll never know" (2009: Vol. 1, n.p.). Chuck differs from Vladek in the extent of his silence. Art knew that his parents had been in the camps and knew some of what had happened from overhearing conversations and his parents' offhand comments. Carol has no knowledge of her father's wartime experiences at all; Chuck has never said a word. Thus, unlike with Art and Vladek, there is no basic information on which Carol can build a version of events and, as such, no frame of reference to explain her father's mood swings and unusual behavior.

Tyler only becomes aware of her father's wartime experiences many decades later, when he unleashes the story in a rambling telephone call. The first words of his revelation are "RIVERS OF BLOOD!" (2009: Vol. 1, n.p.). Later in the text, Tyler writes:

> Those rivers of blood still course through his veins. And through my veins too it seems. So the war was never really buried under tons of mental concrete. Rather, it was an active shaper of life, affecting moods and outcomes . . . more than anyone ever knew. (2009: Vol. 1, n.p.)

She appears to recognize the impact of her father's experiences on his life, as well as her own. Her reference to him as a "caustic agent" shows Tyler's awareness of the dissolving, destructive nature of trauma. In referring to her father, rather than the experience itself, however, she binds him inextricably with his experience; he becomes the experience. However, within the text itself, Tyler is unable to create a link between her father's experiences and her life. The overarching narrative of the trilogy follows Tyler as she creates a scrapbook of her father's war photographs. But, unlike the other texts in this chapter—which are more seamless in their movement between narrative strands—*You'll Never Know* sets up a stark split between the war narrative and the contemporary narrative. Although the text as a whole is arranged like a scrapbook, in landscape format and printed on heavy paper, the war narrative is uniform in presentation on the page: three blocks of text and three images are arranged like photographs with captions. There is no strong relationship between text and image; although the image would be meaningless without the text, the text does not rely on the image. The war sections of the narrative are separated by introductory splash pages, stating the dates and location of each section. The split between narrative strands is marked, not only by these splash pages, but also by the difference in presentation style. The fact that Tyler keeps this narrative physically separate from the rest of the text shows that she is unable to link this history to her own and also to her father's postwar life.

What is striking about *You'll Never Know* is not Chuck's war memories themselves, but the way they sit in relation to the wider narrative of his marriage and later life, as well as his relationship with his daughter and her troubled family life. It is evident that Tyler sees a link between her failed marriage, depression, and general dissatisfaction and the character of her father. It is less clear whether she links her father's many negative qualities (and occasional abuse) to his wartime experiences. The separate presentation of the war narrative suggests that while Tyler is aware that his experiences were traumatic, she has not fully grasped the importance of these events on his overall character, as well as hers. By the end of the text, Tyler has not reached any sort of resolution with her father. The text ends with Tyler's trip to Arlington National Cemetery and an overwhelming sense of the pointlessness of war, represented by the emptiness and stillness of the Second World War memorial.

• • •

Although the father is the most visible parent in *Maus* and *Vietnamerica*, the mother is not entirely absent. However, there is a difference between the type of involvement the father has in the narrative and the involvement of the mother. I suggest that this difference is, on a basic level, due to the amount of input the mothers in these texts have in the public sphere. The social situations in which these texts are set make it clear that the role for the mother is to make them a home and raise children, whereas the father is the breadwinner and family protector. Thus, the father is not only more exposed to the events of the conflict, but also far more publicly visible. The mother's role of homemaker does not make her experience of the traumatic conflict easier; rather, it puts different stresses on her. That the creators of these comics are mostly men does not necessarily suggest that they are unable to relate to their mothers' experiences, but it is an important fact to consider when analyzing these texts. I return to this issue in the Excursus.

In *Vietnamerica*, Dzung's narration frames each section, guiding the reader through the text's many chronological leaps. The narrative panel is a single square panel on a black bleed page, in which Dzung is preparing dinner while telling the family story; many of the narrative captions throughout each section contain Dzung's first-person narrative, presented in a distinctive cursive font that is used solely for her words to distinguish them from the other dialogue. In her story, she is left behind to take care of the family while the men (first, her brother Vinh, and then her husband, Tri) are conscripted or imprisoned. Dzung's responsibility as the daughter of the family to is care for her mother and younger siblings. It is she who must support the family when her brother is shot. Dzung is the one who mediates Tri's behavior towards his children and their new life in the US. Not only does she have the responsibility of raising the family, but she also provides a buffer between her husband and children. As I explain more fully in Chapter 5, Tri Tran was traumatized by his upbringing and experiences in an ARVN prison during his first marriage; he brings this trauma into his life as a father. The traumatized and traumatizing parent, in this text, is Tri, while Dzung, as I have already mentioned, is the buffer to intercede between husband and children; Dzung has the qualities to make her a perfect foil to Tri's somewhat abrasive personality.

In stark contrast to Dzung, Spiegelman's mother, Anja, is mostly absent from the text of *Maus*. Despite this, she has a massive influence on her son. It is crucial to remember in analyzing the character of Anja that the accounts of her are mediated through the memories of Art and Vladek; Anja herself has no voice in the text. "Prisoner on the Hell Planet," which I discussed in Chapter 2, is a frank description of her death and funeral, written relatively soon after the event. This is the closest that the text gets to resolving any of Spiegelman's issues regarding his mother. Vladek's narrative discusses his courtship and marriage to Anja. She is presented as intelligent and gentle, but also very frail and unstable. She takes large amounts of medication and, just after the birth of her son, Richieu, suffers from severe postpartum depression. The narrative suggests that by 1939 Anja was extremely unwell, both mentally and physically.

Anja's fragile mental state seriously affects her ability to parent her children. While I do not wish to suggest that parenting is ever easy, parenting during an event such as the Holocaust offers challenges that no one can anticipate. In 1941, Anja and Vladek have the opportunity to send their son away to a safe house with the son of a friend but Anja violently refuses (2003: 83). Despite overwhelming evidence that their situation is dire, Anja refuses to let go. Although it is not her fault that her son dies, her desperation to cling on to her child has negative consequences. Anja's behavior is not rational; the portrayal of a desperately clinging and mentally fragile woman who is unable effectively to care for her child is the overarching image of her presented in the text. For this reason, it is more likely that her desperate behavior is linked to her poor mental health. Throughout Vladek's narrative, Anja appears rarely but each appearance portrays her as childlike, weak, frail, and in need of constant care and protection. She repeatedly discusses suicide, foreshadowing her successful suicide in 1968. However, she does not exist outside of Vladek's narrative of her. With the exception of "Prisoner on the Hell Planet," Art does not talk about her. Elmwood suggests that this is because "his memory of her is disabled by the trauma of her suicide" (2004: 708). Such is the depth of his grief that Art is unable to remember his mother in any way other than as the woman whose suicide dramatically affected him. Elmwood writes: "Anja's appearances in *Maus* strongly suggest that her suicide is Art's central trauma, in that he reaches considerably less resolution with regard to her suicide than he does with Vladek's alienating wartime experiences" (2004: 705).

Anja and Vladek's traumatization leads them to create a traumatic environment for their child. A parentally created traumatic environment—one that leads to similar symptoms in the child—is reminiscent of the "schizophrenogenic parent" in the work of psychiatrist Theodore Lidz (1985). Lidz examined how the socialization of the parents affected the development of schizophrenia in their children.[3] However, the use of Lidz's work comes with a large disclaimer. His case studies, conducted in the 1970s and early 1980s, were mostly traditional nuclear families in which the father was responsible for financially supporting the family, while the mother was a homemaker. Because of this narrow (and now largely obsolete) focus, his work can seem essentializing to contemporary readers, especially as the traditional nuclear family is becoming less common and more women are engaged in employment outside of the home. Furthermore, it appears there is more than a little misogyny in the ease with which he lays blame at the feet of the mother but largely ignores the father. Nevertheless, Theodore Lidz's work on familial causes for schizophrenia laid the groundwork for contemporary studies into the family situation for the incubation, diagnosis, and treatment of mental illness.

He deduced that a schizophrenic child's inability to act independently, develop a stable self-identity, and engage in normal intimate activities was due to the defective interaction between the parents (Lidz, 1985: 119). Lidz writes of the schizophrenogenic mother: "Her psychotic and strange concepts remain unchallenged by the husband [and] they create reality within the family." While Lidz is discussing a specific psychiatric disorder in parents, the phenomenon he identifies has notable similarities to the situation that appears in families affected by traumata. The "strange" concepts of the parents, caused by their traumatic past, are unchallenged by those around them and, as such, these concepts become "reality" for the family; Lidz refers to this as a *folie en famille* (1985: 43). The incubation of such "strangeness" might well be compounded in many cases where the parents' social circle is comprised of others who have survived similar traumatic experiences, as is the case with Spiegelman's parents. For the child, the home situation clashes with the "outside world," creating both confusion and alienation. The child may be aware that their home life is not normal or healthy, because of their experience of the rest of the world, but they are unable to change their situation, alienating them from both their parents and the rest of the world. Thus, these parents might be described as "traumatogenic"—their relationship with each other, the child, and their surroundings creates an environment that is a petri dish for traumatic symptoms in the child.

"Prisoner on the Hell Planet" can be seen as a case study for the "traumatogenic parent"; it vividly depicts the amount of pressure that is put on Art, the "replacement child" (Gordon, 2004: 14). Anja's tight hold on her son (he refers to it as her "tightening the umbilical cord") shows that she is unable to

Fig. 4.1. *You'll Never Know Book I*, Carol Tyler, 2009. Courtesy of Fantagraphics Books.

form a typical mother-son relationship with him. Not only is she extremely possessive, but she also expects him to be her confidante and supporter. Art represents a post-Holocaust generation that Anja believes provides a level of support that Vladek, himself traumatized, cannot provide. Art is a troubled young man who admits to having spent time in a psychiatric hospital. He would be unable to provide succor to his mother, even if she had not been through the trauma of the Holocaust; he is a young man in need of his parents. The fact that his parents are emotionally (and often physically) unavailable to him, with Anja being paradoxically *too* available, is traumatizing in itself. Therefore, the parents are traumatized by their experiences in the Holocaust and their son is traumatized by his parents' inability to be parents *because* of their Holocaust experiences. The trauma of one generation is transferred to the next. In Spiegelman's case, he places a huge weight of blame for his mental distress on his parents.

In contrast, Tyler places the blame for her traumatization, not on her parents, but on Hitler. In an abstract sequence of images at the end of the first

Fig. 4.2. *You'll Never Know Book II*, Carol Tyler, 2010. Courtesy of Fantagraphics Books.

volume of *You'll Never Know*, Chuck chases after his hat, which has been blown away by wind. He comes across a large sign, flanked by crows, before seeing Hitler holding his hat. The sign, written in German, translates as "I abuse them so that their children suffer . . . and their suffering fills me with pride."[4] That Tyler is willing to remove the burden of blame from her father shows that she does not believe he acts as he does on purpose but that his behavior is a result of his wartime experiences. The phrase on the sign is multi-leveled. On a basic level it states that the aggressors in the war aimed seriously to affect their enemies. Writing this text in German (and in a Teutonic font) makes it clear that Tyler sees Germany as the aggressor, keeping her father's experience of war firmly in the European theatre. The addition of Hitler stating that he takes pride in the children's suffering suggests that, though the suffering of future generations was not a motive, it was an "added bonus" as far as the aggressors could see. The inclusion of the figure of Hitler as speaker of the second phrase, rather than a second sign or an unattached speech bubble, gives the blame a human face, one that is already widely associated with evil and suffering. This page gives Tyler a person to blame for her suffering and that of her father, exonerating him. Chuck doubts this, claiming, "war's got nothing to do with it. I'm just an ornery bastard, that's all."

At the end of the second volume, Tyler suggests that the transgenerational transmission of trauma has not spanned one generation but two. Her daughter, Julia, nearly jumps from a second-story window as a result of psychosis and delusional thinking. Rather than suggesting there is a genetic component to this (Julia's father and Tyler's estranged husband is Justin Green, creator of *Binky Brown Meets the Holy Virgin Mary*, which details his struggles with OCD and scrupulosity), Tyler again places the blame with Hitler.[5]

Hitler, portrayed with the wings of the Nazi *Parteiadler*, states that Julia is "*Meine Bleibendes Vermächtnis*" ("my lasting legacy"). Not only is Hitler delighted that Chuck's trauma became Carol's, but he is "ecstatic" that it is Julia's, too. Tyler attributes responsibility with neither Chuck, nor Julia, nor Justin, but places blame firmly at the feet of the cause of the initial trauma. Despite his cantankerous and often hurtful behavior, Tyler does love her father and feels no resentment to him for his actions towards her. However, in placing the blame for her father's traumatization and subsequent problems at the feet of Hitler, she is deflecting attention away from those who can act on it and work to ameliorate the situation. Hitler is a symbolic figurehead for Chuck's trauma and that of all those who suffered as a result of their involvement in World War Two. Although her blaming Hitler allows Carol to forgive her father and reconcile their relationship, it also suggests that both she and Chuck are unable to truly begin to work through their traumata and reach a more satisfactory, healthy resolution. Because of this inability to fully reconcile, Tyler reaches no conclusion with her father. She sees herself as a bent sapling, unable to straighten out. This matter is not resolved in the text.

"Not my Parents' Life"

Tran and Spiegelman were both born in different countries than their parents: Tran in the US and Spiegelman in Sweden. Not only does this give them access to a different nationality (though Spiegelman does not claim Swedish citizenship), it also removes them completely from their parents' home country and places them from birth in a very different culture. The parents then raise the child in an alien culture. The child does not share the same culture as the parents, alienating them from their parents and their familial past. For Tran, the cultural gap between him and his parents is enormous. His portrayal of his teenage self is very much as an American, often playing computer games, with little interest in visiting Vietnam and learning about his family. Although his parents want him to know about his past, they also place blocks in his way by refusing to talk to him about their experiences. Dzung says, "I tell you these things, but you'll never understand"—how can GB understand when he has neither the frame of reference nor basic information to build on? His parents' inability to explain their experiences, due to both the mental blocks caused by trauma and the desire to protect their son, causes their son to lose interest in his past, choosing instead to assimilate himself fully into American culture.

On a more basic level, there is a language barrier between Tran and his parents. By his own admission, Tran speaks "enough Vietnamese to read a menu and no French" (2014: personal communication), while his parents speak Vietnamese first, French second, and English third.[6] Their English is not as good as Tran's; indeed, they were learning to speak English while he was learning to speak. While the text does not explicitly state it, there is a suggestion that Tran finds this linguistic barrier both frustrating and amusing. As anyone who has learned a second language will know, it is usually the idioms and nuances of the language that are most difficult to learn. As Tran does not understand his parents' language and they do not fully understand his, the result is linguistic distance between them.

The most striking rejection of Tran's family history is shown in his decision to change his name. As a young child, he decides to change his name from Gia-Bao to GB, as "nobody at school, even teachers, ever say 'Gia-Bao' right" (2011: 99). The rejection of one's name, especially when the name is deeply significant to the parents, is a rejection of one's cultural history. Tran is moving away from the history of his parents in the Anglicization of his name. This is not a straightforward issue. The image on the inside cover of the book itself suggests that Tran struggles with his desire to be American and his desire to remember his cultural heritage. He juggles with a number of labels (literally represented in the image), while his Vietnamese name flies out of reach.

The struggle that Tran faces is the seeming incompatibility of Vietnamese and American cultures. Throughout *Vietnamerica*, it appears that Tran rejects his Vietnamese heritage completely, even during the passages describing his 2006 visit for his grandmother's funeral, where he appears reluctant to engage with the culture. However, the very end of the text negates this idea, showing that Tran does indeed wish to find out about his heritage. The book on the Vietnam War given to him by his father for graduation—in an awkward attempt to connect with his son—ends up buried in a box. It is his discovery of the book—and the epigraph that he had not previously seen—that prompts Tran to make the journey to Vietnam and to discover the history of his family. In this respect, then, Tri's attempt to connect with GB fails when he is eighteen, but is successful when he is thirty and leads to the creation of the text. However, as with Tyler, Tran does not reach any resolution of the issues of alienation and tension between him and his father; the scars of his father's

Fig. 4.3. *Vietnamerica*, GB Tran, 2011. p 268. © Penguin Random House.

traumatic experiences are not relieved in the text; nor are father and son able to discuss the barriers between them. The tier of Tran and the telephone uses gutters to split the panel rather than keeping the image as a bandeau panel. The black gutters form a barrier between Tran and the phone, representing the difficulty that Tran has in communicating with his family. The next page shows a bandeau panel of Tran reaching for the phone, showing that he has overcome this first barrier and intends to attempt to overcome others.

Spiegelman faces a similar issue of linguistic difference between him and his parents. He was raised in America, speaking English. His parents are both shown to speak Polish, German, Yiddish, Hebrew, and English, the implication being that both of them speak English very well. As with *Vietnamerica*, Spiegelman writes the entire text in English. However, he uses different linguistic patterns for the past narrative and the present narrative. All dialogue within the past narrative is written in grammatically correct English, replacing Polish, while indicating when other languages are being spoken. Few phrases are included in the original language, usually ones that are easily understandable by an Anglophone reader (the most common of these is "Heil Hitler!"). However, for all of the dialogue between Art and Vladek, as well as the narrative captions that accompany the Holocaust narrative, Spiegelman writes in a strange, transliterated half-English, suggesting that Vladek's English is good, but not perfect; many grammatical constructions and idioms are confused or incorrect. Spiegelman speaks some Polish—he refers to this as "passive Polish" instead of a serious grasp of the language—but gives no indication that he can speak any of the other languages. This limits his linguistic ability to English, a language which, as I have already stated, his parents speak well but not fluently. Spiegelman must wade through his father's cracked English in order to communicate with him; he gives no indication as to how much he feels is lost in translation.

The language that evades Spiegelman the most is the cultural language of Judaism, which he rejects in his twenties. Although he had his *Bar Mitzvah* and was raised in a Jewish household, Spiegelman moved away from the religion, maintaining a secular Jewish identity as "an atheist Jew" (Spiegelman in Schneider, 2010: 23).[7] This is a language of culture rather than words. Spiegelman is unable to understand his parents' experiences because he has little experience of the cultural background, an issue that is exacerbated by Art being brought up in the US. He cannot understand the cultural framework on which his parents' experience hangs. Andrew Gordon suggests that Spiegelman and other children of Holocaust survivors who were raised in the US "became educated beyond their fathers, rebelled against paternal restrictions and, in assimilating to America, became only vestigially Jewish" (2004: 15). His parents' decision to emigrate to America and raise their son in what they consider a safe and comfortable environment also distances him from his family history, as is the case with Tran, and creates distance and barriers between parent and child.

The most famous aspect of *Maus* is the animal metaphor that forms the basis of the narrative. The use of different animals to represent different groups remains unspoken within the narrative (that is to say, at no point does a character say, "Oh crikey, I'm a mouse"). Spiegelman references the long tradition of "funny animal" comics, while also playing with the cat-mouse trope. Spiegelman's use of such a striking metaphor raises many issues of identity and self-identification. However, before discussing this, it is important to note that one aspect of this metaphor has faced much reproach: Spiegelman has been widely criticized for depicting Poles as pigs. Robert Harvey argues that the animal metaphor "plays directly into [Nazism's] racist vision . . . threatening to erode the text's moral underpinnings" (2008: 244). However, Spiegelman's reasoning is that pigs exist outside of the "cat and mouse" food chain and that the depiction of pigs is not necessarily a negative one: "Look at Porky and Petunia Pig . . . I'm unhappy that so many readers thought it was OK to use vermin for Jews but not pigs for Poles" (Spiegelman in Bolhafner, 1991: 97). The nationalist animal metaphor crumbles with cats and mice. The cats are supposed to represent Germans, but Spiegelman does not make a distinction between Germans and Nazis. Rather than making distinctions between Nazis, Germans, and German Jews, the first two are classed as one group; any Jewish character, regardless of their nationality, is portrayed as a mouse. Spiegelman is aware of this problem, discussing it most explicitly in relation to a German Jew in Auschwitz—is he German (cat) or Jewish (mouse)? In making all Jewish characters mice, Spiegelman suggests that Jewish identity cancels out national allegiances. Vladek repeatedly refers to "the Poles" without acknowledging that he is also a Polish citizen by birth and family heritage. Rather, he draws a strong demarcation between Poles and Jews. At one point, Vladek and Anja wear pig masks to pass as Poles—even though they are Polish. The fact that Spiegelman chooses pigs is of special interest here, as pigs are not kosher animals and are therefore considered unclean. Hillel Halkin writes:

> The Holocaust was a crime committed by humans against humans, not—as Nazi theory held—by one biological species against another. To draw people as animals is doubly dehumanizing. (Halkin, 2005: 140)

At the beginning of the second volume, Art is trying to decide how to draw Françoise, his French wife, who has converted to Judaism. Art's objection to making Françoise a mouse is that she is French, yet he makes other Jewish characters into mice without question. Furthermore, he draws himself as a mouse but there are several other animals that could be used: he was born in Sweden (represented as a reindeer), to Polish parents (pig) but is now American (dog). The discrepancies here are never resolved within the text. Spiegelman's animals are uncannily humanoid. Baker writes:

> The smallest expanse of naked flesh other than head and hands may invite the reader to focus directly on the awkward conjunction of body parts. *Maus* is full of such instances: Vladek as a prisoner bathing naked in a river [and] Art sitting on his bed dressed only in his Y-fronts. (1993: 142)

Each animal is drawn with human hands and bodies; the reader must reconcile the humanoid qualities of the characters, remembering that each character is an animal, while also understanding that Spiegelman's metaphor is imperfect by design. In an interview with the *Comics Journal*, Spiegelman says:

> Ultimately, what the book is about is the commonality of human beings. It's crazy to divide things down the nationalistic or racial or religious lines. And that's the

whole point, isn't it? These metaphors, which are meant to self-destruct in my book—and I think they do self-destruct—still have a residual force that allows them to work as metaphors, and still get people worked up over them. (Spiegelman in Bolhafner, 1991: 98)

The self-destruction of the metaphor on which the narrative hangs assists in the creation of the text and the representation of trauma. The awkwardness of humanoid animals representing ethnic and national groups that negate the collective identity of human beings—in a comic that discusses an event in which ethnic and national segregation became, quite literally, a matter of life and death—both jars with and complements the disjointed memories of Vladek, the conspicuous absence of Anja, and the dysfunctional relationship they both have with Art. Although this metaphor has many flaws and does not hold up perfectly under the pressure of the narrative, its weaknesses become strengths as they highlight the many blatant shortcomings of such segregational methods. The lack of resolution maintains the confusion and discomfort of the text. Amid this confusion, the original problem remains: how is the son, who is removed by nationality and culture from the experience of his parents, meant to be able to come to terms with his parents' experience and the effect it has had on him, while struggling at the same time with issues of national and religious identity and an event that is incomprehensible? The conflicts of identity that Spiegelman faces are unresolved. Spiegelman is haunted by the shadow of his parents' experiences and their identity as survivors. In his 2011 commentary on *Maus*, Spiegelman is honest about the fact that his identity has become so bound up in his parents' lives that he is unable to separate it from himself (2011: 9).

The identity that Spiegelman has constructed for himself is based on experiences that are not his own. His trauma has been spawned from events for which he was not present but which are nevertheless not separate from him. Vladek and Anja are traumatized by events that they experienced but were unable to process. Dora Apel writes: "Experience that has not been processed cannot be narrated, constituting trauma, not memory" (2002: 56). By this reckoning, then, Spiegelman is as traumatized as his parents, though he has no frame of reference for this trauma. For both Spiegelman and Tran, the crisis of identity they experience is caused by traumata that they do not undergo first hand and do not understand. In these texts, both creators show that the traumata of their parents have been transmitted to the children; it is for the child to reconcile the experience of the parents with their own experiences in such a way as to make sense of it and to use this knowledge to find their place within their own family and heritage.

Human Identity and Journalistic Distance

Through the publication of his eleven books, Maltese-American comics artist Joe Sacco has created a genre. Comics journalism "fuse[s] documentary and autobiographical methods, dramatizing the tensions between personal revelation and public political and social discourse" to allow Sacco to "rethink his own notions of prejudice and pain, and to convince others to do the same" (Scherr, 2013: 19–20). Sacco works ethnographically, living within his subject area and interacting with the local people on a far deeper level than many other journalists would normally do. What he aims to do is not only to provide a journalistic account of conflict and its aftermath in places like Palestine and Bosnia but also to make visual what Whitlock calls "webs of narrative: micronarratives of familial life and macronarratives of collective identity, codes of established narratives that define our capacities to weave individual life stories" (Whitlock, 2007: 11). What Sacco does in his storytelling is not present a grand, overarching view of the conflict in its entirety but instead considers the micronarratives of personal histories, examining how a national (or international) conflict is experienced at the level of the individual, paring these with macronarratives of national and ethnic identity and, finally, the collective identity of humankind. In this discussion, I consider Sacco's work in general, while making specific reference to *Palestine* (2001) and *Footnotes in Gaza* (2009).

Chute claims that "Sacco visualizes history based on oral testimonies he solicits from others, in a sense producing an archive from non-archived material" (2011: 108). By tapping into populations largely ignored in the mainstream press, he is able to create nuanced narratives of traumatized persons. Furthermore, his use of the comics form allows him to do things that other forms would not allow. As I mentioned in the Introduction, Edward Said praises Sacco's (and, by extension, comics') ability to say what other forms do not and to "[defy] the ordinary processes of thought, which are policed, shaped and re-shaped by all sorts of pedagogical as well as ideological pressures" (Said in Whitlock, 2006: 967). The freedom from pedagogical and ideological pressure that Sacco can find within the comics form not only allows the speakers within his text to be literally pictured within the text, creating a face-to-face encounter with the reader, it also negates a key aspect of trauma theory. For Chute, "[Sacco's] most forceful intervention ... is the visual register, which rejects the absence that trauma theory has for so long demanded" (2016: 223). As I have previously mentioned, the fact that comics *is* able to visually create traumatic affect on the page goes some way to disproving the absolute suggestion that trauma is unrepresentable.

It is this representation of personal histories on the page and his own relationship to these histories that forms a central theme in Sacco's books. His works are "explicitly journalistic yet simultaneously function as a memoir of the author's experience as a journalist" (Chute, 2011: 108). Sacco appears as a character within the books, a caricature with large lips and blank spectacles. It is these spectacles I wish to focus on because they provide a way in to reading the character of Sacco. In a previous article, I discussed the use of spectacles as a double-framing device that allows the artist to use physical characteristics as representative of psychological state. In Derf Backderf's 2012 comic *My Friend Dahmer*,

> the clouding of Dahmer's spectacle lenses represents points within the text at which he allows his own self-creation to overcome that which is socially expected of him and become the key focus of his life . . . That spectacles create a separate frame within the overall frame of the image can shift the focal point within the image. (Earle, 2014: 8)

In Backderf's work, the use of spectacles is tied to the identity of the character and is used to manipulate the comics frame through a double-framing device. Unlike Backderf's Dahmer, Sacco's eyes are never seen behind his spectacles. Several scholars have suggested various reasons for Sacco's blank frames. Rocco Versaci suggests that the "cartoonish style" of Sacco's drawing represents alienation from his surroundings (2007: 119); Wendy Kozol sees his blank glasses as indicative of his status as an avatar (2012: 167). In an interview with the *Guardian*, Sacco admits that, while "it is deliberate now, it certainly wasn't in the beginning. If you look at the first few pages of *Palestine*, you'll see that I didn't used to be able to draw at all!" (Sacco, in Cooke, 2009: n.p.). He goes on to add:

> Also, back then, I really was more like a tourist than a reporter and I suppose the way I drew myself reflected that. But some people have told me that hiding my eyes makes it easier for them to put themselves in my shoes, so I've kind of stuck with it. I'm a nondescript figure; on some level, I'm a cipher. The thing is: I don't want to emote too much when I draw myself. The stories are about other people, not me. I'd rather emphasise their feelings. If I do show mine—let's say I'm shaking [with fear] more than the people I'm with—it's only ever to throw their situation into starker relief. (Sacco, in Cooke, 2009: n.p.)

Sacco is aware of his initial artistic difficulties and the strengths of these particular artistic choices as narrative devices. However, the most compelling comment in his interview is his belief that he is a cipher and that his stories are not about him. While it is possible to say that Sacco is a minor player within his own stories, this is not to say that they are not about him. He provides a central thread that ties together all his works. His physical presence, albeit as a cartoonish avatar, places him as a character within the narrative, whose reactions are available to the reader. Therefore, to say that he is "nondescript" is not accurate. His character is both the glue for the narratives across all works and a litmus paper for the artistic affect within the texts. As often the only Western character in the text, Sacco becomes a stand-in for the Western reader; our reactions to what the book presents are measured against Sacco's reactions and emotions. Because it is the eyes—the organ of epistemology—that are appropriated for our own, his identity becomes our own as he stands in for us within the narrative; his spectacles are blank to allow us to implant ourselves onto him. Sacco can simultaneously keep his distance from the events of the narrative and also draw the reader in. As Tristram Walker writes, "The 'white screen' of the spectacles and the gutter may allow for our own interpretation and imagination but ultimately we are guided in deciding the degree of brutality between frames by the images and written narration provided by Sacco" (2010: 76).

Sacco's texts are undoubtedly texts of trauma, but where he sits in relation to that trauma is very different than the other comics in this chapter. At no point does he wish to suggest that he has been traumatized by his experiences, nor does he attempt to appropriate the traumatic experiences of others. In this respect, I could suggest that Sacco remains unaffected by witnessing and hearing huge amounts of firsthand testimony. However, this is too simplistic. True, he does not necessarily discuss his personal reaction to what he sees and hears, but that is not the only way in which a text can be a "trauma text," as I have mentioned previously. The representation of trauma in Sacco's comics can be read through the lens of what Mark Seltzer terms a "wound culture—the public fascination with torn and open bodies and torn and opened persons, a collective gathering around shock, trauma and the wound" (1998: 1). Sacco shows wounds and bodies repeatedly within the texts. In *Palestine*, "Sacco shows how wounds can be used to foment a sense of belonging and national pride, especially among a people who have lost so much" (Walker, 2010: 79). Walker goes on to write that

> the images that he presents are often horrific. However, he shifts his work away from that of the shock artist feeding the fascination of a wound culture. He contextualizes the horrors within their own political and historical frames but, more important, he looks deeper than the grand sweep of history and finds the people

affected by the trauma. It is by bringing attention to their individuality that we can begin to identify with them as people and not just canvasses for wounds for our fascination. (2010: 86)

The vivid depictions of wounds do not aim to shock or to titillate but to bring attention to the physicality of conflict—the viciously torn bodies that make up so much of the corporeal reality so often ignored or marginalized by the press. Sacco is placing the trauma of the experience directly onto the individual, broken body, allowing the trauma to remain with the person and not become a mere "cipher of victimhood," to use Bennett's phrase (2005: 64).

Sacco wants to give a voice to marginalized communities who have been largely forgotten by mainstream media, a fact most clearly seen in *Footnotes in Gaza*. Sacco collects testimony about two events in 1956, massacres in Khan Younis and Rafah in the Gaza Strip in which nearly 400 Palestinians were killed. He is working on conflicts that are intensely bound up in questions of national and ethnic identity, but it is not these ethnicities which are the major focus of the narratives. Charlotta Salmi suggests that "Sacco is more concerned with his own entanglement in the material he depicts, and the implications for how his audience may come to read or receive the stories he tells" (2016: 8). His narratives are not didactic; they provide an outlet for unheard testimony and open a dialogue between witness of event and reader. Sacco's work "becomes a conduit for the traumatic experience, a co-authorial artefact giving itself over to become, like Joe's spectacles, a black screen for its projection. [In these narratives] we can form through witnessing and sharing trauma, an affirmation of another identity, not just that we are all perhaps 'Palestinian, Muslim or Bosnian now' but that we are all human connected by something more fundamental than national boundaries" (Walker, 2010: 82, 86). For Sacco, comics is a form that not only gives voice to the marginalized but also allows witness and reader to come together in the space of a page to consider the nature of identity in the shadow of tremendous violence and how we position ourselves in relation to it.

• • •

Rip Van Winkle wakes up from his long slumber to find that he is himself and yet not himself; his fundamental identity has been changed by an event he had no control over or involvement in: the American Revolutionary War. Although the day-to-day existence of Rip and his neighbors has changed very little, their basic identity has transformed from subject of a monarchy to citizen of a republic. Just as the Revolutionary War changed the identity of

Rip, the experience and survival of a traumatic conflict can radically change the personal identity of those it affects. The trauma does not affect only the direct victims, but is also transmitted across generations; traumatized individuals can become traumatizing parents, leading to traumatized children and grandchildren. The three texts discussed in the first part of this chapter are all written by artists whose parents survived traumatic conflicts and were affected by these experiences in ways that affected them into later life and, more importantly, affected the way they parented their children. These texts are not only chronicles of family history and family trauma, but also of the artist-child's representations of them working through their trauma and that of their parents. Furthermore, by using the comics form to create their representations, these artists are able to harness specific aspects of the form to assist both the creation of the text and also the development of artistic affects for the comprehension of the reader. In contrast, in the works of Joe Sacco, the artist keeps himself separate from the experiences he represents, while allowing the reader to witness through his blank-framed spectacles. Trauma is positioned on the body as wounds that maintain the personal integrity of traumatic experience, while also speaking to its undeniability. Elaine Scarry writes: "The physical pain [here reimagined in the wound] is so incontestably real that it seems to confer its quality of 'incontestable reality' on that power that has brought into being" (1985: 27). Readers approach these wounded bodies on the page, mediated through a disinterested narrator, who aims to bring to the fore questions of our collective human identity and not the segregating labels that are so crucial to the conflicts he depicts.

5

Moving in Four Dimensions

> Perhaps it is our perennial fate to be surprised by the simultaneity of events, by the sheer extension of the world in time and space.
> —**Susan Sontag**, *Regarding the Pain of Others* (2004)

One basic fact about the nature of comics gives it something that cannot be found in any other narrative medium. In comics, each narrative event occupies its own space on the page and within the book; the specific spatial relationships between panels correspond to (or contrast with) the temporal relationships between narrative events.[1] Thus, more so than with a traditional literary text, the physicality of the comic is a major factor in its reading, as I touched on in Chapter 2. The movement of time mimics the reader's movement through the pages and often the turning of the pages mimics the events within the text, as I discussed in Chapter 1. The physicality of comics reading—at the most basic level, the turning of the page—further contributes to comics emerging as a unique form. If I then consider that comics is able to manipulate temporal awareness in many ways that are not available to any other narrative medium, my contention that comics is a form well-suited to traumatic representation is further supported. This manipulation of temporal awareness is not solely in the hand of the comics artist but also the reader. It is for the reader to decide how long to take over each panel, each page, and even how quickly to turn the pages. Putting this much power over the timescale of the narrative in the hands of the reader means that not only does the reader have to work much harder than, for example, a filmgoer, but that each reader will read the story differently, giving temporal emphasis to some panels over others and changing reading speeds at different times. Tom Gunning expresses this beautifully when he writes that "the power of comics lies in their ability to derive movement from stillness—not to make the reader observe motion, but rather participate imaginatively in its genesis" (2014: 40).

To suffer a traumatic rupture is often to have one's sense of time abused, to suffer a serious temporal rupture. Indeed, for many individuals it is one of the most noticeable symptoms of a traumatic rupture that they lose their grip on time; their sense of personal chronology is severely disrupted. For Freud, writing in *Moses and Monotheism*, this disjunction in personal timekeeping can occur at the very first instance of the traumatic rupture (2001a: 67). It is at this moment that the difficult relationship between time and trauma begins, for, as Freud writes, the complete psychical effects of the traumatic rupture do not necessarily happen immediately—there is a delay; Freud refers to this as deferred action (2001a: 68). Thus, the amount of time that may pass before the trauma's full effect is felt can vary greatly between individuals.[2] However, it remains the case that trauma is, as Caruth contends, a "break in the mind's experience of time" (1996: 61). Freud suggests that this break is not caused by the quantity of traumatic stimuli, but by the mind's lack of preparedness:

> We may, I think, tentatively venture to regard the common traumatic neurosis as a consequence of an extensive breach being made in the protective shield against stimuli. This would seem to reinstate the old, naïve theory of shock . . . and we still attribute importance to the element of fright. It is caused by lack of any preparedness for anxiety. (2003: 31)

The protective shield is not engaged in time; the threat to the self is recognized one moment too late. Furthermore, returning to Caruth's original definition of trauma as an event "experienced too soon . . . and therefore unavailable to consciousness" (1996: 4), if trauma exists separately from human consciousness and comprehension, then it has never been known fully or, indeed, understood and has therefore not existed *in time*. It is this lack of temporal understanding and direct experience that causes the traumatic rupture and leads to the development of traumatic symptoms. I reiterate my initial point: time—and the fracturing thereof—has an effect on all other symptoms of the traumatic rupture.

This chapter discusses time in relation to both trauma and comics, bringing these two areas together in analysis of representations of traumatic time in comics. I work specifically with GB Tran's *Vietnamerica* (2011) and the Marvel series *The 'Nam* (1986–93). These two comics, though centered on the same conflict, differ in both style and focus. First, I note that *Vietnamerica* is a family narrative that spans several generations, while *The 'Nam* covers considerably less temporal ground and none of the characters' genealogy. Secondly, Tran's artistic style owes much to his father's past as a watercolorist, making it markedly different from the mainstream "house style" that is used in *The 'Nam*. The third major difference is that Tran's story concentrates on the Vietnamese, the occupied, rather than *The 'Nam*, which looks solely at the American forces, the occupiers. Moreover, *The 'Nam* was created specifically with the Comics Code Authority in mind, narrowing the options of the creators to a large degree, as I have already discussed. The constraints of both CCA and Marvel's "house style" combined create a text that ignores many aspects of the soldiers' experience of Vietnam (notably swearing and drug usage) but does not stifle representations of the intense trauma that many endured. In my analysis of these works, I pay particular attention to the use of analepsis and multiple analepsis, framed narratives, and metalepsis.[3] Although these tropes are employed across many different literary and comics genres, their usage here contributes to the representations of trauma within the text; each trope is used in a very specific way, with the overarching purpose of chronological destabilization, mimicking a traumatic rupture.

Further to this, I look at two specific instances of representations of photographs in two comics. These photographs are famous and, as such, their inclusion in the comic can be seen as a far more obvious collision of the "real world" and "comics world" than simply including the events in a storyline. I also look at the inclusion of superheroes, paying particular interest to what Umberto Eco discusses in his essay "The Myth of Superman" (1997): that superheroes cannot intervene in actual events because they would change the course of history. I use the (similar but independent) work of two theorists to complement these analyses: Thierry Groensteen's "spatio-topical system" and Mikhail Bakhtin's "chronotope."

Theories of Time in Groensteen and Bakhtin

In *The System of Comics* (2007), Groensteen argues that the basic unit of the comic is the panel. Although it is possible to break down each panel into smaller units, "for the particular subject that is comics, the operativity of the micro-semiotic is revealed to be, in practice, extremely weak" (2007: 5). Rather, the analysis of comics begins to become possible at the "level of relations between the units . . . the level not of the ropes, but of the knots" (2007: 5). With this in mind, Groensteen posits the "spatio-topical system" of the comic, which gives much emphasis to the placement of panels in relation to each other. Removing all words and images so the page is pared down to the "grid" of the frames (a stage of the creation process referred to as *quadrillage*) leaves a framework on which the "language of the comic is written" (2007:

28). In short, before the addition of image or word to the hyperpanel, we can see already that the positioning of frames is of extreme importance to the creation of the comic.

For Groensteen, there are four main parameters that govern the "general architecture" of the hyperpanel. First, the height of each tier of panels should be taken into consideration as "a tier stands out better if . . . its height differs from that of the others on the page" (Groensteen, 2007: 63). Similarly, the width of the gutter (Groensteen uses the term "interstices")—both horizontal and vertical—has an effect on the visual scaffolding. The location of bubbles (speech or thought) can drastically alter the whole page. The convention is that bubbles are placed in the upper part of the panel and "a different position, if it is anarchic, will scramble the apparatus of the layout" (2007: 63). Such breaking of convention, given the "anarchic" (I hesitate at this term and prefer "chaotic") effect it can have on the layout, is common and, indeed, to be expected in trauma comics. Finally, Groensteen discusses "the number of panels that make up the tier, in the absolute terms and relative to the quantity of panels that are included in neighboring tiers." He argues that tiers containing a lot of panels—or panels of unusual shape—are more likely to be eye-catching and to demand "narrative interest" than tiers containing two panels of equal size and shape. It is at the level of the tier, rather than just the panel, that true interpretation can begin (2007: 63).

Earlier in his text, Groensteen writes, "the position of a panel on the page corresponds to a particular moment in the unfolding of the story, and also in the process of reading" (2007: 35). This is echoed over and over in comics theory. McCloud writes:

> Time can be controlled through the content of panels and the transitions between panels. As unlikely as it seems, the panel shape can make a difference in our perception of time. . . . Ever notice how the words "short" or "long" can refer either to the first dimension or to the fourth? In a medium where time and space merge so completely, the distinction often vanishes. (1994: 101–102)

The relationship to which McCloud alludes is examined at great length in Mikhail Bakhtin's concept of the "chronotope" (1978: 493–528). Bakhtin writes that "the essential conjunction of temporal and spatial relationships artistically assimilated into literature shall be called the *chronotopos*" (in literal translation "timespace"). For Bakhtin, as for McCloud, there is an "indissoluble connection between space and time" (1978: 493). The chronotope works on three levels:

First, as the means by which a text represents history; second, as the relation between images of time and space in the novel, out of which any representation of history must be constructed; and third, as a way of discussing the formal properties of the text itself. (Vice, 1997: 201–202)

On the most basic level, it would be entirely feasible to look at comics through the lens of the third chronotopic level only—the work as being bound up in space-time connections by the very virtue of its form. However, the first chronotopic level is of equal importance, as the comics discussed here find their inspiration in actual events. Thus, the historical time of the event and the physical space of the page become inextricably linked. Furthermore, such events become chronotopic in their own right. For example, as I stated previously, "9/11" has taken on a chronotopic meaning as it refers to both the time in which the event happened but also the place where it occurred. In this sense, prepositions of time and place often become equivalent—Kurt Vonnegut writes that he was "at Dresden," instead of the more typical "in Dresden" (1991: 19). This construction only makes sense if it is acknowledged that the event is chronotopic—Dresden as a location in both space (city in Eastern Germany) and time (February 13–15, 1945). In terms of historical events, the chronotope "provides substantial basis for the showing and depiction of events . . . thanks to its particular solidification and concretization of the distinguishing marks of time in defined areas of space" (Bakhtin, 1978: 521).

Bakhtin's chronotope, then, gives us a framework by which "time [can] thicken [and become] artistically visible [and] space [can become] charged and responsive to the movements of time" (1978: 493). Using this framework gives both comics creators and readers a structure on which to hang both their timescale and their representations of historical events. Traumatic representation, which thrives on atypical temporality and chronological inexactitude, still adheres to Bakhtin's concepts, as there remains a strong link between time and space. For *American Widow* and the 9/11 charity comics, the chronotopic meaning of "9/11" becomes artistically observable. The spatial movement within the comics is limited, keeping all action firmly rooted in the geographical center of "9/11." Similarly, the vast majority of the comics are set on the exact day. Bakhtin uses the example of a road narrative as having a clear chronotopic outline. However, unlike in a road narrative, there is little movement within these comics, making the chronotope of each individual comic narrow. In a road narrative, distance traveled and time passed are inseparable.[4] Sue Vice uses the example of *Thelma and Louise* and the line "I'm trying to put some distance between us and the scene of our last goddamn crime!" (1997: 214). In the charity comics' depictions of 9/11 there is very little movement and time appears to stagnate. Bakhtin, referencing a similar chronotope in Flaubert's *Madame Bovary*, calls this "thick, sticky time, which oozes in space" (1978: 520). It is this oozing time that the reader encounters throughout much traumatic representation within comics. The traumatic rupture of representation—the creator's inability accurately or adequately to reproduce the traumatic event—gives rise to clotted or fractured temporality. Traumatic chronology is often presented as fractured. One of the more explicit examples of this is Vonnegut's *Slaughterhouse-Five*, in which the protagonist is a time-traveler. In other texts, chronology can be seen as clotted; the movement of time ceases and seems unable to progress at all. Brian Michael Bendis and Scott Morse's silent comic "Moment of Silence: A True Story" demonstrates this (Bendis and Morse, 2002: 8–12). The eight-page comic shows seven views of the same man, holding his arm in the same position, with no movement of time whatsoever. Rather than an elongated chronotope that spans much time-space, the traumatic creates a chronotope that mimics the trauma that it represents.

Stories within Stories—Analepsis and Framed Narratives

GB Tran's 2011 family narrative *Vietnamerica* recounts the multigenerational story of his family history, starting with his grandparents' (specifically, his grandmothers') experience of the French colonial presence and First Indochina War. The text follows three levels of narration: the historical background of his family, the postwar experience of the two younger generations, and Tran's 2006 visit to Vietnam for the funeral of Thi Mot, his maternal grandmother. The first narrative layer—the historical background—does not work chronologically and relies heavily on analepsis. Tran's mother, Dzung, acts as the narrator for a single scene-setting panel before the narrative shifts back. Although this framing happens throughout the text there is one section which utilizes a specific (and iconic) comics style that does not feature in any other part of the text. Tran uses *ligne claire* to illustrate the flashback-within-a-flashback narrative of his father's imprisonment by the ARVN (2011: 68–91).[5]

In this section, the first flashback (to Tri's imprisonment) uses dark coloration and black gutters, combined with crosshatching, crowded bubbles, and onomatopoeia, to create an atmosphere of uncertainty. However, the darkness and confusion of the images contrast sharply with the uniformity of the paneling, beginning with equally sized and spaced bandeau panels (2011: 69).

Fig. 5.1. *Vietnamerica*, GB Tran, 2011. p 71. © Penguin Random House.

Uniformity of panels generally suggests a steady and mechanical passage of time. This may be the case—Tri cannot know how much time has passed—but this stability of timeframe serves to destabilize the narrative as a whole; it is disconcerting because it jars uncomfortably with the content of the images. The relative size of each instance of onomatopoeia to the rest of the image within each panel suggests two things. First, that the sound represented is extremely loud and second, that the room in which the activity is taking place is small and cramped. As is common in the comics form, the writing style corresponds to the noise itself; the artist writes the sounds as he wants them to be read in order to evoke certain emotions and sensations within the reader. This brings the textual style into direct involvement with the meaning of the words, furthering the onomatopoeic effect.

The second flashback occurs while Tri is in his cell and takes him back into his early life, hence "flashback within a flashback" (I will refer to this as the "flash-flashback"). This occurs three times and it is here that the *ligne claire* comes into play. A trigger in the flashback takes Tri into the flash-flashback. The ARVN guards refer to him by his full name, Tran Huu Tri, which moves the narration back to Tri's first day at school and the occasion of his meeting his best friend, Do (2011: 71). Each flash-flashback starts on the right-hand side of the page, creating a stark contrast between the two pages. The cleanness and rich, bold color of *ligne claire* seems childlike compared to the roughness of the preceding images. By starting the flash-flashback on the right-hand side, rather than the left, which would require a page-turn, the shift in time is very fast. It happens in the time it takes the reader's eye to move up the page. Were it presented on the left-hand page, the shift in time would take longer—the time it took to turn the page. Not only would this remove the bold contrast between pages, it would also give the reader more time to pause before moving further back, removing the shock of the sudden time shift and allowing for anticipation of what was about to happen, replacing shock with anticipatory fear, as Freud and Breuer describe in *Studies in Hysteria* (2000: 57). Additionally, *ligne claire* uses emanata, especially in the case of someone being punched, to demonstrate the individual's physical state. This, coupled with a heavy use of onomatopoeia, is typical of the form.

Ligne claire is more than just an artistic style. It carries with it tremendous iconic weight, thanks to its associations with Hergé and *Les Aventures de Tintin*. In choosing to use this style, Tran will be aware of these associations. Earlier in the text, while discussing his father's childhood in a small Vietnamese town, a panel shows him being presented with a copy of *Le Lotus Bleu*, the fifth book of the Tintin series (2011: 38). This panel acts as a brief hint of what is to come, as well as testifying to the influence of Hergé on both Tran's development as a comics artist and Tri's life as an artist. In a later panel, Tran's mother fumes over his father's inability to throw anything out and, holding two Tintin books, she says, "He's a grown man! When does he ever read comics?" (2011: 142). The inclusion of Hergé and the watercolorist style of Tran's artwork both refer to the impact of the French colonial presence on the development of Vietnamese artistic identity, as represented in Tran and his father.

Bruno Lecigne argues that "the ideological efficacy of the *ligne claire* lies not in what is chosen for depiction, but in the idea that the world is legible" (Lecigne in Miller, 2007: 19). *Ligne claire* is a lens through which the world attains some level of clarity and comprehensibility. Laurence Grove writes that many artists "reject *ligne claire* precisely to suggest that life is not always clear cut, and that the violent ambiguities of society can indeed be worthy of artistic portrayal" (2010: 183). However, it is precisely *for* this reason that Tran uses it here. The story contained within the *ligne claire* flash-flashback is not a pleasant, happy childhood memory—in many ways, it suggests that Tri had a horrible childhood, fraught with disappointment and negative experiences—but it is important to remember that this is what Tri remembers while locked in a small, dark prison cell. Although his memories are not entirely happy, the lens of *ligne claire* makes them appear clean, putting this narrative in stark contrast to the cold and dark reality of his situation.

Tran's use of triggers for each of the three flash-flashbacks is not only an innovative method of moving the narrative back in time, but also a technique which mimics the triggering of memory and subsequent regression to memory that occurs in a traumatic rupture. It is, of course, common to everyone to find that certain stimuli will trigger a memory, but this is often more pronounced in an individual who is undergoing—or has undergone—great stress. In this respect, the suddenness of the narrative time shift mimics the shifting of personal chronology that can occur in a traumatic rupture. At the other end, when the flash-flashback moves forward to Tri in his cell, the *ligne claire* panels become increasingly thin, with a bandeau panel being sliced into sections, creating the effect of a stuttering filmstrip on a projector. This gives the impression that Tri's memory is faltering. Tran plays with this idea most explicitly in the last tier of *ligne claire* panels, in which Tri's thoughts are shown as a stream of slides in a thought bubble. The structuring of this section with multiple analepsis allows Tran to explore key events of his father's past, as well as the effect of these events on his older self—while also illustrating the nature of memory and traumatic regression.

· · ·

The 'Nam is not a typical mainstream comic series. Although published by Marvel and created in line with the house style and the CCA, the series does not follow the formats laid down by the majority of Marvel series. It is a misconception that all mainstream comics involve superheroes; the majority do. There are no regular superhero characters in *The 'Nam*. Moreover, mainstream comics may deal with convoluted story arcs but they do not typically handle political issues on the same level as *The 'Nam*. This particular series is noted for its use of a variety of narrative devices. The most striking of these is the use of letters as a means of creating a distinctive narrative voice. *The 'Nam* includes two issues in which the letter device is used as the framework for the entire issue: "From Cedar Falls, with Love" (November 1987) and "Notes from the World" (February 1988). Both stories are centered on Ed Marks, who acts as the "author" of the letters.

In "From Cedar Falls, with Love," Marks writes to his parents from a small village in Vietnam (2010: 28). The opening page of the issue sees Marks and fellow soldier Rob Little receiving mail in the aftermath of Operation Cedar Falls and then beginning to write replies.[6] The majority of the issue uses Marks's reply as captions for the images, which are presented without any bubbles or internal dialogue; the captions remain outside of the frame of the image at all times, creating an immediate distance between the words and images in the mind of the reader. The artwork for these panels lacks the sharp lines that are present in the rest of the issue. This lack of clarity is most evident in the rendering of faces, which appear to become more generic and anonymous than in the rest of the series on the whole. The transitions between these panels follow the lead of the captions and, as such, are not fluid at all. However, the fact that they follow the letter's narration means that the transitions do not jar for the reader as much as they would if the images did not follow the letter device.

The style of writing that comprises the captions reads exactly as a letter from a young son to his parents would. It is colloquial and fluid, makes occasional offhand comments ("You sure do get hungry in the bush!") and, most importantly, is peppered with parenthetical explanations of army slang, directed at Marks's mother: "Over here we move around in slicks (that's slang for helicopters, Mom) all the time" (2010: 30). The fact that Marks so often makes corrections to the letter suggests that it is handwritten, and composed quickly. For example, at one point Marks writes "this is army talk for whatever the Brass, sorry, the officers, have in mind" (2010: 33). Were this not a handwritten letter, the corrections would likely have been removed. Their inclusion substantiates the story's contention that Marks is writing this in the "bush."

The most arresting feature of this issue of *The 'Nam* is the degree of disconnection between the words and images. Marks describes the events of Operation Cedar Falls to his parents in plain language that is ambiguous in its meaning. His descriptions are not inaccurate but they fail to fully describe the horror and violence that he witnesses. The vast majority of the panels and their associated captions include this disconnection. At one point, Marks describes his job as "helping to cordon the perimeter," which sounds innocuous but is accompanied by an image of a Vietnamese man on a bike being shot in the back with an M14 rifle. In the next panel, he writes that "it wasn't an easy job but on the whole we managed to do it" (2010: 36). Again, the choice of words is calm and measured but the accompanying image is of marine aircraft dropping bombs and the subsequent explosion. If one chose to read only the captions, one would receive a calm and carefully sanitized account of what happened—not incorrect but by no means the truth. Reading the images alone, one receives a disorganized visual report of the same event with no censoring, but also no explanation of the images.

Although it would be correct to suggest that Marks's not fully accurate letter is his attempt to protect his parents (especially his mother, who evidently has little knowledge of military life) from the reality of his tour of Vietnam, this is only part of the matter. It is also a way of protecting himself. If he memorializes this event in a letter to his parents in these carefully chosen words, that is how it will remain in his memory. Thus, Marks is creating this softened rendering of events for himself as much as for anyone else. Moreover, at this point in the story arc, Marks is "short," having less than one month left in Vietnam before his tour is over. It is highly likely that the reason Marks writes with such blandness and lack of emotion is because this is how he sees it. Throughout the series, the character develops from a naïve and easily startled young man into a "combat veteran" (2010: 28). For Marks, as with so many soldiers, his key concern is his own survival and the survival of his fellow soldiers. The disjunction between images, then, is not only a break in the relationship between image and word in Marks's letter but also in his perception of events. The amount of traumatic stimuli that Marks has encountered during his tour has caused a traumatic rupture to occur but he is not currently experiencing explicit symptoms of this. Rather, he is still in what Freud terms the "incubation period" (2001a: 67), the period of delay between the traumatic event and the onset of explicit traumatic symptoms. The narrative gives no indication as to whether Marks goes on to develop serious traumatic symptoms.

There is an awareness of the limitations of this narrative device within the comic itself. After witnessing the death of another soldier from gunshot Marks says, "I keep forgetting . . . My brain keeps blocking it out . . ." In the next panel, he stares at a blank piece of paper, thinking, "How do I tell my folks about that?" (2010: 45). It is with this thought that Marks concludes his letter with well wishes and love. There are no words to explain the death in any way that will be accessible to either Marks's parents or his own comprehension, and so the event is passed over. The fact that the event is present in the comic outside of the letter narrative attests to the inadequacy of this narrative device—or, indeed, any—to make full sense of such events.

"Notes from the World" uses Marks as a letter-writing narrator in a different way. Rather than writing from Vietnam to his parents in America, he is writing from America (namely, South Carolina) to Rob Little in Vietnam. The panel used to introduce the letter device is drawn as an airmail envelope (2010: 100). Unlike "From Cedar Falls, with Love," there are no breaks in the letter narrative; it runs without interruption to its end and then the narration moves back to Rob reading the letter in Vietnam. Marks explains his experience of leaving Vietnam and flying back to the US, spending time with his parents and then returning to duty at Fort Jackson. As with "From Cedar Falls, with Love," the artistic style of the letter panels lacks clarity of line and color, but not to the same extent. Additionally, unlike the previous issue, "Notes from the World" uses captions that are integral to the frame of the image. There is no physical disconnection between words and images in this comic. Indeed, there is little detachment between the captions and the images throughout the whole of Marks's letter. There is one section which has very few captions, in which Marks visits his old girlfriend to find that she has a baby (it does not say whether the child is Marks's), but he only briefly writes about this: "I decided to go and see my old girlfriend . . . the less said about that fiasco, the better" (2010: 106).

There is a disparity in levels of separation between word and image in these two comics. For the most part, the image and words match perfectly. This comic makes no great demand of closure on the reader. Rather, it is a description of the difficulties faced by returning soldiers. Marks can speak more openly because he is writing to a fellow veteran who will understand his situation better than most. He ends the letter with a claim that he is going to write about his experience in Vietnam as this can only be done "by someone who understood what it's really like" (2010: 114). While this is a noble endeavor, the reader is left questioning whether this will ever be possible, given the innate unknowability of traumatic experience and the difficulty in transcribing it into a coherent narrative, as made plain by Marks's earlier attempt at an explanation in "From Cedar Falls, with Love."

Long Distance Chronology

The most temporally sophisticated issue of *The 'Nam* is "Auld Acquaintance" (2011: 120–41). The story is set in late February 1968, just before the end of the Battle for Hue, the longest battle of the Vietnam War. However, though the amount of time covered is no longer than an hour, the location covers thousands of miles, from Vietnam to the US and back again several times. The issue opens with three soldiers—Clark, Ice, and Aeder—discussing the lack of honest reporting on the events in Hue. Clark mentions his experience of finding a Viet Cong mass grave. Although this recollection takes only two panels, it is accompanied by inset captions and the frame has a wavy outline to suggest a dreamlike state of memory. Ice is disturbed by the fact that this detail is not mentioned in any press release. With his loud declaration of "If they lie to us about what's goin' on, what do they do back in the world?" (2011: 122) the narrative shifts to Columbia University in New York City, where Ed Marks (now free of the army and a student) is watching the television news, which states the same information that Ice and Clark were debating in the previous panels. The panel's main caption states "at that same time" to make the reader aware that these events are happening concurrently, albeit 8,500 miles apart.

Marks discusses the televised coverage of the news, which he believes to be unequivocal truth, with a university professor. Marks's anger at the professor's extreme antiwar stance causes him to snap a pencil in half (2011: 127). The narrative moves again, to the Philippines, where "Top" Tarver (First Sergeant Tarver) breaks his "substandard military crap pencil" (2011: 128). Tarver discusses the events in Hue and his time in Vietnam with Corporal Lewin, flashing back to his time with Rob Little. After this, the narration moves again—this time to Rob Little on a rifle range in Fort Bliss, Texas. Here the linking image is less explicit. It is a close up of Tarver's face followed by a close-up of Little's. Both are African-American and are drawn similarly, save for Tarver's characteristic gold teeth. On the rifle range the topic of discussion is the ongoing Battle in Hue. Rob drinks a bottle of coke and the action moves once more, this time to a meeting "somewhere in America" of various employees of comics companies discussing the possibility of holding a convention for comics fans. This is a reference to the first San Diego Comic-Con (now the largest and most famous comics convention in the world) in 1970. This mini-story seems to jar with the others in this issue. The only link to *The 'Nam* is the presence of the character Thomas, who was a private in Vietnam for several issues and is identifiable by his extreme clumsiness.[7] Thomas spills his coke (this is the link to Rob Little) and ruins a stack of comics, holding them up by their soggy corners. Again, the narrative shifts, this time to an unidentified location and a group of soldiers discussing the progress of the American troops in Hue. Sergeant Crews concludes that the American forces "will lose this war ... and in the press too" (2011: 137). The final shift of narrative is, again, to an unidentified location (the image detail implies a hospital) and a character called Frank T. Verzyl, who is catatonic from his experiences in Vietnam.[8] The last tier of the issue contains two panels: the first shows Verzyl's doctor saying, "I don't think the war will ever end for this one," the second gives a close-up of Verzyl's frozen and terrified face and the nurse's reply of "and for a lot of others, doctor, too many others" (2011: 141). This exchange stands as a comment on the prevalence of severe trauma in veterans of the Vietnam War.[9]

Aside from the linking images that move from one mini-narrative to the next, the entire issue is tied together with a single narrative concern—the media coverage of the ongoing Battle of Hue. The differing opinions of each set of characters, as well as the different types of media reporting that are mentioned, are the catalyst for this discussion. The artistic style is consistent throughout each mini-narrative. Furthermore, of the seven mini-narratives, five contain analeptic panels as the characters relate past experiences. This use of a specific narrative technique creates continuity between each individual narrative. The chronotope of this story is geographically wide and temporally narrow. There is no indication of how much time passes, but each shift in narrative is accompanied by a caption that suggests the events either occur simultaneously or occur one immediately after the other. Thus, the amount of time it takes the reader to construct the narrative is roughly the amount of time that the events of the narrative take. The temporal structure allows the reader to interact with the narrative on a temporal level—the reader moves through the narrative at the same speed as the action is happening. Conversely, the atypicality of this chronotope is disorienting. The reader is expected to jump from place to place, across a wide geographical distance, in the turn of a page, with no indication as to when this jump will occur. The thread of discussion that runs through each section is the only thing the reader has to tie the narrative together. This puts a strain on the reader, who has to construct a coherent narrative. Although this is the case in all comics, it is more pronounced in "Auld Acquaintance," as the reader is forced to move through each section quickly and make the jump between sections as smooth as possible in order to maintain the narrative, with very little assistance from the narrative itself. In a traumatic narrative, the idea of being forced—or coerced—into reading becomes particularly pertinent. The individuals within the narrative are forced into certain situations and their viewing of such situations is coerced, rather than voluntary; furthermore, this coercive viewing returns in the psychological aftermath of the event. Placing the reader in a similar position of coercive reading heightens the affective nature of the reading experience and influences the creation of the traumatic chronotope.

The Intrusion of History

The first level of the chronotope relates to the text's representation of history and how the chronotope "serves to assimilate real temporal (in the extreme, historical) reality" into literary texts (Bakhtin, 1978: 493). This use of the chronotope makes it possible "to reflect and introduce into the artistic plane . . . substantial elements of historical reality" (1978: 523). When an actual (historical) event is incorporated into a text it is chronotopic. As with the creation of the chronotope of Dresden mentioned previously, the inclusion of an event marks it as a particular place in both space and time. However, even in texts which find their basis in historical events there is still an overarching fictionality to them. Although the supra-event is real, the minor events and activities of the text may not be.

There is a trend gathering momentum in artistic representations of conflict for including "actual" information. By this, I am not referring to the works of artists such as Joe Sacco, who use the comics form to create journalistic narratives and give voice to marginalized communities, as I discussed in the previous chapter. Instead, what I am referring to are the photographs and video footage of the event spliced into the narrative in an attempt to lend it an air of accuracy and historical credibility. A clear example is the recreation of Robert Capa's photographs of the D-Day landing in 1944 in the film *Saving Private Ryan* (1998). There is an assumption that what the camera tells us is unvarnished truth. For the most part, when speaking of conflict photography, this is true, though it is important to add that very few photographs of conflict were completely unposed prior to the Vietnam War, which marked the beginning of the war photographer as a "hands-off" observer. That said, it is important to note here that claiming a photograph is a true and accurate record of an event is problematic. Roland Barthes discusses the relationship between connotation and denotation, arguing that in photography the two are distinct from each other (Barthes, 1977: 15–51); John Fiske claims succinctly, "denotation is what is photographed, connotation is how it is photographed" (1982: 91). Barthes writes:

> Denotation is not the first meaning, but pretends to be so; under this illusion, it is ultimately no more than the last of the connotations (the one which seems both to establish and close the reading), the superior myth by which the text pretends to return to the nature of language, to language as nature. (1974: 9)

Hence, the photograph that is taken at face value as being an honest representation of a moment in time should, instead, be viewed as a representation of the event. However, the inclusion of photographs in comics does not necessarily consider this and instead uses the photographs to cement the comic's narrative arc into a wider historical event. Bruno Latour contends that "the more the human hand can be seen as having worked on an image, the weaker is the image's claim to offer truth" (2002: 18). Although the human hand is indeed at work in the creation of a photograph, it is nowhere near as evident as in a comic; this belief in photograph as truth sits as a false-opposite to the "weaker" comics form.

Simone Weil (2003) attests that violence turns anyone subjected to it into a "thing"—photography does the same (2003: 7). Photographs capture an event, a person, or a place, crystallizing it into a single, consumable image. It is in part due to photography's ability to encapsulate and crystallize that certain images of conflicts become "the image" of that particular event. However, this is not a simple case of picking the "best" or "favorite" photograph. Sontag writes:

> Photographs that everyone recognises are now a constituent part of what a society chooses to think about, or declares that it has chosen to think about. It calls these ideas "memories"... What is called collective memory is not a remembering but a stipulating: that *this* is important, and this is the story about how it happened, with the pictures that lock the story in our minds. (2004a: 76–77)

The locked-in picture becomes an icon: the uncaptioned image, endlessly repeated—a stand-alone representation of the event. Furthermore, it becomes a chronotope. The still image of a split-second of an event becomes, in that singular time and place, the event itself. Taking this into consideration, I look at two famous photographs and their subsequent comics representations: Richard Drew's *The Falling Man* (2001) and Eddie Adams's *Saigon Execution* (1968). I consider how each sits in relation to the chronotope and, furthermore, how each works as a chronotope in the wider narrative of the comic.

As a chronotope, "9/11" is very narrow. Not only is the temporal aspect confined, even by its name, to one day (although the aftermath was not over so quickly), but the spatial aspect has also been narrowed, with many people forgetting that the events of 9/11 were not just those that occurred in downtown New York City, but also in rural Pennsylvania and Washington, DC. Regardless, the chronotope of 9/11 does not take this into account and so it has become crystallized as the events of mid-morning in New York City on September 11, 2001. Because of this, many of the most famous photographs of 9/11 are of events that happened during this narrow time-window.

. . .

There are twelve photographs in the series taken by Richard Drew that have been labeled *The Falling Man* (2001). They were taken as a man fell from the upper floors of the North Tower. Although there is much speculation, he has never been officially identified. This photograph is one of the most hotly debated of all those taken on that day. The *New York Times* only printed the photograph once due to the barrage of complaints.[10] The photographer himself noted that many people were commenting to him personally that they found the image "too disturbing" (Drew, 2010). The objections of the public about this image's publication stem not only from concern for the victim's family but also a concern for themselves. Several thousand people were in the towers at the time of the impact; several million people were in New York City. For the residents of New York and the US, this photograph is a threat of what could happen, what might happen. The objections, then, were an objection to a glimpse at a possible, devastating future through an image of a definite and traumatizing present. There are many references to *The Falling Man* throughout *American Widow*. Torres includes a full-page representation of the photograph (2008: 197). However, she picks one of the less well-known photographs of the series, where the man is not falling against a backdrop of the building. That she chooses to show the figure as a tiny and barely perceptible mark on an otherwise mostly empty page is visually startling. The expanse of white space is vast and void-like, the tiny figure falling parallel to a very basic drawing of a building. The lack of visual information on the page draws the eye to the figure, despite the size, as it appears at first to be a smudge on the page. It is only upon realization of what the mark represents that it becomes clear that this is a rendering of Drew's photograph. This page is not presented as a bleed. Instead, it is kept constrained within a frame to emphasize the photographic nature of the moment paused in time (and, as a chronotope, time-space).

Soon after the event, Torres believed her husband to have jumped. She writes, "You said, 'Fuck it, I'm out of here.' And that was that" (2008: 46). However, at no point does the text substantiate this claim. That said, it is a recurring motif throughout, coming to represent the tragedy of the event and the desperate decisions that had to be made: to jump or not to jump. On the page before the "Falling Man" image, Torres writes, "The Medical Examiner said it took you eighteen seconds to fall. What were you thinking?" (2008: 196). This is a complex comment. Is the medical examiner definitely talking about Eddie or is he speaking in general? When Torres asks "what were you thinking?" is she meaning it in the sense of "what on earth was going through your head to make you do that?" Or, more literally, "what was going through your mind as you fell?" The meaning remains ambiguous. Torres's use of *The Falling Man* in the text resonates with what Jonathan Safran Foer says when he talks of the photograph as representing "a twenty-first century Tomb of the Unknown Soldier" (2007: 153). The photograph has become an icon for grieving families. Regardless of whether Eddie is the Falling Man or not, the inclusion of the image in *American Widow* is further testimony to the permeation of this image in the visual memory of 9/11. Furthermore, it keeps the chronotope of 9/11 firmly centered on this one place and this one time.

Unlike the chronotope of 9/11, which is concentrated on the tight and narrow area of sixteen acres and several hours, the chronotope of the Vietnam War is wider, although temporally difficult to define, due to the transition period in the mid-1950s, when the French forces left (signaling the end of the First Indochina War) and American forces moved in. That said, the official dates of the Vietnam War are accepted as November 1, 1955, to April 30, 1975. The spatial boundaries of the conflict do not entirely correspond to the name, as the conflict spread into Laos and Cambodia. This aside, the spatial and temporal parameters of the Vietnam chronotope are considerably wider than that of 9/11.

Previously I mentioned the lack of posed Vietnam War photographs. It is entirely true that very few were posed by the photographer, but there are other people capable of setting up a shot, aside from the person behind the camera. Eddie Adams's world-famous (and Pulitzer Prize-winning) photograph *Saigon Execution*, taken in February 1968, shows the chief of the South

Vietnamese national police, Brigadier General Nguyen Ngoc Loan, shooting a Vietcong suspect in a street in Saigon. We do not doubt the un-staged nature of this image. However, "it was staged—by General Loan, who had led the prisoner out to the street where journalists had gathered; he would not have carried out the summary execution there had they not been available to witness it" (Sontag, 2004a: 53).

Adams's photograph captures the moment of the impact of the bullet at point blank range. The prisoner's face is turned to the side in a grimace but he has not yet begun to fall. The general's arm is still outstretched. Of this, his most famous photograph, Adams is recorded as saying:

> They walked down to the street corner. We were taking pictures. He turned out to be a Viet Cong lieutenant. And out of nowhere came this guy [General Loan] who we didn't know. I was about five feet away and he pulled out his pistol, shot him [the VC prisoner] in the head and walked by us and said, "They killed many of my men and many of our people." I kept making pictures. (Adams, 1969)

This photograph became one of the most important images of the antiwar movement, adopted as a representation of the excesses and injustices of war, although Adams disagrees with this, stating that it is more accurately a representation of the unfathomable decisions one is required to make during wartime.

As I discussed previously, *The 'Nam* is careful to follow a rigid temporal structure which mimics the standard US Army tour of duty. This allows the writers of the series to place the characters into actual historical events without causing disruption to the comic's timescale. This gives the creative team more flexibility as to what they can include in terms of actual landmark events throughout the conflict. Hence, in Issue 24, the story arc involves the Tet Offensive and the moment of Adams's photograph. The issue ends with a full-page image (Murray and Golden, 2011: 93).

The image fills an entire page but is not presented as a bleed, as with Torres's representation of *The Falling Man*. This is a double-frame image—two images presented one inside the other. The camera lens serves as an inner frame for the restaging of Adams's photograph, reflected in vivid color. This is a major change from the original, which is presented in black and white. The bold colors here are typical of the mainstream style to which *The 'Nam* vigorously subscribes. The outer frame shows the camera itself being held by—it is assumed—Adams, though the image includes little of his face. The image appears cramped, as both hands are visible, holding the camera tightly. Adams's mouth is open as he speaks, suggesting an expression of shock. The

Fig. 5.2. "Beginning of the End" in *The 'Nam Volume 3*, Murray and Golden, 2011. p 93. © Marvel Entertainment.

name of the camera brand is clearly displayed, not only for realism's sake (the brand would be visible on the camera, of course) but also to remind us that without technology pioneered by Leica this type of photojournalism would not be possible.

The speech bubble in this frame gives rise to questions of terminology. Adams shouts, "Holy . .! Suu, keep shooting! Just keep shooting!"[11] But is it to Suu that Adams aims the command to "keep shooting"? "Shoot" as a photographic term is first noted in the 1890s (OED, 2012). This is the same time that another firearms term, "snapshot," also entered photographic discourse. The movement of these two terms from one distinct discourse to another may be coincidental, but it does show an awareness of the camera's ability to take something of its target, as a weapon might. If this reading is reversed to suggest that Adams is not talking to Suu but to General Loan, the words have a decidedly different meaning. Shooting a prisoner makes for good photographs—award-winning ones in Adams's case. To quote a popular maxim of the American press: "If it bleeds, it leads." The image and the speech give no indication as to which reading is intended. It is for the reader to decide for themselves.

The use of the double-frame is not common in comics. This format shifts the reader's focus. We are not only watching the events take place but we are also watching the watchers; not only are we given the action, but also the reaction. For a readership which was not present at this event, the shifting focus allows us to understand the position of the observers: Adams is evidently shocked and fascinated by this event—the reader is prompted to feel likewise. However, there is also an aspect of meta-narrative here. The reader is reminded, through the frame of the camera's lens, that what is shown is mediated by someone: in the case of this image, by Adams; in the case of the wider text, by Murray and Golden. The unique insight that draws us towards the traumatic experience captured here on film and paper also pushes us away with a coarse shove, reminding us of the mediated nature of everything shown. I take up the issue of mediation and relationships between representational levels in the final chapter of this book as part of a wider discussion of postmodernism.

This image is metaleptical; the interplay of many narrative levels and the double-frame allows for this to occur. If Adams is the creator of the image-event, he sits at the extradiegetic level, in the position of the image's narrator. This is attested to by the fact that Adams's hands and camera frame the image as a whole and thus create the double-frame within the hyperframe. The image-event itself—the action within the narrative—exists at the metadiegetic level. Adams, as photographer, is creating the story, choosing how to frame it and take it at the precise moment of his choice. The photograph itself, as encapsulated in the camera's lens, is the story being told. The collision of extradiegetic and metadiegetic narratives creates metalepsis.

The temporal aspect of this photograph's chronotope is narrow—only the split second of the camera shutter's movement to capture the image—and this in turn narrows the spatial aspect. However, the overarching chronotope of Vietnam encompasses a broad spatio-temporal area and this photograph does not condense it. What it does do, however, is to allow an intensely iconic event to act as a foothold for readers, rooting the text in its historical context and giving validation to the historical accuracy of the rest of the text. Thus, the inclusion of this photograph has a different function within the whole text to Torres's representation of *The Falling Man*. Whereas Torres's personal history—and the unknown final acts of her husband—are inextricably tied to the photograph, *Saigon Execution* ties a whole cast of characters to a conflict, though not necessarily to the event photographed.

• • •

A photograph typically relies on an audience—it is not a common occurrence to take a photograph of something and then hide it away, although the trope of hiding a precious photograph appears consistently throughout literature and art. The concealing of a photograph until a certain time—after a death or a key event—is often seen in narratives of mourning and loss. These instances are generally exceptions to the norm, and the displaying of a photograph in a public place (be it a physical display in an exhibition or a reproduction in the media) moves the image into the public sphere. An event that had previously been viewed by a limited number of people can (almost instantly) be viewed by millions of people internationally, despite their having little or no direct link to the photographed event or person whatsoever. In this respect, a photograph can act as a bridge between the public and private spheres. What is, at its basic level, a photograph of a man being shot becomes representative, in the act of viewing, of a much wider conflict. In these representations of conflict, traumatic temporality, which can be both fractured and frozen, unites all viewers in the frozen moment of the photograph; time becomes collective and connects.

This creation of a collective traumatic time is not strictly metaleptical. Although the image-narrative begins to exist on a separate narrative level to the event itself by the fact it becomes a representative image of a much wider event, the collective trauma that arises from it pauses time. Temporality becomes both cohesive and coagulated. The image is a freeze-frame of the event. In this respect, photographic representations of conflict span the public and private spheres to create a traumatic chronotope that is, paradoxically, both sticky and fractured, disconnecting and reconnecting.

Invasion of the Superheroes

Moving away from the textual temporal relationships that are contained within tiers and hyperpanels, there is a wider issue at hand that comes into question when reading mainstream comics, especially superhero narratives. How can superheroes be involved in historical events, especially war and conflict, when their super powers would surely guarantee that their "side" achieves an unequivocal victory? It is a recurring theme throughout the mainstream comics universes that superheroes are unable to intervene in actual historical events: "generally serialized comic books (and superhero comics especially) are predicated upon the exclusion of history in the sense that characters cannot directly intervene in history" (Cooper and Atkinson, 2008: 60).

Although the superhero genre has experienced a healthy and stable popularity following the resurgence of the genre in the 1970s, since 2001 this popularity has increased greatly. DC and Marvel combined are worth an estimated $400 million (Hughes, 2013: online). For many, this rise in popularity since 2001 (or, more specifically, since 9/11) signals a desire for escapism and safety, epitomizing the "need of the 'average' American to escape from the very real horrors of international unrest and terrorism whose epic moment was 9/11" (Roberts, 2004: 211). For others, the repetition of widespread urban destruction in post-9/11 mainstream comics and filmic adaptations suggests a desire to recreate the events in a medium that gives us control: "This time, the terrorists don't win" (Smith and Goodrum, 2011: 488). In Freudian terms, what happens here is that shock—that which is uncontrollable and uncontrolled—is replaced with anticipatory fear—that which is controllable (Freud and Breuer, 2000: 57). The ability to be in command of the events of the narrative, despite what is known to be the "true" ending, gives back the control that is lost in the shock of a traumatic rupture.

There is an issue of cultural saturation at hand here. American popular culture is so deeply imbued with superheroes that they have become a cultural staple. It goes without saying that the superheroes will save the day at the end of mainstream comics, though there will undoubtedly be perilous obstacles to overcome first. It is expected that there will be a superhero come to the rescue. As such, this desire for a hero has (understandably) filtered into the cultural imagination. The fact that this is wholly unlikely is an unpleasant shock. I am not suggesting that Western society (and America in particular) is naïve enough to think that Superman is a real person who will save the day. Rather, the lack of this level of altruistic heroism in typical everyday life is a rude awakening to a society which has constructed great narratives around these very qualities. Thus, the desire to replace shock with anticipatory fear cannot occur in reality because the situations that would allow this to happen (the arrival of a superhero) do not exist.

In 1990, in an attempt to boost dwindling sales, *The 'Nam* introduced the Marvel superhero the Punisher for two issues in a story arc entitled "The Punisher invades The 'Nam," which was reborn for a three-issue arc in 1992. These three issues follow a flashback of Frank Castle (alias Castiglione) and his tour of Vietnam. The Punisher was enjoying a brief burst of popularity and it was thought that this crossover would draw current Punisher fans to the series. The choice of this particular character was based on more than just current sales figures. Castle's character is a classic antihero. Following the mob-ordered murder of his wife and children, Castle, a marine and Vietnam veteran, becomes a vigilante, employing both war weaponry and martial arts training to apprehend his targets (Dougall, 2009); I return to the issue of Castle's motivations in the Excursus. It is Castle's military background that seems the most obvious reason for his selection for *The 'Nam*. However, a character who remorselessly punishes the "enemy" and acts only "for the good" (in this case, the American military) adds a dimension of revenge upon the VC and NVA that would be absent in interactions with other characters.

When it was first conceived, *The 'Nam* was carefully constructed to work alongside actual historical events and typical army tour chronology. The addition of the Punisher skews this attempt at a realistic chronology. Even though Castle is not a "super" hero, as he has no superpowers, his extremely high pain tolerance and skill in armed and unarmed combat removes him from the ranks of the ordinary soldier. In the first story arc, Castle is sent on a one-man mission to kill a VC sniper called "The Monkey," a feat he manages to accomplish with very little difficulty. This is in direct contrast to the rest of the arcs in *The 'Nam*, which, if not representing actual military maneuvers, depict plausible scenarios. Thus, not only does the inclusion of the Punisher affect the temporal structure of *The 'Nam* by the fact that he is a (semi) superhero, but it also affects the realistic nature of the narrative and the continuity therein.

"The Punisher invades The 'Nam" is not the only interaction of mainstream Marvel characters with the series. While the Punisher's story arcs detract from the series' continuity, the involvement of Iron Man, Captain America, and Thor in Issue 41 ("Back in the Real World") does not. Rather, these characters exist on a different narrative level, being part of a "what if" daydream by a character who has been reading comic books. Iceman, a well-respected sergeant, is packing to leave Vietnam at the end of his fourth tour and finds a stack of comics belonging to Private Aeder.[12] Iceman imagines that Thor disrupts a VC ambush by altering the weather, Captain America uses his shield to destroy a bomb at the American embassy, and Iron Man blows up two missiles before they hit two American planes. Following this, the three capture Ho Chi Minh from a rally in Hanoi and take him to Paris to negotiate. Iceman and a fellow soldier, Martini, laugh about this, saying, "That's the way wars should be fought!" (Murray et al, 1990: 19). However, the men make it clear that they are aware of the fictional nature of these daydreams and the complete inability of superheroes to exist, let alone intervene. They are considered as amusing "what if" scenarios, suitable for escapism and entertainment alone.

In the case of "Back in the Real World," the inclusion of superhero intervention is not simply for the purposes of entertainment. The responses of the soldiers—that war is not how popular media displays it and superheroes could not exist in war because then there would not be war—stands as testament to what Eco discusses in his essay when he writes that superheroes would win the war outright and so cannot be put into war situations in any realistic sense. Keeping the superheroes within the realm of the fantastical maintains the realism of *The 'Nam*. It also allows the series to work in the opposite way to superhero narratives. By removing the events which allow shock to become anticipatory fear, it allows the narrative to remain as realistic as possible. By removing any chance of a typical mainstream conclusion, the reader must move through the text with the same level of unknowing and uncertainty as the characters.

Keeping superheroes from intervening allows the badge of heroism to fall on the characters that the reader recognizes as real and deserving of it. The final panel of the issue shows Iceman's helicopter leaving Vietnam, while his two colleagues wave him off and the heads of the three superheroes are in the background. The message of this panel is unambiguous: Real heroes do not wear capes and are imbued with a modesty that removes the self-importance that is often characteristic of many superheroes. The several hundred short comics collected into anthologies to raise money for 9/11 charities take this issue of heroism and "superheroism" in a similar direction. "Unreal" (Seagle, Rouleau, and Sowd, 2002: 15–16) uses Superman to illustrate the fact that "the apparent failure on the part of superheroes is diverted . . . by endowing non-superheroes with superhero-like qualities" (Smith and Goodrum, 2011: 495). It is the rebranding of heroes that is seen in "Unreal" that becomes the overarching aim of these four publications. The ultimate heroes—the men of tomorrow with superhuman ability and incredible gadgetry—are rendered powerless. Their place is taken by what Joe Kubert describes as "ordinary men and women engaging in extra-ordinary acts of heroism" (2002: 214). In a text that aims to make heroes of "mere mortals," the powers of superheroes *must* be removed. There is no way that ordinary people can compete with superhuman abilities. However, "[superheroes'] status is diminished by the heroism of people who do not possess superhuman powers and whose efforts therefore have to be ranked more highly" (Heinze, 2007). Tim Sale's one-page comic reworks the "superhero in a telephone booth" cliché to place the power in the hands of the New York Fire Department (Sale, 2002: 70). A young boy changes from a Superman T-shirt to one bearing the acronym "FDNY." Of this, Cooper and Atkinson write: "The transformation is complete with the readers accepting the movement from the mythic figure of the superhero to the localized fire fighter" (2008: 71).

In these comics, superheroes cannot save the day even if they wish to; the flexible temporal scheme of the mainstream comics universes does not comfortably allow for the inclusion of historical accuracy. However, superheroes are not rendered completely defunct. In *New Avengers*, Cap is scathingly referred to as "the soldier—the man out of time" (Bendis and Djurdjevic, 2010). This is a reference to the fact that he had spent the previous sixty years frozen in the depths of the ocean. However, it also makes a wider comment on the position of both soldiers and superheroes. Speaking of Cap as a soldier and, to use Kurt Vonnegut's term, a man "unstuck in time" with no temporal home; he is a man whose importance is not bound to any one period in history (Vonnegut, 1991). If the need for soldiers is not time-bound, there will always be a need for them. This statement becomes a comment on the perpetual nature of man's involvement in conflict.

The 9/11 charity comics make clear the point that the input of superheroes is limited to witnessing the events. In one comic, Superman's dog, Krypto, shares his water bowl with some police rescue dogs (Loeb, Pacheco and Meriño, 2002). As Umberto Eco suggests, to incorporate historical events into the narrative universe of superheroes imposes great limitations; so much of the superhero universe is written and rewritten in different ways, but it is not possible to do this with actual events (Eco, 1997: 123). Thus, the superhero can only be a witness; he cannot participate because that would potentially change the course of events. On countless occasions Superman has been able to redirect massive objects using only his superhuman strength so why not a plane *en route* to New York? Instead, "the act of witnessing is the only form of action" open to these characters (Cooper and Atkinson, 2008: 69). This inability of superheroes to act in times of conflict is to be expected, given the temporal guidelines that govern their intervention. If they were able to intervene then this would remove any sense of realism. For *The 'Nam*, this would affect the entire creative ethos of the series. For the post-9/11 comics, it would mean that the "real heroes" lost their position as superheroes took over. In both cases, it would mean that the events of the comic would be altered in such a way as to allow anticipatory fear to create a safe, controllable narrative. This would neither be accurate, nor a viable representation of a traumatic experience.

• • •

For Art Spiegelman, one of the key aspects of comics is

> the fact that moments in time are juxtaposed. In a story that is trying to make chronological and coherent the incomprehensible, the juxtaposing of past and present insists that past and present are always present—one does not displace the other the way it happens in film. (Spiegelman, 2011a: 165)

Comics, then, is a form in which, by its very nature, time can move in a variety of chronological patterns. Whereas in film the viewer sees one period of time at once, in comics the reader can see all panels on the page (or double-page spread) at a glance. This fact alone alters the way in which comics as a form works on a temporal level. Spiegelman goes on to define comics as "an essentialized form of diagramming a narrative movement through time" (2011a: 168). This definition speaks to the reduction that goes into the creation of each narrative arc and each panel—the selection and construction of each moment and its relationship to those around it. Applying the filter of traumatic representation to a form with an already atypical relationship to time exacerbates the existing temporal issues. As this chapter discusses, issues of temporality and personal chronology are crucial factors in the development of a traumatic neurosis. For many sufferers of a traumatic rupture, the chronological disruption is the most debilitating and obvious of the symptoms that are experienced. This disruption is also one of the easiest to be represented in the comics form, as I have already explained, due to the comics form's grammatical thread—the transitions and movement of time across the gutters. The recreation of the trauma is heavily reliant on the fact that so much of the construction of the narrative's chronology is dependent on the reader.

6

Postmodernism vs. Comics and Trauma

Moe: It's po-mo! Postmodern! Yeah, all right, weird for the sake of weird.
—Groening et al., *The Simpsons* (2001)

In the previous chapter, I discussed the issue of time in relation to both comics and trauma; the relationship between the three is complex. Often it is the symptoms of temporal disruption that are the most obvious and destabilizing. The ability to manipulate time is central to the comics form. In this chapter, I reconsider time, trauma, and comics in the light of postmodernism. My discussion calls on the work of several key postmodern theorists, especially Jean-François Lyotard, Fredric Jameson, and Linda Hutcheon. I consider the issue of history and its relationship to trauma in general, as well as traumatic representation in comics. Prior to this, however, I wish to give some consideration to the question of whether comics can be seen as a postmodernist form.

In my introduction, I argued that many aspects of modernist art, especially panelization and aspectival viewing, are equally important for comics. That a comics reading of *Guernica* is possible gives weight to my suggestion. While I do not contend that comics is a strictly modernist form, many of the features of comics time discussed in Chapter 5 appear to have more in common with the temporal issues typically found in postmodernist art, especially in relation to nonlinear postmodern chronology and complex hermeneutic codes. The question, then, is whether it is possible to reconcile these formal aspects between ideas of the modernist and postmodernist; the problem is further compounded by the fact that many of the traits fundamental to the comics form are also found in postmodernist literature. For example, in Chapters 2 and 5, I discussed the importance of the material comic book in narrative development. This is not unique to comics; a body of literature known as ergodic literature shares this relationship between material form and narrative. Espen Aarseth writes:

> In ergodic literature, nontrivial effort is required to allow the reader to traverse the text. If ergodic literature is to make sense as a concept, there must also be non-ergodic literature, where the effort to traverse the text is trivial, with no extranoematic responsibilities placed on the reader except (for example) eye movement and the periodic or arbitrary turning of pages. (1997: 1–2)

BS Johnson's *The Unfortunates* (1969) and Mark Danielewski's *House of Leaves* (2000) are two of the most well-known texts of this type. *The Unfortunates* is presented as twenty-seven unbound sections in a laminated box; only the first and last chapters are so labeled. The reader may read the remaining twenty-five sections in any order. Similarly, *House of Leaves* is a sprawling work of ergodic literature, containing a huge amount of footnotes (many of which contain further footnotes) that force the reader to decide how they move, quite literally, through the pages. This text also uses different colors for certain words (blue for "house," for example) and references to certain characters; different fonts are used to differentiate between characters. It is for the reader to decide how to interpret these aspects of the text and how much importance to place on them in relation to the creation of narrative movement. Considering the demands ergodic literature places on the reader and the range of devices used in its creation, it is easy to categorize this as a subset of postmodernism. However, these devices and the participation of the reader are not unusual for comics. Therefore, is comics a postmodernist form because it works in a similar way to postmodern literature? An affirmative answer could be found in the fact that comics seemingly rejects the distinction between high and low culture. Fredric Jameson writes that a key feature of postmodernism is "the effacement of some key boundaries or separations, most notably the erosion of the older distinction between high culture and so-called mass or popular culture" (1998: 2). However, before answering this question, I wish to consider the relationship between modernism and postmodernism.

In terms of the words themselves, the prefix "post" is confusing. It is evident that postmodernism identifies itself as something that is "not modernism," but the actual meaning of the prefix is ambiguous.[1] This ambiguity immediately signals the complexity of the relationship between the two. In his 1971 work *The Dismemberment of Orpheus*, Ihab Hassan presents the differences between modernism and postmodernism in a table. The opposites presented appear to present a clearly defined line between the two, but underneath the table Hassan writes, "the dichotomies this table represents remain insecure, equivocal. For differences shift, defer. Even collapse; concepts in one vertical column are not all equivalent; and inversions and exceptions, in both modernism and postmodernism, abound" (1971: 269). Hassan is aware of the

Table 2 – Précised from *The Dismemberment of Orpheus*, Ihab Hassan, 1971: 269.	
Modernism	Postmodernism
Purpose	Play
Distance	Participation
Creation	Deconstruction
Paranoia	Schizophrenia

difficulty—indeed, the impossibility—of creating a list of binary opposites between modernism and postmodernism because they are not clear opposites but share many bonds. I have précised the table to include four pairs.

• • •

These four aspects of the table show the extent to which the modernism/postmodernism divide is by no means as clean as one may first think. The comics form is invested in both play and participation—the participation of readers is of utmost importance to the form and there is a distinct playfulness inherent in many of the tricks of narrative construction; reader and writer are involved in a game of sorts. Furthermore, given high modernism's rejection of popular art forms (playful art, if you will), comics is clearly excluded. However, this depends on a particular (narrow) reading of modernism to which I do not subscribe. The binary opposition that Hassan sets up between paranoia and schizophrenia is the most difficult to consider in the table because, especially in the light of trauma, they are not opposites but two facets of one phenomena. The notion that the relationship between modernism and postmodernism involves continuities—in particular, the idea that postmodernism belongs to the history of modernism—is found in many theoretical discussions of the subject, especially those put forward by Linda Hutcheon and Jean-François Lyotard.

For Hutcheon, "postmodernism is both oedipally oppositional and filially faithful to modernism" (1989: 88). Here both ends of the spectrum are represented. In describing the opposition of postmodernism to modernism as "Oedipal," Hutcheon references Freud's interpretation of the Oedipus myth (and subsequent development of the Oedipus complex) and the apparent desire of the son to usurp the father's position, while understanding that this is not possible, instead viewing the father as a rival and object of jealousy. The modernist father, then, is placed as the binary opposite to the jealous postmodernist son who develops ways of distancing himself from the father; at the same time, the postmodernist son remains faithful to the father and maintains the relationship between them. Thus, in this one relationship there is a clear continuation—as in the preoccupation with aspectival viewing—and opposition—as in high modernism's rejection of popular art and postmodernism's embracing of it.

Hutcheon's concept of the dual nature of the modernism/postmodernism relationship echoes Lyotard's essay "Answering the Question: What Is Postmodernism?" in which he writes, "[Postmodernism] is undoubtedly a part of the modern" (1991: 79). Lyotard does not see postmodernism as a separate entity at all but as something that can emerge within the modern at any time, as a natural reaction to modernism. He writes:

> The postmodern would be that which, in the modern, puts forward the unpresentable in presentation itself; that which denies itself the solace of good forms, the consensus of a taste which would make it possible to share collectively the nostalgia for the unattainable; that which searches for new presentations, not in order to enjoy them but in order to impart a stronger sense of the unpresentable. (1991: 81)

What is central to Lyotard's understanding of the postmodern is that it has not broken away from the modern (and does not necessarily desire to) but moves beyond what is "good" and known solely for the purposes of creating new methods of representation in order to demonstrate, paradoxically, the unrepresentable. Hutcheon's and Lyotard's works create a description of postmodernism that allows comics to remain closely affiliated to modernism while still acknowledging the relationship between aspects of the form and aspects of postmodernism. There are texts within the arena of comics that break with the basic practices of the form in a way that could allow them to be called "postmodern comics." In the introduction to a collective comic, *Le Coup de Grâce*, the authors write: "We long for startling transitions, improbable links, new kinds of narrative associations. We find conventional narrative functions boring and stifling. . . . Meaning does not lie in clarification" (2006: ii). These comics seek to push boundaries in a similar way to postmodern literature; though this would be cause to refer to them as "postmodern comics," the issue of linkage and deconstruction prevents this categorization from being clear cut. A comic that does not subscribe to the basic rules of transitions will be difficult, if not impossible, to read. However, "this new kind of comic art disrupts the expectations and habits of readers of traditional comics" (Groensteen, 2013: 31).[2] The clearest example of this new and experimental comic art is seen in Chris Ware's 2012 *Building Stories*, a comic presented as fourteen individual pieces in a box that the reader quite literally constructs for themselves. Groensteen suggests that new ways of thinking about comics has produced heightened awareness that "[it] is not ontologically destined only to perpetuate a canonical model dominated by the categories of narration and legibility, but that its constituent features—the association of text and image, the spatio-topical apparatus for the display of images—lend themselves to the exploration of new forms, new configurations, new ambitions" (2013: 31).

Although it is often the case that that which is new and innovative is automatically labeled as "postmodern," this can be a misnomer. That said, it is not far-fetched to see the break with CCA guidelines (c. 1970s) and the move beyond "house styles" as similar to Lyotard's denial of the "solace of good forms." Comics can be most clearly seen as postmodern through the lens of Lyotardian postmodernism, which does not deny the relationship with modernism but which also moves beyond the more constricting aspects of it.

• • •

Before moving onto discussions of time, I wish to draw attention to a short comment in Jameson's *Postmodernism* (1991) which raises a number of questions in relation to this argument on conflict and modernism/postmodernism. He writes that Vietnam was the "first terrible postmodernist war" (1991: 44). Although this statement receives no explanation from Jameson, many critics have speculated on what he may have meant. Michael Bibby writes:

> To modify the war as "postmodernist" implies that the war is yet another phenomenon of postmodernity. The war, in this sense, is read as exhibiting the traits of a general historical, cultural condition already identifiable. If we can attach a qualification to the name of the war, it must be because that which qualifies it supersedes it, gives it shape, definition, morphological precision. (1999: 148)

It is necessary for me, at this point, to briefly mention the difference between postmodernity and postmodernism. The former refers to the social condition that became prevalent in the 1950s and in which we have remained, according to some thinkers, ever since. Antony Giddens suggests that postmodernity is the social and historical period out of which grows the second term, "postmodernism" (1990: 4). Postmodernism is the cultural phenomenon—the artistic, literary, and political movement—that results from postmodernity. It is the cultural output of the late twentieth century. As Lucas Carpenter observes, the postmodernist lens is applied to the war and specifically the literature it spawned (2003: 31). In this he is combining both postmodernity (the condition in which the war existed) and postmodernism (the art that it engendered). He writes that "some writers . . . tried to accommodate Vietnam within the realistic-naturalistic, 'war is hell' model of the American war novel . . . while others realized that Vietnam demanded a very different kind of narrative paradigm" (2003: 31–32). As I argued in the introduction, Vietnam marked a profound shift in the literature, film, and (perhaps most importantly) journalism of war.[3] While many of the narratives of Vietnam exhibit traits that would lead to their categorization as postmodernist, these traits are also found in narratives of trauma. The coming together of postmodernism and the shift in war experience after Vietnam was fortuitous; the similarities between traumatic representative techniques and postmodernist techniques make the two forms difficult to distinguish. If I contend that Jameson's statement refers not to the presentation but the experience of the Vietnam War, this opens up the war beyond the art it produced. Taking a Lyotardian position, Carpenter states that Vietnam "squelches whatever remains of the Western metanarrative of history that accommodates war as a possible inevitable form of primal human collective behavior" (2003: 32). Indeed, for Carpenter, Vietnam was instrumental in giving rise to postmodernism as it was a "chaotic quagmire with no clear boundaries and no easily identified enemy" (2003: 35). By this reckoning, "postmodern" is a label that can be given to certain kinds of experiences that exist outside of a comfortable Manichean paradigm and rework the metanarratives through which so many of us view the world and categorize our experiences; this is a category which includes trauma. Moreover, this is a way of considering postmodernist experiences that is not dependent on any one historical time. Typically, it is claimed that postmodernism "began" some time after the Second World War and is still in operation in the twenty-first century. Thinking of postmodernism as something that is not time-bound suggests that any experience that fits the criteria given above can be considered a postmodernist experience. This collection of "postmodernist experiences" could include in this any number of wars, genocides, and revolutions, going back, perhaps, to Malory, Beowulf, or even Homer. The postmodernist experience, one that has moved beyond the temporal constraints of modernism while not fully severing the relationship, is very close to the experience of a traumatic rupture and it is in this close relationship that there is a well-defined link between trauma and postmodernism most clearly. Thus, the three concepts of this chapter—comics, postmodernism, and trauma—are certainly linked but the triangular relationship is a complex one. The key to their linkage is time.

The previous chapter was an extended discussion of the importance of time to the basic mechanism of comics and the disrupted temporality usually occurring in traumatic ruptures. Postmodernism has a tempestuous relationship with time for many reasons, including its ability to be a (roughly) time-bound concept and also one that is not governed by its historical position whatsoever. Jameson uses the case study of E. L. Doctorow's 1975 novel *Ragtime* to consider the particular way in which postmodernism attempts to represent both time and history. He describes the specific declarative sentence structure that Doctorow favors while stating that the effect is not really one of the condescending simplification of children's literature, but rather something more disturbing: "The sense of some profound subterranean violence done to American English, which cannot, however, be detected empirically in any of the perfectly grammatical sentences with which this work is formed" (1991: 24).

Doctorow, according to Jameson, attempts to construct a tense that does not exist in English—a specifically verbal past tense—"whose perfective movement . . . serves to separate events from the present of enunciation and to transform the stream of time and action into so many finished, complete, and isolated punctual event objects which find themselves sundered from any present situation" (1991: 24). This tense causes time to clot in a similar way to the clotted temporality seen in traumatic ruptures.[4] More crucially, though, Jameson claims that *Ragtime* is a clear example of how "the historical novel can no longer set out to represent the historical past; it can only 'represent' our ideas and stereotypes about that past. . . . We are condemned to seek History by way of our own pop images and simulacra of that history, which itself remains forever out of reach" (1991: 25).

The stagnation of time (and, therefore, history) seen in *Ragtime* becomes an excellent example of Jameson's central postmodernist concern of "historical deafness"—the inability (or unwillingness) to think historically. Postmodernism's denial of metanarrative and the theories of "wholeness" that were important to modernism leaves theorists to make sense of the present age without the tools and structures that once governed critical thought. Jameson suggests that this "depthlessness [leads to] a consequent weakening of historicity, both in our relationship to public History and in the new forms of our private temporality" (1991: 6). He considers the breakdown of temporal consciousness and the signifying chain in relation to Lacanian understandings of schizophrenia. He writes:

> Lacan describes Schizophrenia as a breakdown in the signifying chain, that is, the interlocking syntagmatic series of signifiers which constitutes an utterance or meaning. . . .] Schizophrenia is a rubble of distinct and unrelated signifiers. (Jameson, 1991: 26)

The schizophrenic, rather like the postmodernist, "is reduced to an experience of pure material signifiers . . . a series of pure and unrelated presents in time" (1991: 27). The postmodernist loss of historicity and historical consciousness resembles schizophrenic detachment. What remains is a complete disconnection from our history; to attempt to root ourselves leads to the realization that images and icons are endlessly referential: "Absolute and absolutely random pluralism . . . a coexistence not even of multiple and alternate worlds so much as of unrelated fuzzy sets and semiautonomous subsystems" (Jameson, 1991: 372). Each element is a free-floating image, with no meaning beyond itself.

The key to the signifying chain is not the links themselves but the linkage—that which binds each link to the overall chain. The content of the chain may not have been changed significantly (or at all) by the condition of postmodernism; it is a change in the glue that binds them. Jameson's postmodernism would see the chain dissolved completely into individual signifying units and trauma works the same way, especially in relation to Herman's contention that trauma is the "intense focus on fragmentary sensation, on image without context" (1992: 38). It could be suggested that each image that forms part of the traumatic memory correlates to a single link within the signifying chain and, in a traumatized mind, each link is to a great extent left single and floating without reference. If the aim of healing a traumatic rupture is to reconnect the floating signifiers of the traumatic event and thus provide understanding and assimilation into the conscious mind, the aim of the trauma artist—to create a piece of art that represents and to some extent reproduces the traumatic event—is congruent. However, in reconnecting divided signifiers, something specific is being done to postmodernism. Attempting to reassemble fragmented experience and reverse temporal dislocation might be said to resist the postmodernism which typically accepts that this recreation is not possible. The aim of both healing and trauma art is to rebuild fragmented experience; in relation to postmodernism, this is closer to the return of a modernist search for the ultimate reference point. Timothy Lustig and James Peacock summarize the apparent relationship between postmodernism and trauma:

> The influence of postmodernism might also do something to explain a feeling that "trauma" has recently become a less compelling topic for writers and critics alike because it carries certain implications about human subjectivity and wholeness which are incompatible with a postmodern take on selves variously described as fractured, plural, elusive, performative or provisional. Recovered memories, traumas overcome or "cured" by catharsis and therapy connote a view of individual sovereignty increasingly open to question. (2013: 9)

Although a traumatic rupture may be a postmodernist experience, the healing and artistic process is not. In line with a modernist attempt to reconnect brokenness—an endeavor that is usually futile—the artistic process depends on at the very least an attempt to reconcile schizophrenic signifiers.

Groensteen's arthrology is an essential concept for consideration in the light of the breakdown and recreation of the chains of signification that occurs in the creation of traumatic art. Groensteen states: "Demonstrating that meaning is inherent to the image is not something that directly speaks to comics, since it is between the panels that the pertinent contextual rapports establish themselves" (2007: 107). The signifying chain is thus of utmost importance. The point can be seen further in the claim from Aron Varga Kibedi that comics is a form whose narrative creation is dependent on "the juxtaposition of images to generate narrative" (1989: 96). Postmodernist breakdown of signification would undermine the basic functioning of the comics form.[5]

It is possible to view the comics form from a reverse angle—to say that it is not primarily a connected form but a broken one. Pierre Mason calls comics "the stuttering art" in reference to the brokenness of the form and the repetition of images that makes narrative construction possible (1985: 72). Mason's comment implies that comics can be seen as broken first and connected second, rather than, as is more common, the other way around. In this respect, then, the postmodernist insistence on the death of unity and wholeness is the starting point of the comics form, which then moves beyond this to synthesize unity within the form through the reader and the use of transitional movement. Whether or not the objective is achieved is dependent in large part on the reader. Reading becomes "more like a deliberate act than a reflex activity" (Peeters and Samson, 2010: 125). As the comics reader has, by the very nature of the form, a considerable input into the creation of the narrative flow, the narrative and meaning construed therein may differ from person to person. This can be plainly seen in the creation of a readership that is akin to the reader Barthes desires in "The Death of the Author" (1967). Barthes states that a text "is not a line of words releasing a single 'theological' meaning (the 'message' of the Author-God) but a multidimensional space in which a variety of writings, none of them original, blend and clash" (1977: 146). The removal of author opens the text to freedom of interpretation for the reader. Comics reading, by this definition, is a poststructuralist (if not also postmodernist) enterprise.

. . .

Comics, postmodernism, and trauma are all concerned with time and temporal ruptures. In trauma, these are ruptures of the mind; for comics, these are ruptures of the gutter, splitting images apart for the reader to suture together. Jameson is acutely aware of postmodernism's interest in rupture. It "looks for breaks, for events rather than new worlds, for the tell-tale instant after which it is no longer the same; for the 'When-it-all-changed,' as [William] Gibson puts it, or better still, for shifts and irrevocable changes in the representation of things and of the way they change" (Jameson, 1991, ix). Postmodernism, however, does not seek to heal the ruptures. Rather, it is aware of the difficulty in healing rifts and does not strive for unity and wholeness, preferring to acknowledge brokenness. This returns us to the quotation from Malcolm Bull in the introduction to this book, in which he contends that psychical unity is not and should not be the aim. That traumatic art and comics do strive for some modicum of wholeness makes a strong relationship between these three concepts difficult, though a preoccupation with temporal ruptures does forge a basic relationship between the three.

The texts I discuss here are all invested in historical time and "actual" events. Both trauma and postmodernism cast doubt on the accuracy of historical remembrance and the ability of art to represent it. As Timothy Melley writes, "Trauma has seemed a valuable model of history not because it represents postmodern indeterminacy, but because it seems to promise unparalleled contact with the past in all its original immediacy and fullness" (2003: 108). He refers to Caruth's point that, for Freud, the neurotic repetition is nothing but the "*unmediated* occurrence of violent events" and "the *literal* return of the event" (2003: 108, emphasis in original). However, Melley makes it clear that there are major flaws with this view of traumatic memory. A truly unmediated return to the event is impossible, due to the nature of memory, which is likely to be imperfect regardless of its traumatic nature. A traumatic model of history is "a model in which physical or emotional wounds distort or destroy memories" (Melley, 2003: 121). To see trauma as a model for history is to accept that history is a flawed and imperfect concept that in no way promises truth or delivers closure. As I have previously discussed, to postmodernist thought history is a deeply problematic concept; the view of history as being a study of objective fact and truths collapses when considering history as a narrative that is dependent on the experience of the writer. History should not be given a privileged position of authority over literature. In her 1988 book *The Poetics of Postmodernism*, Hutcheon coins the term "historiographic metafiction" to refer to texts that "attempt . . . to demarginalise the literary through confrontation with the historical" (1988: 108); these texts seek to break down the borders between history and fiction—which Hutcheon calls "notoriously porous genres" (1988: 106)—and combine aspects of the fictional alongside historical figures and documentation to problematize history's position of authority. The presence of history in a postmodern text "is always a critical reworking, never a nostalgic 'return'" (Hutcheon, 1988: 4). The majority of the texts herein are not strictly examples of historiographic metafiction, though they do contain information regarding historical events. However, there is distinct use of historiographic metafiction techniques in *The 'Nam* and in *X-Men: Magneto Testament* (henceforth referred to as *Testament*), a 2009 "origin story." It is these two texts I consider here.

• • •

Testament is a five-part story that outlines the history of Max Eisenhardt, who becomes Magneto, a central villain of the Marvel (and specifically X-Men) universe. This comic follows his experiences growing up as the youngest child of a middle-class Jewish family in 1930s Nürnberg, amid the infamous rallies. Max faces institutionalized bullying at school before leaving Germany with his parents several days after *Kristallnacht*, heading for the Warsaw Ghetto. His family is shot trying to escape and only he survives, before being taken to Auschwitz, where he works as a member of the *Sonderkommando*. He escapes the camp during the revolt of October 7, 1944. The comic has been painstakingly researched to make it as accurate as possible, using sources from a number of Holocaust organizations. What is most striking about this comic in relation to Hutcheon's work on historiography is the contrast of fiction and fact as displayed within a single panel. The events of the text follow a series of key milestones of the Holocaust; throughout, Max is shown interacting with the events (though never influencing or affecting them). The end of each event sequence shows a series of aspect-to-aspect panels, with white-on-grey caption boxes explaining the historical event behind each sequence. Although the rest of the comic uses caption boxes, they are black with white text; the grey of the history captions removes them from the narrative thread of the overall comic, creating a distinction between the fictional narrative and the historical facts that underwrite it.

The fact that the caption boxes establish a distinction between "actual history" and "fictional history" suggests both Hutcheon's historiographic metafiction and Jameson's concern with the pastiche and simulacra that becomes postmodernist history. In a Jamesonian sense, *Testament* is a pastiche of superhero mythology, mainstream comics art, and history textbook. The fierce insistence of writer Greg Pak to create a text that is as accurate as possible, while also being sensitive to those involved, is emphasized by the inclusion of a series of very detailed endnotes, which repeatedly declare the writer's desire for historical precision or delicacy. Their inclusion suggests that this text is setting itself up as a document of history. The evident desire to break down the boundary between, in this case, fictional comic and historical document is very much in line with Hutcheon's historiographic metafiction.

The superhero is, to put it crudely, as fictional as it is possible to be. To read a narrative that centers on fantastical events occurring in a world not unlike our own requires a considerable suspension of disbelief. For a superhero comic to purport to be a historical document is a bizarre assertion. However, looking through a postmodern lens, the fact that *Testament* attempts to span diverse genres indicates the postmodernist breakdown of genre boundaries. This is another example of the continuation from modernism to postmodernism. Modernism is wary of genre boundaries. Arden Reed, among others, claims that modernism is interested in "genre blending" and hybridization.[6] In this respect, the designation of *Testament* as "superhero comic" is problematic. Although the artwork is in line with the Marvel style, the narrative itself contains barely any "superheroism." Furthermore, the inclusion of painstakingly researched historical events is not typical of the superhero genre. Thus, there is a blending of superheroes and nonfiction that, in turn, distances the text from both genres. Magneto is, in effect, alienated from his own genre by the historical interjections; he is a superhero stranded in a world in which he has no power.

• • •

The Holocaust has become a common plot event in both literature and film. Art Spiegelman claims that the Holocaust "is the perfect hero/villain paradigm for movies. It's replaced cowboys and Indians" (Spiegelman, 2011: 70); he uses the coinage "Holokitsch." Kitsch (or the "kitschification of culture") is seen as one symptom of postmodernism. Jean Baudrillard offers a definition of the term "kitsch":

> The kitsch object is commonly understood as one of that great army of "trashy" objects, made of Plaster of Paris or some such imitation material: that gallery of cheap junk—accessories, folksy knickknacks, "souvenirs," lampshades or fake African masks—which proliferate everywhere, with a preference for holiday resorts and places of leisure. (2004: 109–10)

Kitsch simplifies and trivializes complex ideas by breaking them into clear-cut stereotypes. Furthermore, it tends to be oriented to the masses and thus mass consumption; the aim is generally seen to be profit-making. Baudrillard states:

> To the aesthetics of beauty and originality, kitsch opposes its aesthetics of simulation: it everywhere reproduces objects smaller or larger than life; it imitates materials (in plaster, plastic, etc.); it apes forms or combines them discordantly; it repeats fashion without having been part of the experience of fashion. (2004: 111)

Kitsch has "its basis in consumer society" (Baudrillard, 2004: 110). Holokitsch is that which takes the events of the Holocaust and reduces them to something consumable, though often in different ways. Spiegelman states:

> The Holocaust has become a trope, sometimes used admirably, as in Roman Polanski's *The Pianist*, or sometimes meretriciously, like in Roberto Benigni's *Life is Beautiful*. Almost every year there's another documentary or fiction film up for some Academy Award in this category. Then there are lots of sentimentalized documentaries about life in the shtetl or World War II. (2011: 70–73)[7]

Holokitsch, then, is not necessarily a purely negative designation but can also be applied to works that have some value beyond their consumer nature. As the case of Binjamin Wilkomirski shows, the legacy of the Holocaust is one that some individuals have attempted to appropriate for themselves.[8] The two cases are undoubtedly different, but the reasons for Pak and Di Giandomenico's appropriation of a survivor identity for Magneto are not too far removed from the reasons that Wilkomirski lied about his identity. In being a survivor, Magneto is afforded a courage and traumatic history that few other life events could give.

• • •

In his 2003 comic, Joe Kubert appropriates a Holocaust survivor past but in a different way. Kubert was born in 1926 to a Polish family; the family immigrated to New York City in 1928. Had they stayed, he and the rest of the family would have likely been moved to the Warsaw Ghetto; Kubert would have been sixteen at the time of the ghetto uprising. In *Yossel*, he narrates the story of the eponymous character who lives the life Kubert may have lived in different circumstances. Yossel is a talented young artist, who takes part in the planning and implementation of the uprising. The two characters—Yossel and the (not present) figure of the young Kubert—are as similar as it is possible for them to be. Kubert recreates his past as if his parents had not moved. After growing up in the small Polish town of Yzeran, Yossel's family is taken to Warsaw. His skill as an artist is noticed by the Nazi guards, who have him draw for them every day. In exchange, he receives small gifts from them. He gets involved with a group of young men, assisting in the planning of the uprising in 1943. Following the narrated flashback of a rabbi who has escaped from Auschwitz, the young men plan the uprising and, subsequently, are killed.

The narrative of *Yossel* is told in layered analepses. The initial layer of narrative is of Yossel in the Warsaw sewers, drawing on scraps of paper with a stub of pencil.[9] Brad Prager claims that the movement of time is carefully constructed to assist in avoiding conflict between narrative levels:

> Kubert's comics jumps in time [but] *Yossel* steers clear of the present. In this way, his work avoids staging a confrontation between the past as a point represented, and the present as the point at which the author affirms that his work is only a representation. (2010: 117)

The material presentation of the text, raw sketched drawings printed on rough grey paper, mimics the drawings that Yossel makes. Prager writes:

> The regularity and precision of his text stands in stark contrast with the rough, imperfect images, and the juxtaposition of the two recalls an issue specific to the representation of such atrocities: Kubert's decision to represent the horrors of the Holocaust imperfectly constantly reminds readers that the images should not be taken to stand for authentic Holocaust experience. This is not a story as depicted by a witness—and, even if it were, looking at them is a far cry from being there. (2010: 118–19)

The roughness of the artwork, juxtaposed with the seriousness of the subject matter, corresponds to a breakdown in the boundaries of high and low art. In contrast to other works of Holocaust art and their seeming hagiographic status, *Yossel* is a piece of "low art," seeking neither to beatify nor to "kitschify"; this creates a potential boundary that the narrative—and the interplay of artwork and content—dissolves.

While in the sewer, he draws the story of his childhood—one analeptical level. Within this flashback is the story the rabbi tells of Auschwitz—a second analeptical level. Layered narratives and multiple analepses are two ways of manipulating chronology that can be seen as typically postmodern. However, there is a larger temporal issue at play in *Yossel*. The fact that this work consciously replays a history that "did not occur but could have" makes it a work of "allohistory."[10] Survivors are wont to think "what if?"—this is the core of

Fig. 6.1. *Yossel*, Joe Kubert, 2003. p. 43. © DC Comics.

"survivor guilt"—and "for this reason it is unsurprising that comics that deal with the Holocaust are particularly likely to cross into the allohistorical space between what was and what might have been" (Prager, 2010: 117).

The creation of an allohistorical narrative of Kubert's past creates an alternative personal history that alienates both the writer and reader from the "actual" history. Kubert's depiction of his younger, alternative self creates a distinction that leads to *Verfremdungseffekt*—a sense of alienation between factual and fictional. This type of allohistorical text, in which an individual places themselves in an alternative, nightmarish situation, becomes an outlet for the guilt that may be felt by those who did not witness the events.[11] The alienation that this guilt engenders mimics the postmodern breakdown of historicity. Instead of being a cultural phenomenon, however, in this respect it is concentrated in the example of one individual's allohistorical pseudo-self.

So far in this chapter I have shown the extent to which comics, trauma, and postmodernism are linked in a curious and complex relationship by the mutually occurring factors of temporality and temporal disruption. The timescale of comics is central to the creation of the narrative and the temporal symptoms are often the most obvious and debilitating aspects of a traumatic rupture. These two points are straightforward and largely self-evident. However, the addition of postmodernism is the complicating factor. Comics has much in common with postmodernist art but is not easily categorized as a postmodernist form. It is through the relationship between modernism and postmodernism that the argument for comics as postmodernist is best viewed. Thus, if we agree with Hutcheon and Lyotard that postmodernism is a continuation of modernism, comics can be seen through a postmodern lens. Both *Testament* and *Yossel* clearly demonstrate how issues of complex temporality in texts can be read in a postmodern sense.

• • •

In my introduction, I discussed Malcolm Bull's contention that modernism is concerned with aspectivalism and the preoccupation with multifaceted viewing that forms the artistic basis of much modernist art (especially Cubism). Looking at a subject from multiple angles adds another facet to ideas of time in modernist art. A Cubist image of one subject from multiple angles suggests one of two things. Either, in the case of Duchamp's *Nude Descending a Staircase No 2* (1912), that the subject is in motion and the artist attempts to capture the movement in the piece, or, in the case of Braque's *The Guitar* (1909), that the subject is being viewed from a multitude of angles all at once. Typically, these varying perspectives are layered on top of one another. However, in his

2008 comic *Judenhass*, Dave Sim combines comics panelization, photorealistic art, and multiple perspectives. *Judenhass* is a nonfiction comic in which Sim presents a selection of anti-Semitic quotations from prominent figures, superimposed over images of Holocaust victims. The quotations move chronologically from the first century CE to the early twenty-first century; this rough timeline forms the narrative thread of the comic. Sim's contention is that the Holocaust was "inevitable" and he attempts to show the prevalence and depth of anti-Semitism over the past 2,000 years.

With the exception of the opening pages' sketches of Auschwitz and the concluding image of Pope John Paul II at the Western Wall in Jerusalem, each page of *Judenhass* shows an image of the Holocaust, rendered as line drawings, from multiple perspectives but, unlike the previous examples from Cubism, each different view is contained within separate panels. Each image is therefore repeated across the page instead of being repeated on top of itself. There are no alterations made to the image in each panel; they are exact copies of each other. The image below, which spans three pages in the comic, shows the increase in panel size that occurs across the pages until the ending image of the sequence, which shows the full photograph. The final page is presented on the left-hand side of the page, meaning the horrific extent of the complete image arrests the reader directly after a page turn. The increase in the panel sizes allows Sim to reveal the final image incrementally as the reader moves across the page.

The repetition of the image across three pages suggests a visual representation of the Freudian repetition compulsion. Earlier in this chapter, I discussed Melley's consideration of Freud and his criticism of Freud's suggestion that the return to the traumatic event is "unmediated" and is a "literal return of the event" (2003: 108). Melley is right to argue against the literal return of the traumatic event. His contention is that traumatic memory is "as open as ordinary memory to influence, suggestion and contamination" (2003: 111). The return is thus not unmediated and not literal. The images above are a clear example of the mediation that is at play in the creation of—and return to—traumatic memory. A single image is repeated; this image represents the traumatic event. The repetition of the image represents the compulsion to return. However, the fact that the image is altered in each panel—whether by perspective, artistic differences, or position on the page—suggests the mediation of the memory by external and psychological factors, the same factors that affect ordinary memory. This three-page section is a comics rendering of the psychological mediation that is at play in the repetition compulsion. These pages can also be read in relation to their affective properties. The original photograph from which they are drawn is harrowing to say the least; the

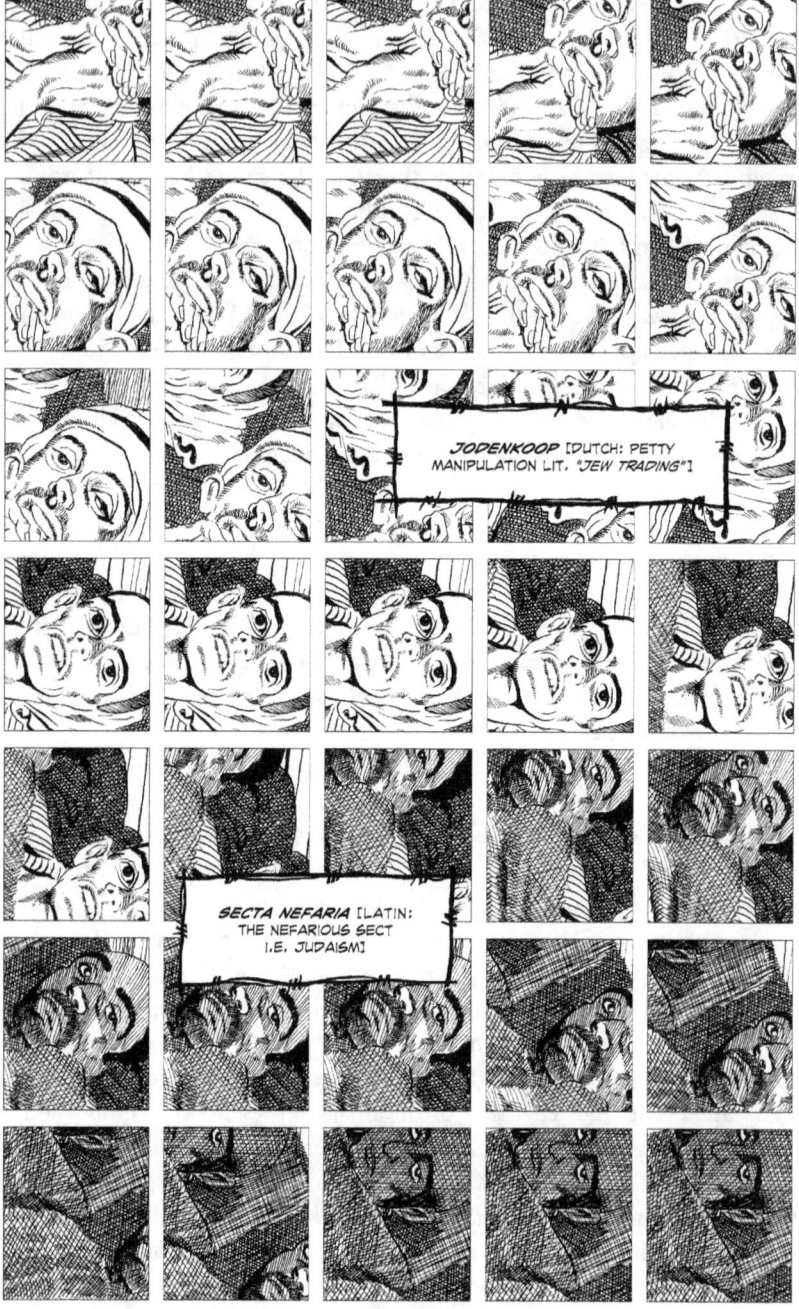

Fig. 6.2. *Judenhass*, Dave Sim, 2008. pp. 18–20. Courtesy of the artist.

starkness of the human bodies, their extreme wastage and fragility, elicits a shock response from most viewers. It is likely also to provoke feelings of sadness, disgust, anger, and horror. The repetition of the image—and the fact each separate image focuses on a small section of the original, magnified—amplifies the traumatic affect. The viewer is bombarded with the image, which fills the page over and over. Sim aims to create an intense affective response, not by using bold, brashly colored images, but by multiplying the image itself. The image is kept black and white to allow it to speak for itself, as the photograph does, without considerable alteration by the artist.

Judenhass best exemplifies the issues faced when attempting to categorize comics as modernist or postmodernist. It is a clear example of the coming together of modernist multiple viewing and comics presentation techniques. The bland penciled artwork is far removed from the high-contrast mainstream style that typifies comics art. Both modernist and postmodernist concerns are represented. Furthermore, *Judenhass* is a strictly nonfiction comic and demands to be seen as one, with its long explanatory introduction and use of quotations, with no dialogue or narrative direction. For a form in which even nonfictional texts are considered fictional, simply because they are comics, the structure of *Judenhass* helps to break down the preconceived ideas of what a comic should be and allows for comics to be considered fictional or nonfictional where appropriate. A clear example of the implied fictionality of comics can be seen in Marjane Satrapi's *Persepolis* (2000), which was ranked at number five on *Newsweek's* "Top Ten Best Fiction Books of the Decade," even though *Persepolis* is autobiography rather than fiction. Comics is bedeviled by its past as a disposable form that was known for sensationalism and escapism; comics is still thought of as being superhero floppies. Although critical and academic interest in the wider comics world is growing, this low opinion remains. Regardless, a large percentage of the best-selling and highly acclaimed comics are most accurately categorized as memoir or reportage. The postmodern lens which advocates a breakdown of high and low art is an excellent way of looking at comics as a whole, as it allows for all genres of comic to be considered on an equal level.

• • •

In *Worlds of Hurt*, Kalí Tal claims that trauma literature cannot be viewed through a postmodernist lens. She writes:

> The approach of most postmodern critics is inappropriate when applied to reading the literature of trauma. Postmodern critics have been concerned with

the problematics of *reading*. As professional readers, it is in their interest to put forward the argument that any text, properly read, can be "understood." Those among them who do not claim to be able to divine the author's intent simply claim that an author's intent is irrelevant. It's obvious that this approach won't work for the literatures of trauma. The act of *writing*, though perhaps less accessible to the critic, is as important as the act of reading. (1991: 17–18)

Tal claims that postmodernists do not have an interest in the writer. Although this may be corroborated by Barthes in "The Death of the Author" (1967), Tal creates a schism between reading and writing that does not exist. Although postmodernism does not give much credence to authorial input, it does not exclude it completely. Tal is explicit in her belief that "literature of trauma is defined by the identity of its author" (1991: 17). She writes that "survivors have the metaphorical tools to interpret representations of traumas similar to their own [whereas a non-traumatized person] does not have access to the meanings of the sign that invoke traumatic memory" (1991: 16). By Tal's reckoning, trauma literature should only be written—and can only be truly understood—by survivors. This is a bold, yet flawed, statement. Although individuals who have experienced a traumatic event may wish to write about their experience (and may be encouraged to do so), this is not to say that they would be better able to create a piece of art that represents and mimics the symptoms of a traumatic rupture than a non-traumatized individual. As I have repeated throughout this book, this is the aim of affect, which also allows the trauma artist and reader to experience emotions that are related to trauma—such as fear, shock, and disgust—without conflating the traumatic event itself to its representations. To claim special preference for traumatized "trauma artists" undermines the scope of human imagination. Tal writes:

> Accurate representation of trauma can never be achieved without recreating the event, since, by its very definition, trauma lies beyond the bounds of "normal" conception. Textual representation—literary, visual, oral—are mediated by language and do not have the impact of the traumatic experience. (1991: 15)

She is correct that representation is mediated by language and visual tradition. To some extent, she is also correct that accurate representation cannot be achieved without recreating the event. However, it is evident that this is impossible. The event *cannot* be recreated, so other representational strategies must be employed. These strategies are often congruent with postmodernist artistic techniques. Thus, contrary to Tal's beliefs, trauma can be viewed through a postmodernist lens. Furthermore, if trauma can be seen as a postmodernist experience—one which forces us to rework the paradigms and metanarratives that govern our world view—the postmodernist lens becomes even more pertinent. Lyotard ends his essay "Answering the Question: What Is Postmodernism?" by stating: "The answer is: Let us wage a war on totality; let us be witnesses to the unpresentable" (1991: 82). Lyotard's postmodernism is aware of the need to witness to the unpresentable; the most unpresentable subject matter is the traumatic. The fracturing of traumatic experience is congruent to the fractured postmodernist world view, the "war on totality." Compounded with the fractured nature of the basic comics form, postmodernist strategies are highly appropriate for the creation of traumatic narratives.

Excursus[1]
XX Comics in an XY World

Herstory, *n.*
Punning alteration of history *n.* (fancifully reinterpreted as *his story*, implying that history has in the past been viewed predominantly from the male perspective), with *his-* replaced by her *adj.*
—***Oxford English Dictionary*** (2016)

As I write, a storm is raging in the comics world, centered on Angoulême, a town in western France and home to the International Comics Festival (*Festival International de la Bande Dessinée d'Angoulême*). In December, the short list for the festival's *Grand Prix* was announced with great fanfare. The winner of this award—one of the most prestigious in comics—acts as president of next year's festival, draws the poster, and is also invited to prepare an exhibition of their work. The shortlist for 2016's award contains thirty names, none of them women. Almost immediately, there was uproar and the international press began to report on the matter. The *Smithsonian Magazine* suggested that the *Grand Prix* at first ignored, and then denied the existence of, female comics artists; the BBC denounced the festival as "marred." Advocacy group *BD Égalité* claimed that "it all comes down to the disastrous glass ceiling; [female artists are] tolerated, but never allowed top billing" (2016: n.p.) and ended their statement with a witty one-panel comic, drawn by Florence Cestac, the only woman (so far) to have won the *Grand Prix*.[2]

In response to the considerable press coverage and debate, the festival's board issued a statement on their website. The statement was less than satisfactory. It states that the *Grand Prix* is an award which crowns an author for all of his or her work and contribution to the history and evolution of comics. It went on to say:

Fig. 7.1. Florence Cestac, 2016. Courtesy of the artist.

The last three winners embody the nature of this prize. Their names are Willem, Bill Watterson, Katsuhiro Otomo.... These artists have been creating for several decades. When one goes back that amount of time to observe what role men and women played in the field of comics, it is clear that there were very few recognized female authors at the time. If we take a closer look at Franco-Belgian comics, which we know best, and observe its main comics magazines, such as *Tintin*, *Spirou*, *Pilote*, *Á Suivre*, *Métal Hurlant*, *Fluide Glacial*, it is objectively much faster to count their female authors (almost on the fingers of one hand) than their male authors. The Festival cannot revise the history of comics. (2016: n.p.)

But, as Tom Spurgeon reminds us, we can and should revise history. He writes, "It's actually very easy to rewrite the history of comics. It happens all the time. You rewrite history by putting people on these lists" (Spurgeon in McCubbin, 2016: n.p.). That the festival is unable to see the ways in which their shortlist is deeply flawed and no longer an accurate representation of the comics world is both surprising and unsurprising in equal measure. On the one hand, it is surprising that any major arts organization can be so narrow-minded as to think that women can be so casually ignored. On the other, given how hugely biased comics is in favor of men—both as creators and characters—it is no surprise at all. Comics, perhaps more acutely than any other narrative art, has long been harshly divided, with (mostly) male creators and characters remaining in the spotlight, while female creators and characters stand at the margins.

Jane Tolmie suggests that "there is a seemingly unproblematic and unproblematized awareness that the comics world is defined by a masculine ethos" but that the use of almost exclusively androcentric language "naturalizes and normalizes the masculine ethos to the point that it disappears from view, which has the inevitable effect of marginalizing women artists/writers as exceptions to the rule" (Hatfield in Tolmie 2009: 82). She claims that some of the most influential comics (and comics studies) are "produced and analyzed almost entirely by men, in relation to men and for men, but never in those or any other explicitly gendered terms" (2009: 82). It seems nearly impossible, then, for female comics artists to be considered equal to men when the very underpinnings of the form are so loaded with androcentricity.

The purpose of this excursus is not to provide a detailed analysis of a wide corpus of comics by and about women. *Comics, Trauma, and the New Art of War* is about how comics engage with stories of real wars and the traumata engendered by them; there are not a great deal of comics by or about women that deal with this specific context, although I discuss a small selection here. Rather, I wish to address more general concerns about the representation of women within the comic text and also the position of women artists within the field. To this end, I address three central issues. I begin by considering the representation of women in combat. Throughout this book, I have noted that female characters tend to be stuck in traditionally feminine roles (Torres as mother and widow; the women of *Vietnamerica* as homemakers; Anja in *Maus* as a fragile hysteric). I return to this discussion and introduce Russell Braun and Garth Ennis's *Battlefields* as a counterpoint to my earlier analyses. From this, I open a conversation about women as artists. What concerns are female artists writing into their work? Finally, I return to the original issue of women as second place in the comics world and what it means for contemporary comics.

• • •

The history of women as players in major conflict is a complicated one. Although women have played a role in the military for many centuries, it has usually been in secretarial, support, and caring positions; the role of women in active combat has been hotly debated and remains controversial. Since the 1970s, most Western armies have begun to enlist women for active duty in all branches of the military. In the Second World War, the British army allowed women to be "employed as spotters, predictors, height finders, radio locators and radar operators. They were also active on searchlights and in-hit confirmation. But men alone loaded and fired the guns," as killing the enemy was considered too masculine (De Groot, 1997: 436). Similarly, the US military has been accepting female recruits since 1917; the passing of the Women's Armed Services Integration Act in 1948 made women a permanent part of the military. At present, 78 percent of army positions and 99 percent of air force positions are open to women, providing they pass psychological and physical screening. Despite this, studies are divided on the efficacy of mixed gender units, with some claiming that the inclusion of women is detrimental to the unit as a whole.[3]

A further issue that is raised in relation to mixed combat units is that of sexual harassment and assault, often couched in the ugly rhetoric of "boys will be boys." A recent comment on this topic—and one that is especially high-profile—comes from 2016 Republican presidential nominee Donald Trump, who posted on Twitter:

> 26,000 unreported sexual assults [sic] in the military—only 238 convictions. What did these geniuses expect when they put men & women together? (2013: n.p.)

This is an extremely troubling comment—to suggest that sexual assault is an expected byproduct of male-female co-employment is worrying on many levels—but it does tap into a common theme in both conversations about, and representations of, women in conflict.[4] Gender politics becomes conflated with discourses of violence and sexuality, with rape becoming a primary weapon of war. This type of talk, typified by Trump's tweet, is both incredibly harmful to women and does a great disservice to men. It is the same apologist discourse that claims that "boys will be boys" is an acceptable justification for violent, offensive, or generally "bad" behavior; all that these phrases really do is oversimplify complex, socially ordered, and learned behaviors in order to excuse gendered violence and aggression.

One of the simplest explanations for the limited numbers of female protagonists in American comics of conflict is that women have long been bit players on the military stage; if women have not been taking up the roles, it is natural that they will not be depicted as frequently within comics representations of conflict. This is a fair comment, though it is not accurate to suggest that women do not write comics about trauma. Indeed, some of the most beautifully constructed comics by female artists that have been published in the past forty years have dealt with deeply traumatic subjects. In her 2010 book *Graphic Women: Life Narrative and Contemporary Comics*, Hillary Chute provides chapters on the works of Aline Kominsky-Crumb,

Phoebe Gloeckner, and Lynda Barry, all of whom take as their starting point the traumatic (and often sexually violent) childhoods that form the bases of their books. The marginalization of female comics artists within the comics world has much to do with the silencing of these narratives of sexuality and trauma. Kominsky-Crumb is a fine example: "Her underwhelming reception contrasts markedly to that of her husband, cartoonist Robert Crumb, who has been canonized exactly for writing the darker side of (his own) tortured male sexuality" (Chute, 2010: 31). Furthermore, Chute writes that

> given the (gendered) suspicion of memoirs generally, and especially of the supposedly "extreme" or too divulgent memoirs of women, this may also explain why the idea of such memoirs with the additional element of the visual does not easily win attention. The visual register is often seen as "excessive." (2010: 5)

Women's narratives of sexuality and trauma are considered "excessive" almost regardless of their exact content; men's narratives are rarely considered in this light. It begs the question of how men's narratives of similar issues need to be presented to be labeled likewise. As the primary focus of this book is the specific field of conflict trauma, I do not discuss the above mentioned texts here. However, I do wish to highlight their importance and offer Chute's book as a suggestion of further reading which discusses the issue of women's trauma and comics.

There *are* a number of comics that do deal with women's role in active combat. I discuss two in particular in this excursus: Garth Ennis and Russell Braun's *Battlefields* (volumes 1, 6, and 8), which concentrates on the Soviet Air Force 588th Night Bomber Regiment, a female bomber regiment of the Second World War, and Miriam Libicki's *Jobnik!* (an autobiographical comic describing her time in the Israeli Army).[5] The central difference between these two texts is that one is written by two men and the other by a woman; although both deal with historical events, Libicki's text is explicitly autobiographical. I examine both these texts in due course but before doing so, I wish to return to the texts already analyzed here.

Both *American Widow* and the *You'll Never Know* trilogy present explicitly gendered views of the conflict they represent; similarly, the female characters in *Maus* and *Vietnamerica* are contained within stereotypically female roles. A simple analysis of this would suggest that this is how it actually was—that these women did exist within these roles and, as the comic aims to represent the events with some degree of accuracy, they are presented "truthfully." I do not wish to dispute the veracity of the representation. The underlying question is that of the social positioning of women. These narratives present the male characters as interacting within the public sphere of the conflict, while the women remain within the domestic, private sphere. It is not the text itself but our socially influenced readings of it that suggest that these roles are in some way "less than" the male, public role. *American Widow* is a particular victim of this: Torres's story is intimately bound up in her identity as mother and wife. She cannot (and does not wish to) be separated from these obviously female roles. These are the lenses through which Torres constructs her identity and her story. However, by considering her comic as "women's comics," we devalue the text. Yes, Torres is female and is telling her own, personal story, but that is not to say that her story has any less importance than that of men in similar situations. So often stories which deal with motherhood and issues of the private, domestic sphere are labeled as "women's texts"; it is rarely the case that narratives that deal with questions of masculinity are labeled "men's texts." These so-called "women's stories" are not lesser in substance: narratives of the private sphere can and do tell us as much about the complexities of conflict and the experience of trauma as any other. The most balanced way to consider this would be to consider these narratives the other side of the coin, so to speak. In *Maus*, *Vietnamerica,* and *You'll Never Know*, Vladek, Tri, and Chuck interact in the public sphere as mediators between the conflict event and their personal community, whereas Anja, Dzung, and Hannah/Carol exist in the private sphere as representatives of the domestic reality of the conflict. It should not be that women are tacked on the end as afterthoughts, but that they represent a separate dimension of the conflict within the comic.

Ennis and Braun took the Russian all-woman night bomber regiment as their focus for three story arcs in the *Battlefields* series. Volume 1, *The Night Witches*, is set on the Eastern front and concerns the origins of the regiment and their first raids. Volume 6, *Motherland*, focuses on the star pilot, Anna Kharkova, and her new assignment in a squadron defending the Russian front. Finally, Volume 8, *The Fall and Rise of Anna Kharkova*, covers Anna's postwar imprisonment in a Siberian labor camp. When asked why he wished to focus on this particular regiment, Ennis answered:

> In the case of the Night Witches, I was drawn to the exceptional nature of the characters involved. Young women in their late teens or early twenties, piloting obsolete biplanes on night-bombing missions against a vastly superior force, that's interesting enough—but when you consider the bullshit they had to put up with from their male counterparts, and even worse, the potentially ghastly consequences of capture that they faced, the story becomes downright fascinating. (2008: n.p.)

For Ennis, the gender of the participants makes this story all the more powerful; this is an opportunity to tell a story of women and conflict that exists almost entirely in the male-dominated public arena. The comic itself does not shy away from representing the harshness of the regiment's male coworkers or the potentially negative opinion they have of these women. In the induction, their (male) superior officer states:

> I don't ask for you and I don't want you. I think the notion of women aircrew is a joke; I think women combat fliers are a worse joke; I think women assigned to the base alongside my fighter squadron are the worse joke of all. My squadron—who are currently out of sight laughing, by the way, because they know I've got to stand here in front of you and perform this ludicrous duty—my squadron are engaged in trying to stop the Nazis, which is hard enough in the first place, without you lot showing up and getting in the way with your ... your ... your female requirements. (Ennis and Braun: 2009, n.p.)

Guards-Major Aleksandr Lukin's words sit as a useful introduction to women in conflict comics in general: the idea that "female requirements" (however that can be interpreted) will get in the way of the conflict plot. As I have shown throughout this book, conflict comics are not straightforward narratives of conflict; they are, instead, nuanced and often intensely personal. That this is something only considered in relation to women in comics says a great deal about the androcentricity of the form. However, Lukin is shown to be wrong in his estimations, when the Night Witches are successful during many night raids, despite their substandard equipment. The resulting text is a remarkably feminist exploration of the regiment that allows credit to rest with those who earned it, regardless of their gender. The female characters are often depicted as fun and frivolous—at one point chasing each other in a silly game—but any suggestion that this is the summation of their character is sharply contradicted at the end of the first installment. Having been shot down by a German nightfighter, Anna is stranded close to a German encampment. Although she has been found by a sympathetic German soldier, Graf, who is trying to help her escape, she does not understand German and so stabs him to death and escapes into a blizzard. As she stabs him, her eyes are fixed and in the background; ghost-like images of her deceased fellow pilots represent her driving force in the moment. Rather than cowering or displaying stereotypically feminine traits, Anna shows herself to be brave and unflinching. The final page of the comic shows her marching into the blizzard, her stare fixed and aggressively determined, wielding a large rifle.

Accompanying this image (and the previous two panels) are white, rectangular text boxes that contain a quotation from Guards Captain Nadezhda Popova, the inspiration for the character of Anna in the comic. Popova's quotation reads:

> Sometimes, on a dark night, I will stand outside my home and peer into the sky, the wind tugging my hair ... I stare into the blackness and close my eyes and imagine myself once more a young girl up there in my little bomber.... And I ask myself "Nadezhda—how did you do it?" (Popova in Ennis and Braun, 2009: n.p.)

Not only does the inclusion of this quotation lend gravity to the situation as it grounds it in historical fact, as with the grey text boxes in *Magneto: Testament*, but it also reminds the reader that such acts of heroism and courageous action are not bound by gender; both men and women are able to act with extreme bravery in the heat of battle. The German soldiers' less-than-heroic actions and lack of honorable conduct affirm this point.

In his interview, Ennis coyly mentions the "potentially ghastly consequences of capture" (2008: n.p.). Rape and sexual violence are among the most widely used weapons of war leveled against women in combat zones, both military and civilian. A 2004 *Médecins Sans Frontières* report states that the charity first came across rape as a weapon in the 1990s: "In Bosnia systematic rape was used as part of the strategy of ethnic cleansing.... Women were raped so they could give birth to a Serbian baby" (2004: n.p.). *MSF* estimate that 500,000 women were raped during the Balkans conflict. This is by no means the first instance of rape as a weapon. As far back as antiquity, rape has been used to control and demean women. Kelly Dawn Askin describes the war rape of women in ancient Greece as "socially acceptable behavior well within the rules of warfare," with the women being seen as "legitimate booty, useful as wives, concubines, slave labour, or battle-camp trophy" (1997: 21). A central voice in any discussion of sexual violence and war rape is Susan Brownmiller. In her seminal 1975 text, *Against Our Will: Men, Women and Rape*, she writes:

> War provides men with the perfect psychological backdrop to give vent to their contempt for women. The maleness of the military—the brute power of weaponry exclusive to their hands, the spiritual bonding of men at arms, the manly discipline of orders given and orders obeyed, the simple logic of the hierarchical command—confirms for men what they long suspect—that women are peripheral to the world that counts. (Brownmiller, 1975: 165)

For Brownmiller, war gives an opportunity for that which is innate in man's psyche to become reality. She suggests that the military is an intrinsically male institution, designed to accommodate and play into essentialist ideas of masculinity. It is also a situation wherein perpetrators of rape are likely to remain unpunished. Although rape as a weapon is widely denounced as a crime against humanity—and the UN Security Council adopted *Resolution 1820* in 2008, which states that "rape and other forms of sexual violence can constitute war crimes, crimes against humanity or a constitutive act with respect to genocide" (2009: n.p.)—it is incredibly difficult to punish given the scale of the act and the complexity of prosecution for these types of crimes. As Brownmiller writes, "Men who rape are ordinary Joes, made unordinary by entry into the most exclusive male-only club in the world" (1975: 25). War rape gives average men a way to be "something."

In *The Night Witches*, the German soldiers on the ground capture a Russian girl (although it is never explained, it is likely she is a local peasant and not a pilot as they believe); she is taken to a dilapidated barn by the platoon and is repeatedly raped. The narrator, Graf, shrouds the act in euphemism by stating "man by man, in the gloom of an abandoned cellar, the squad damns itself" (2009: n.p.). Graf is standing watch outside the barn but is called inside where the squad leader, *Feldwebel* Scholz, forces him to rape the girl.[6] Despite the girl being the main focus of this section of the comic, she features very little as a physical presence on the page. E. Ann Kaplan suggests that the refusal to frame women even in the most important scenes of their life is something that is not uncommon in the visual arts. She refers to a 1928 King Vidor film in which the woman is not shown at all during the birth of her son. Instead, the father, male doctor, and male child are the focus (Kaplan, 2013: 3). To be removed from one's own experience on the basis of sex is common; the focus remains androcentric. The rape scene is an entirely male act; the girl is wholly insignificant.

Graf claims he is unable to commit rape and so Scholz kills the girl, before forcing the younger soldier to spend the night with her naked, maimed corpse. Graf says, "Some time before dawn it occurs to me what Scholz is trying to do: make me hard enough to survive the war in Russia. Make me into enough of a beast, so that one day I might just make it home" (Ennis and Braun, 2009: n.p.). While this is a basically accurate summation of the scene, it is not the only reason for the act, nor does Graf's justification adequately justify the rape and murder of another human for what amounts to "training purposes." Rather, the rape is an attempt for the (unsuccessful) German soldiers to regain control of their landscape and reassert their power as men.

Unable to seize this power in a military arena—and finding themselves under threat from female pilots—rape is a logical choice of action for this reassertion of power. It returns us to Brownmiller's suggestion that rape makes ordinary men feel exceptional. It also brings this discussion back to my earlier point about the conflation of gender politics with discourses of violence in discussions of war and women.

The Night Witches presents a double-edged view of women in conflict—female pilots, fighting to be recognized as valid by their male colleagues and largely succeeding, placed alongside a vicious rape scene in which the female character is almost unseen, her degradation instead displayed in the actions and facial reactions of the male characters. The text *does* present a nuanced view of women in conflict but, as it was written by two men, it presents a view of women in the military through a male gaze. As such, its ability to understand the deeper experiences of female military personnel is limited. But, as I previously mentioned, comics about women in the military are less common. One of the few autobiographical comics about a female soldier's experience of the military is Miriam Libicki's *Jobnik!* Libicki is an American-Israeli, who served her national service in an infirmary on an unnamed Israeli base. She describes her duties and the relationships she forges with other soldiers in careful, often banal detail; her drawings are rendered in pencil, without color. There are two striking features of Libicki's narrative that I wish to focus on: the extent to which sexuality and sexual relationships play into the narrative and the banality of her role.

In her study of Jewish American women in comics, Tahneer Oksman writes:

> As the narrative reflects from its outset, Miriam's identity is premised in a desire to connect with others. Her sense of self as an outsider is, along these lines, based in her failure to establish meaningful relationships, especially with the men around her. (2016: 198)

The first page of the comic introduces the reader to Miriam's military role and sexual life in her first statement: "I am a citizen of the United States and Israel. And a soldier in the Israel Defense Force. I have had no further boyfriends but significant further sexual experience outside the, uh, context of commitment. All heterosexual" (Libicki, 2008: 4). Miriam is clearly defining herself in relation to other people, as Oksman suggests, be it through nationality, occupation, or sexuality. The text boxes containing this statement are accompanied by snapshots of Miriam engaging in various sexual acts with unidentified men, framed as Polaroid photographs. In her opening section, it

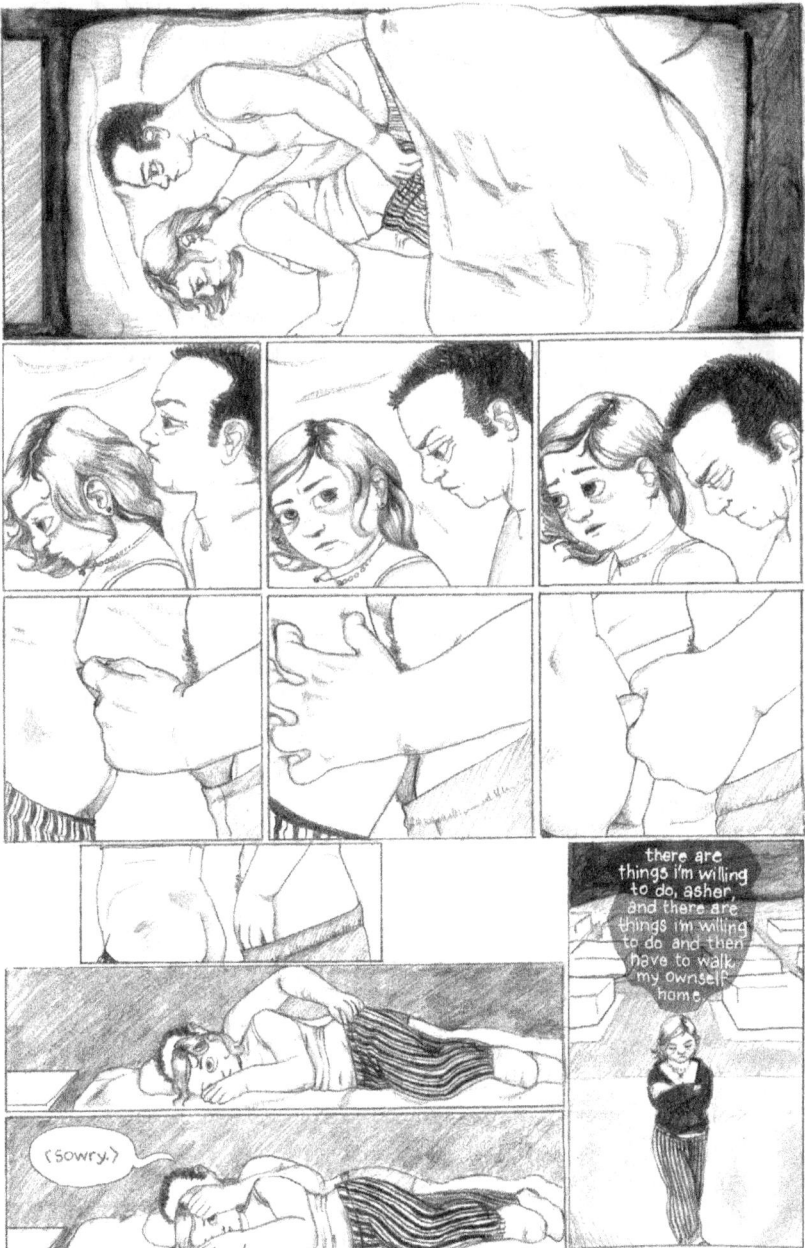

Fig. 7.2. *Jobnik!* Miriam Libicki, 2008. p. 78. Courtesy of the artist.

is the sexual dimension that immediately seizes the reader's attention and this theme continues throughout the whole narrative. Libicki's self-depiction is oddly sensual, her large eyes are often downcast coyly, and she is able to draw the human body in sexual positions with both taste and eroticism. Later in the text, Libicki writes, "Ever since I was five, I knew I was the biggest slut on earth ... but neither my mother nor I could ever get the hang of dressing me right. We didn't have the orthodox-girl sixth sense of *tznuit*" (2008: 100).[8] Miriam lacks the modesty she feels that Orthodox girls should have and so she turns to the opposite: "the slut." In a rigidly defined group, like Orthodox Jewish communities, an inability to fit into expected situations or definitions is likely to make an individual move against the norm and, for Miriam, this is shown in (more overt) displays of female sexuality. Indeed, as Stephen Tabachnik writes, "Her desire to tell the truth about her sexual encounters prevails over any attempt to hold back, and in that sense her artistic side seems to be more important to her than her Orthodox side" (2014: 204).

It is the relationship thread that drives the narrative forward. Throughout the text, Miriam has several short-lived relationships (perhaps it is more accurate to call them "liaisons") with her fellow soldiers. They fall into a pattern: Miriam develops a close relationship in her mind with the fellow soldier, only to be turned down or ignored by him at a later date. This not only speaks to Libicki's naiveté but also to the clear power dynamic between male and female soldiers. The clearest example of this unequal relationship is Miriam's involvement with Asher, a known womanizer. Miriam recounts many nights spent cuddling with Asher (and engaging in other sexual acts). At one point, he attempts to penetrate her anally (Libicki, 2008: 78). The event is depicted in fragmented panels, beginning with a bird's-eye view of the pair spooning on a bed.

In six uniform panels, Libicki shows her frustrated and dismayed face alongside close-up images of her bottom and Asher's midsection. The three panels that show the attempted insertion are concealing. The two white shapes of the bodies clearly show what is being attempted, but the focal point of each panel is Asher's hands. In the first panel, his hand is a fist; in the second, he is grasping her bottom, with clenched fingers that appear to be digging into her forcefully; in the final panel of the three, his penis is grasped in a fist, thrust towards Miriam. Asher's hands being the central point represent the dominance he holds over her in this situation; his rank and gender give him a power over Miriam that translates into the sexual act. When combined with the upper three panels, the act is clearly shown as unwanted, confirming the power inequality. Two further panels, showing Miriam face-on with a blank stare as Asher pulls up her trousers, close the event with a half-hearted "sowry." In the final panel, Miriam walks home in the dark, her body language showing anger, frustration, and also disgust at herself. That Miriam is in this situation is not the issue at hand: it is Asher who initiates and leads the events and he who holds the power in this situation. Miriam's naiveté and desire to fit in forces her into submission in a situation that she is not comfortable with and that she later goes on to state she regrets. While this is not a rape event, it is a coerced sexual act and references the sexual discourse that abounds in discussions of men and women in the military.

Libicki's military term coincided with the Second Intifada (the Al-Aqsa Intifada), commencing in September 2000. News of the Intifada infiltrates the comic throughout the narrative; Miriam is shown listening to the radio or watching television news. Information is presented in jagged-edged bubbles, a common technique for showing that noise is coming from an electronic device. At no point does the comic show footage of the violence, either on television screens or as events within the narrative. In an interview with a Jewish website, she said of her comic:

> I needed to include the news and the Intifada because that's the hook of the story—"teenager making poor relationship choices" is not a great hook. When I use the news bits, it's not my memories I'm working off. Most of these, I don't have a clear memory of where I was when this bombing began or where that treaty happened. I guess it's a very intense way, but Israel is an intense place to be, back then, and even more so now. (Libicki in Roth, 2010: n.p.)

Libicki is writing about her experience of being in the army during a violent conflict, but any violence is secondary to the author's sexual relationships and personal growth. Oksman writes:

> Miriam's gradual dissociation from the daily military violence that surrounds her runs parallel to a passivity in relation to her sexual interactions. This disengagement is figured in images that convey her increasing confusion and defeat in relation to the spaces around her. (2016: 207)

The violence of the conflict is reconfigured into the psychological and sexual dominance that defines her relationships with others. The conflict is there to provide "the hook," but what it also does is emphasize the humanity of the characters and the importance of their personal stories in the creation of nuanced conflict narrative; the two stories sit as parallels to each other.

The sexual experimentation thread of *Jobnik!* is the most interesting aspect of the text. The conflict thread is less interesting—mostly because of the

Fig. 7.3. *Jobnik!* Miriam Libicki, 2008. p. 23. Courtesy of the artist.

nature of Libicki's role. She is a secretary and a noncombatant soldier. Her role is naturally going to involve the banal aspects of conflict and bureaucracy that do not make for a dramatic story. There are moments of humor. At one point, Miriam is asked by her commanding officer to steal a stapler and scissors from another office; at another, she folds paper incorrectly because she was "thinking in English." For the most part, however, her role is in no way intellectually stimulating. Libicki uses the comics form to emphasize the monotony. One of her first duties is to burn folders labeled "H.A.M.A.S., no relation to the Palestinian group. It means classified and secret documents. Mostly medical files" (Libicki, 2008: 14). Traveling off-base to an incinerator in the middle of a barren landscape with a colleague who makes tasteless Holocaust jokes, Libicki documents in detail the burning process. In a full-page image, Miriam empties the ashes of the documents into a pit and drags her equipment back to the base.

In this complex panel, Miriam plays with temporality and overlaps several panels that employ aspect to aspect transitions. The frames of each panel are visible, cutting across the action and providing a dividing line for shading. The difference in shading levels in each panel represents the levels of sunlight—Miriam's task takes her many hours and, by the last section of the panel, bottom right, the shadows are long and the sun is low. The visual density of the image is juxtaposed with the lack of dramatic action, while the carefully intersecting frames highlight Miriam's isolation and boredom.

Military correspondent David Axe writes positively of Libicki's book, and his review describes the awkward relationship between Miriam's soldier role and her sexual development:

> It's a story about war, but its main character is an Israeli Defense Forces secretary who never sees combat—and even describes herself as "unsuited for IDF life." In its heart *Jobnik!*—that's Israeli slang for a non-combat soldier—is a coming of age story all tangled up in the Al Aqsa uprising—a.k.a., the Second Intifada from 2000 to 2005, in which some 4,000 Israelis and Palestinians died. (2013: n.p.)

Axe notes the conflict between Miriam's role in the IDF and her coming-of-age story. This is the central conflict of the narrative; the Intifada is a smaller part of the narrative than Miriam's own struggle to create herself within her role as soldier and as woman. And, as I stated previously, the issue of gender in a conflict setting is conflated, not exactly with discourses of violence and sex, but certainly with sexuality and inter-gender relationships. In both *Battlefields: The Night Witches* and *Jobnik!* female characters are defined by their relationship with male characters, something that can be seen in all of the female characters discussed in this book.

• • •

In 1999, American comics writer Gail Simone founded the website Women in Refrigerators. The name refers to an event in *Green Lantern #54* (1994) in which Kyle Rayner returns home to find his girlfriend, Alex DeWitt, has been murdered and her disarticulated body has been stuffed into the refrigerator. The website consists of a list of female characters who have been raped, tortured, and/or murdered; it consists of 120 names. Simone's list clearly demonstrates that the phenomenon of violence against women is an enduring theme in comics. The list is prefaced with the following note:

> Not every woman in comics has been killed, raped, depowered, crippled, turned evil, maimed, tortured, contracted a disease or had other life-derailing tragedies befall her, but given the following list, it's hard to think up exceptions. (Simone, 1999: n.p.)

The point is humorously made—women's value in comics is found in their position as catalyst for male action, rather than anything to do with their own agency. Rob Bricken agrees with Simone's claims, writing:

> In [superhero comics], men can fly and fight and do heroic things and meet girls and have a secret identity—you know, all the stuff men secretly want to do. Women ... not so much. In fact, outside of comic books specifically written for women, female characters in superhero books have a pretty tough time of it. And by "tough time," I mean horrible, horrible things happen to them. (Bricken, 2008: n.p.)

In recent years, the "women in refrigerators" trope has often been dismissed as lazy writing. The death or suffering of a female character as a catalyst for the actions of male characters devalues both genders. Storylines become ones of simple anger and revenge, rather than tackling more complex themes and giving a voice to female survivors of violence. It is entirely accurate to call this "lazy," as it does not require any engagement with the female characters at all; all that is needed is for them to be known as "Male Character's Girlfriend/Wife/Lover/Female Friend," and their death and mutilation can then be used as a motivator. The Punisher is an excellent example of this trope; his family were killed and the entire storyline of their deaths takes up a very small percentage of the overall *Punisher* narrative arc. Their deaths serve *only* to give the male protagonist reasons for his actions. Indeed, the characters were created for no other reason than to be brutally murdered. The central issue here is that, as I previously mentioned, women's narratives of abuse and violence are often silenced in comics; women's trauma is not given an equal stage to comics of men's trauma.[9] Trauma aside, women's stories are not being told. John Berger famously claimed in *Ways of Seeing* that "according to usage and conventions which are at last being questioned but have by no means been overcome—men *act* and women *appear*. Men look at women. Women watch themselves being looked at" (1973: 47, emphasis in original). Berger's point is repeatedly reflected in comics. Female characters lack agency and appear as decoration; the "women in refrigerators" trope is an excellent example. Women no longer want to watch ourselves being looked at (if we ever did!) Constant violence against women in comics does not suggest that the industry is particularly interested in a large percentage of its readership. Despite what stereotypes would have us believe, some reports suggest that roughly 47 percent of comics fans are female.[10] Of course, much of this research relates primarily to mainstream comics, but the point is valid across the whole genre. It is no longer a case of "there are no women so we need not bother with them." As the furor in Angoulême proves, there are many women who are deserving of accolades but are not receiving them.

In the introduction to the 2007 edition of *The Best American Comics*, Chris Ware is aware that a "frequent complaint regarding these sorts of collections (and even recent museum shows) is that there aren't enough (or any) women in them" (Ware, 2007: xxiii). Although this collection *does* contain a reasonable number of female artists, he adds, "I should state right here that I am not of the cut of cloth to check an artist's genitalia at the door. Nor in the case of this book did I go out in search of a couple of hermaphrodites to even out the score" (2007: xxiii). This is a strange comment to make anywhere, especially in the introduction to a collected edition, and Tolmie reads "the genitalia comment [as embodying] a particular sort of dismissive rhetoric that obscures the cultural processes by which both centre and margin(s) are defined and valued" (2009: 83). Ware's comment says little about the female artists he does include (or women artists in general) but does encapsulate the discomfort around the issue of gender that makes any discussion of it seem less about equality and more about an attack on the dubious meritocracy that lurks behind any selection process. I have no concrete suggestion for how we ought to remedy this and bring more women into the field or to allow women's narratives of trauma to be considered as valid as men's.

The position of women as both characters and creators in the comics world has noticeably improved in recent years, though there is still ground to be gained. Furthermore, comics discussing migration, forced migration, and marginalized peoples are receiving academic attention with increasing regularity, especially within the wider field of postcolonial studies. In a recent special issue of the *Journal of Postcolonial Writing*, the editors present articles on an international range of texts which give voice to marginalized groups and propose the comics form as ideally suited to the creation of these specific types of narratives:

> To read a comic we must cross boundaries by the thousand. The movement from each panel to the next is a border crossing that weaves the narrative in each step. At every turn we must consider our next move and bridge the gap between the panels. The transitional movement we use is about reconciling violence and reconstructing brokenness; post-colonial narrative art seeks to redefine and recreate identity out of a violent and often obliterated past.... We as readers participate in violence, perpetrating it with every movement of our eye across the page. For this reason alone, comics is a form that can handle the stresses and tensions of a postcolonial narrative perfectly. (Earle, Knowles, and Peacock, 2016: 8)

In creating comics as a space for working with narratives of marginalized pain and experience we are opening up this form to new and exciting narrative developments. The increasing visibility of previously unseen artists and their perseverance to tell great stories in engaging, innovative, and beautiful ways encourages new artists of both mainstream and "alternative" comics. It also results in increased visibility of female and ethnically diverse mainstream characters, such as Ms. Marvel and the new incarnation of Captain Marvel.

Conclusion
Considering *Guernica* in the Wake of *Cerebus*

Hobbes: How come we play war and not peace?
Calvin: Too few role models.
—Bill Watterson, *Calvin and Hobbes* (1987)

In May 2010, Comic Book Resources, a comics website, launched a weekly activity on their blog, Comics Should Be Good. The aim was to give space for new and aspiring artists to develop their work. Each week, a new topic was posted and artists would submit single-page works on that topic. In response to the topic "What if?" deviantART[1] user Cynthia Sousa created *X-Men Guernica*—"What if Picasso drew X-Men comics?" This piece mimics the shape and structure of *Guernica*, as well as the color scheme. Sousa reworks the bombing into an attack on the Xavier Institute. The artist posted the piece on her online gallery and received a large amount of feedback, some positive and some suggesting that the appropriation of Picasso's painting was inappropriate and disrespectful. It was not clear what exactly was considered disrespectful: the artist chosen or the subject of the original art being altered. However, both the process that underlies this work and the final piece itself tell us much about the nature of comics, as well as the relationship between comics, conflict, modernism and postmodernism.

In my introduction, I discussed the complex relationship between Picasso's *Guernica* and the comics form. I suggested that the panelization and multi-aspectual viewing link the two and make it possible to perform a comics reading of *Guernica*. The rough narrative that is seen in *Guernica* is also present here, albeit using comics characters. The use of these characters encourages the viewer to reinterpret the painting through X-Men mythology. *X-Men Guernica* uses eight characters in place of the original figures of the painting.

Conclusion

Fig. xx.1. *X-Men Guernica*, Cynthia Sousa, 2012.

To the far left, Rogue cradles her dead brother, Nightcrawler; the siblings are watched over by Beast, who replaces Picasso's deformed bull. Across the center of the image, replacing the prostrate man, is Cyclops, a beam from his visor forming panels within the image. The events are watched by the two witness characters, here reimagined as Storm and Emma Frost; Wolverine replaces the man in the far corner, with his arms stretched to the sky. The most problematic character in this reworking is Magneto, who replaces the gored horse, the large central figure of the original painting. Magneto is usually considered to be a villain and enemy of the X-Men, although he has also been an ally at times during the development of the series. Not only does Magneto's presence here cause disorientation for the viewer, it highlights one of the central features of the X-Men franchise. When first creating the X-Men in the 1960s, Stan Lee was heavily influenced by the Civil Rights movement; he "used science fiction in time-honoured fashion as a potent means of holding a mirror up to society" (Kaplan, 2006: 59). The X-Men characters are all mutants since they possess the X-gene. The basic narrative that runs through all *X-Men* comics is of the mutants working to coexist peacefully with humans. Magneto is the adversary because, despite his desire to protect mutants, he uses violent and extreme methods to do so. Professor Xavier and the X-Men are committed to more diplomatic methods. Their symbolic purpose in the 1960s is not subtle. Just as Picasso's original painting depicts an attack on a specific ethnic group, the Basques, Sousa's work depicts an attack on a subgroup, albeit a fictional one, the Mutants of Professor Xavier's school.

In Picasso's original painting, the victims were anonymous, their deformed faces representing the dehumanization of violence and conflict. In assigning recognizable characters to previously anonymous figures, Sousa eliminates this powerful element of the original work. However, this is also the feature that sets *X-Men Guernica* apart from the original. In Chapters 2 and 5, I discussed the recognition on the part of comics creators that the superhero was unable to intervene in violence and conflict in post-9/11 America. The four comics collections published to raise money for 9/11 relief charities use superhero characters but make it clear that their powers are useless and they are limited to the role of witnesses; the most they are able to do is assist the emergency services in the aftermath. In these chapters, I concentrated on individual superheroes who were depicted as acting alone. The fact that this image shows the impotence and helplessness of a superhero team magnifies their inability to effect change and protection, especially in post-9/11 America. As I have shown previously, the impotence of superheroes has become a common theme in mainstream comics since 2001. The destruction and chaos in the image suggests not only that superheroes are not the invincible übermenschen they are assumed to be, but that we do not want them to be.

The desire for a new type of hero is shown by Cyclops's position in Sousa's work—his dead body takes the place of Picasso's dismembered soldier, though Cyclops does not bear the stigmata as the soldier does. Cyclops is unusual for a superhero of his generation. Although created in the 1960s, at the same time as the antiheroes Wolverine and the Punisher, he is often held up as an archetype of the selfless, ethically driven hero, who possesses excellent tactical and strategic skills. In this respect, Cyclops has much in common with Captain America. Despite his mutation, which allows him to deliver "optic blasts" on any given target, Cyclops has remained a steady influence for "good" in the X-Men universe. The fact that he is one of two dead characters in *X-Men Guernica* (the other is Nightcrawler) suggests that this type of hero has no place in contemporary narratives of heroism. A further point can be made regarding the inclusion of Cyclops in this context. While Cyclops was the clearest embodiment of the desire for peaceful coexistence, he has developed as a character. He has taken more militaristic action and, in the 2012 story arc "Avengers vs. X-Men," moves into criminal activity to protect mutants. His development from perfect soldier to renegade follows a clear narrative arc, in which his basic survival is threatened to such a degree that he is forced into extreme action. Cyclops's change in both personality and moral compass is clearly linked to his experience of traumatic events.

• • •

X-Men Guernica shifts Picasso's work from being an indictment of the violence (whether the Spanish Civil War and the events of 9/11) to a statement about conflict in comics, both thematically and formally; not only is conflict a prevalent theme in all genres of comics, but there is conflict inherent in the formal construction. There is conflict in the relationship between panels as the act of closure is dependent on reader input and thus the panels exist in a fluid relationship that changes with each reading. This focus on conflict opens up a wider discussion of claims that comics and popular culture in general promotes violence. Prior to the 1954 Comics Code, critics such as Fredric Wertham and Sterling North argued that the depiction of violence in comics was excessive and unnecessary. Although this is a consensus that has endured, the criticism remains vague and disorganized. To state that some comics are "too violent" suggests that there is a level of violence that is acceptable but does not suggest how this would be measured or by whom. As with the employment 1954 Comics Code, which has not been in use since 2011, comics publishers have created their own rating systems to inform readers about the nature of the material, especially in terms of violence, sexual scenes, and profanity. Despite the implementation of comics grading systems, artists continue to depict violence; although methods are, in general, becoming more subtle, recent series such as Frank Miller's *Sin City* (1991–2000), and Brian Azzarello's *100 Bullets* (1999–2009) have disregarded old concerns. These series—and a large number of other comics that depict graphic violence—are published by mainstream publishers and have received wide-ranging acclaim.

However, the issue of violence in comics was reawakened in a new guise in 2008, when the Apple App Store refused to sell a webcomic, *Murderdrome*, which had been written specially to showcase a digital comics reading application. Apple claimed that the comic was rejected on the grounds of "objectionable content" (McNevitt, 2009: online). However, the App Store also sells a large corpus of equally violent films and texts—including films such as *Reservoir Dogs*, as well as texts by authors such as the Marquis de Sade—without censorship or warning information. Although many people sent messages of support to the creators and their publisher, Infurious Comics, Apple made it clear that the application and book would not be made available via the App Store. Aside from the wider matter of corporate censorship, the ban on *Murderdrome* suggests two things specific to comics: that the negative reaction to comics has largely died down in relation to print media—print comics are for all intents and purposes "accepted"—but also that the negative reaction has shifted to webcomics. Print comics are afforded legitimacy by the fact they have a recognized publisher and material form; webcomics do not have this protection. However, they are the new frontier, in terms of comics development, and it is from this new era of digital comics production that *X-Men Guernica* comes.

In the late 1930s, *Guernica* represented a larger issue in conflict art: that conflict (and conflict trauma) required new representational strategies and insisted on new artistic and narrative forms. In the modernist period, *Guernica* was new and bold. Now that nearly eighty years have passed since it was painted, its position as a masterpiece of antiwar and trauma art is secure. *X-Men Guernica* might be called a postmodernist piece because it is a parody of the original. In *The Politics of Postmodernism* (1989), Hutcheon states that parody "signals how present representations come from past ones" (2002: 93). In contrast, Jameson sees parody in postmodernism as being "blank parody" (1991: 17). Parody has been replaced by pastiche:

> Pastiche is, like parody, the imitation of a peculiar or unique, idiosyncratic style, the wearing of a linguistic mask, speech in a dead language. But it is a neutral practice of such mimicry, without any of parody's ulterior motives, amputated of the satiric impulse, devoid of laughter. (1991: 17)

Pastiche is "the cannibalisation of the past" and represents a loss of connection to a historical referent. Instead of history, the viewer encounters a series of simulacra: the past as "referent" finds itself gradually bracketed and then effaced altogether, leaving us with nothing but texts (1991: 18). *X-Men Guernica* does not merely mimic without comment, however; the choice of characters not only carefully considers the shape and narrative of the original but creates a new narrative of its own. Sousa's work is not *Guernica*, nor does it try to be. It uses the original to make a bold statement on the ubiquity of violence in comics and contemporary society.

If the objections to *X-Men Guernica* are seen as an objection to the use of Picasso for comics parody, the issue raised is similar to those discussed in Chapter 6—the dissolution of barriers between high and low culture. Postmodernism is acutely aware of "the effacement of the older (essentially highmodernist) frontier between high culture and so-called mass or commercial culture, and the emergence of new kinds of texts infused with the forms, categories and contents of that very culture" (Jameson, 1991: 2). The breakdown of what Andreas Huyssen called "the inherent hostility between high and low [culture]" (1986: viii) works in comics' favor when considering conflict and traumatic representation within the comics form as it opens up discussion on accessibility. The fact that "the categorical demand for the uncompromising segregation of high and low has lost much of its persuasive power" (Huyssen, 1986: 197) means that popular and seemingly marginalized forms are given an equal footing in both the critical and academic arena. That this popular form is able to tackle "serious" subjects means that the themes contained therein will be communicated to a wider audience in a form that is both highly accessible and highly effective.

Within American comics, the move towards serious subject matter has been a slow process, partly due to the mainstream monopoly on comics publishing until the mid-1970s. However, it is possible to see a phenomenon informally called the "Cerebus Syndrome" at work here. The name is taken from Dave Sim's multi-award-winning comic series *Cerebus the Aardvark*, which ran from 1977 to 2004. The series is a sixteen-volume story that follows Cerebus, a misanthropic aardvark; the series began as a parody of heroic fantasy comics but gradually became a platform for any topic Sim wished to discuss. He is especially known for his controversial views on politics and the sexes; these views were voiced loudest in Issue 186 of *Cerebus*, under the pseudonym "Viktor Davies." The Cerebus Syndrome is the name given to this gradual change from parodic and light subject matter to more serious concerns; it is not a static entity but rather the ability to trace a shift in the tone of a piece of narrative art. It can be seen in many popular series, including *The Simpsons* and the *Batman* comics franchise. The readers of the particular comic may be unaware of the shift and only notice it in retrospect. Regardless, the Cerebus Syndrome can be very effective in introducing serious subject matters to an audience that may not otherwise show interest. It is possible to trace a noticeable Cerebus shift in American comics as a whole, from newspaper funnies to superheroes to underground comix to the contemporary American comic. As I have shown, comics has faced a considerable amount of negative reception in both academic critical literature and popular criticism in the media; the history of their reception as cheap entertainment has proved difficult to shift. However, it is precisely because comics is not expected to deal with weighty subject matter that they are effective at doing so. The cultural perception of comics as a form that "doesn't do serious" allows the form to reach a wider and more diverse audience than may be typically possible with text literature or film.[2]

Comics is receiving attention—and being used as serious documentary of conflict and experience—from some fairly unexpected places. The required reading list for new recruits at the United States Military Academy at West Point currently includes Marjane Satrapi's *Persepolis* (2003), which discusses the artist's upbringing in Iran during the Iranian Revolution of the late 1970s. Although I have not been able to discuss this text more fully due to my geographic parameters, Satrapi's text is widely praised as an excellent analysis of the impact of conflict in a young person's development into adulthood. West Point's reading list previously included George Pratt's reworking of the 1960s DC antihero "Enemy Ace," a German flying ace in World War I and II. Pratt rewrites the character as a frail and terminally ill old man, who is visited by a traumatized Vietnam veteran journalist; the comic deals with the interaction between the two men and the traumatic experiences that bind them. While it might be suggested that this recognition of comics by the military can be seen as an indication, not of these comics' acclaim and acceptance, but that they are now facing the deliquescence of their oppositional tendencies, I do not agree. That military training institutions are choosing to use comics for the purposes of training combat personnel is testament to the skill of comics to represent trauma, but that fact also opens up the form to a far more diverse readership, with wider reaching publishing opportunities. Giving these texts a different level of legitimacy—as a military training tool—will open the way for comics to be used in all manner of situations beyond simply educational ones, though their position within education should not be underestimated. To allow these works the legitimacy they rightly deserve—and for this to be recognized in *fora* like West Point—will allow more and more artists to develop narratives of trauma and for these to be considered within the wider comics canon.

• • •

In her 1940 essay on Homer's *Iliad*, entitled "The Poem of Force," Simone Weil writes: "Though all are destined from birth to endure violence, the realm of circumstance closes their minds to this truth" (Weil, 2008: 53). War and conflict—and the violence they perpetuate—are among the oldest and most widespread of human experiences. James Tatum concurs with this when he writes that "the one impulse that has proved as enduring as human beings' urge to make wars is their need to make sense of them" (Tatum, 2004: xi). For this reason, among others, conflicts, wars, and their consequences have been a key theme in art for thousands of years. Above all else, however, conflict art has shown that it is not the event itself that remains with us, but the traumatic imprint that stains us indelibly and affects every subsequent experience. Rather than making sense of wars, the desire of conflict art is to make sense of the trauma they leave in their wake. I have argued that the comics form is ideally suited to representing conflict and, moreover, the trauma that is inherent in conflict. The representation of a traumatic event in any artistic medium relies on the artist's ability, not to recreate the event itself, but to recreate the experience of the event—the trauma that the individual experienced and continues to experience. The specific structural and artistic techniques of comics is able to mimic the symptoms of a traumatic rupture in the formal presentation of the narrative, which in turn is able to mimic the experience of a traumatic rupture in the reader.

It is easy to diagnose the comics form as an instance of the Cerebus Syndrome. The form has undergone massive changes in both artwork and thematic concerns since the earliest publications, moving from cheaply printed fantastical storylines to sophisticated works of art. In this book, I have paid much attention to trauma theory and its wide-ranging sense of its own limitations and possibilities. Bennett claims that "much trauma theory . . . privileges *meaning* (i.e. the object of representation, outside art) over *form* (the inherent qualities or modus operandi of art)" (2005: 4). *Comics, Trauma, and the New Art of War* aims to bring together these two oft-disconnected areas, while also showing that comics is able to do things that other forms cannot because it is intrinsically bound up in a culture of imagination, fantasy, and limitlessness. It is a form that encourages difference and experimentation. It is open to all themes. Indeed, the one thing that comics is definitely *not* is a laughing matter.

Notes

Introduction

1. Although the first aerial bombing raid is considered to be the dropping of a single bomb from an unmanned balloon, launched by the Austrian military in 1849, during the First Italian War of Independence, the first substantial aerial bombing campaigns were the Zeppelin raids on Liège, Antwerp, and London during the First World War. There is no evidence to suggest that these bombings were intended to be attacks purely on defenseless civilians, as is the case in Gernika.

2. It is important to note here that the plural of comic is typically used as a singular (as "politics" is) to refer to the entire form or industry. Hence, I talk about "the comics industry" or "comics creators." This is usually employed to avoid the unintentional consequences of using the adjective "comic," which suggests comedic content. By this definition, then, "comics is" is an acceptable way of discussing the form.

3. Superman is not just a figure obsessed with destruction but also one concerned with nationalism, immigration, and eugenics—all topics that were hotly debated in the late 1930s. Superman is more than just a nationalist figure, though this is a major aspect of the character. He is also an immigrant (an alien from the planet Krypton), created by two young first-generation Jewish immigrants, representative of the huge immigrant population of the United States.

4. For an excellent demonstration, see Matt Madden's *99 Ways to Tell a Story* (2006), in which the artist tells the same one-page story in ninety-nine different ways.

5. Many scholars of the Franco-Belgian tradition argue that a multitude of works, especially those of Hergé, were anthologized long before any American works. However, the first *Tintin* story was published in 1928 in serial form in *Le Petit Vingtième* and was not published as a complete book until 1931.

6. Since the 2011 release of *Captain America: The First Avenger*, the character has become a "flagship figure" for the Marvel universe, especially in film. He has starred prominently in five films since 2011. The character is still undoubtedly a patriotic symbol, but his portrayal is no longer one of overt, uncontested nationalism. Instead, Cap has become reconfigured, still as pro-American, but also grappling with the issue of how to reconcile patriotic feeling with the influence of neo-liberalism and post-9/11 populism.

7. I conducted an informal poll of twenty of my colleagues and students. The question was "*Quick!* Name a war story!" Eighteen of the twenty respondents named a film. One person said *War and Peace*; one said *Band of Brothers* (the award-winning television series).

8. Auerbach's book was translated into English under the title *Mimesis: The Representation of Reality in Western Literature*.

9. Wilkomirski's book was published in Anglophone countries with the title *Fragments: Memories of a Wartime Childhood*.

10. Although the initial publication of *Maus* was in 1986, the three-page comic that Spiegelman wrote prior to beginning the full-length work was published in *Funny Aminals* in 1972. However, as this is not the specific text I am studying—and it differs greatly in content and artistic style—I do not consider this to negate my publication date stipulations.

11. Many of these books (it would be inaccurate to describe them as fiction, though equally inaccurate to label them nonfiction; so often trauma literature blurs the boundaries between the two) have achieved critical acclaim and a wider readership. Others have been made into successful Hollywood films (Gustav Hasford's *The Short-Timers* became *Full Metal Jacket*; Ron Kovic's *Born on the Fourth of July* was filmed under the same title).

12. In 2003, *Time* magazine published an article in which Eisner stated that he did not know that the term had been previously used and he did not take credit for the invention of the term (Arnold, 2003: online).

13. A photo-comic uses photographs or film stills instead of artwork, along with bubbles and captions, to create the narrative.

14. Torres is the writer of the comic but does not draw the artwork, which is created by New York-based artist Sungyoon Choi. According to an interview with comics news website Newsarama, Torres wrote the original script "in Microsoft word using text boxes for the panels. In each box I wrote descriptions of what I thought should go in them along with dialogue and thought balloons. [She] spent a lot of time doodling and found that I was very good at—and enjoyed—conceptualizing the artwork. Too bad I wasn't very good at drawing" (Lorah, 2008: n.p.). Torres decided to make her book a collaborative piece and also decided she wanted a female artist to work with her: "It's hard to articulate the difference between a man's and a woman's work but I knew that a female artist was what the project needed." Of her collaborator, Sungyoon Choi, Torres said: "Some comic art is cluttered, making it a battle to get through each page, but Choi's work was very succinct with a lot of white space and great composition. And it was extremely heartfelt" (Lorah, 2008: n.p.). While Torres did not directly draw the comic's art, she was very much a part of creating each panel's image, mood, and coloration. It is often the case that the writer of a comic receives the vast majority (if not all) of the praise for the work (Alan Moore is a key example; many people do not credit his collaborators at all). However, we must remember that the artists are also engaged in interpretative work around trauma, even if it is not their own. They are working to give voice and face to difficult narratives just as much as the writers.

15. These texts are henceforth referred to as "the 9/11 charity comics" for ease of nomenclature. When a specific comic is mentioned, I will reference it separately.

Chapter One

1. Most notably in *Beyond the Pleasure Principle* (1920) and *Moses and Monotheism* (1939).
2. By way of example, it has been noted that over 150,000 veterans of the Vietnam War committed suicide within five years of returning home. This is nearly three times the number who died in combat. These statistics are taken from Chuck Dean's book *Nam Vet: Making Peace With Your Past* (2012).
3. Its extreme form is "positivism," which was developed (in the modern sense) by the philosopher and sociologist Auguste Comte in his 1848 book *Discours sur L'ensemble du Positivisme*. Comte's positivism argued that society operates on absolute laws just as the physical world does.
4. At first glance, this bleed is reminiscent of Martin Handford's *Where's Waldo?* series, which featured densely packed crowd scenes.
5. "Emanata" refers to the lines around a character's head to indicate shock, drunkenness, or any other number of emotions and states. "Grawlixes" are typographical symbols used to replace words, usually expletives. Both terms were coined by Mort Walker in *The Lexicon of Comicana* (2000).

Chapter Two

1. As an interesting aside, I wish to remind readers that it is highly unlikely that Homer was one man. Rather, many classical scholars have called attention to the very real likelihood that Homer was in fact many poets consolidated over time into the entity known as "Homer." This theory has multiple bases, including the curious etymology of the name itself. Harris (2007) writes that the Greek name *"Homēros"* is identical to the Greek word for "hostage." He states that the name was likely derived from the name of a group of poets called the *"Homeridae,"* which literally means "sons of hostages"—the descendants of prisoners of war. At the most basic level, it is probably more accurate to refer to Homer, not as a "he," but as an "it." Other notable scholars who have written on this theory include Graziosi (2002), Nagy (1996), and Jensen (1980).
2. The name of the great hero and central figure Achilles has its root in the Greek for "grief of the people." In the etymology of his name, Achilles is a "Hero of Grief."
3. Although webcomics are not presented in a strictly physical sense, they still exist in a specially constructed physical space. The construction of webcomics works with the presentation space available, just as print comics do.
4. I take as my model for mourning the Five Stage Model, proposed by Elisabeth Kübler-Ross in *On Death and Dying* (1969). This model is no longer universally accepted; there are other models suggested that secure more widespread assent from specialists. In terms of "popular" models of mourning, however, it is the most well-known.
5. I do not wish to belittle the experiences of those we may class as "trauma by proxy"— I am sure that many people felt very strongly after 9/11 and the experience of witnessing

affected them deeply—but I do wish to make the distinction clear and to remind the reader that we should not conflate the two. Traumatic experience belongs to those who are touched by it directly, and to claim that all who witness it are automatically victims of trauma would be untrue and unfair.

6. The fact the family is drawn as Dalmatians is a reference to the fact that this breed is a popular choice for fire stations.

Chapter Three

1. Blaine was under the command of William Calley, who was convicted of war crimes for his role in the My Lai Massacre on March 16, 1968. Calley was convicted of the premeditated murder of 104 Vietnamese civilians. Blaine was present at My Lai, though he was exonerated of any responsibility for the events at a military tribunal in 1970.

2. It is commonly noticed that the German word *"traum"* ("dream") is very similar to "trauma," though in *traum* the 'au' is generally pronounced /aʊ/, while "trauma" is pronounced with an /ɔː/ sound. However, the two words do not share a common root. Rather, *traum* is derived from the Old West Germanic *"draugmas,"* meaning a deception or illusion (*OED*, 2013: online). The German etymology of *traum* references the phantasmagorical and illusionary aspect that is central to dreaming.

3. See Varvin et al., 2012; Barrett et al., 2013.

4. The average age of a Vietnam soldier was twenty-three (Karnow, 2008). However, this number includes all soldiers and not just conscripts; it is likely that the majority of conscripts were younger.

5. *Parshas Truma*, the specific section of the Torah that comprises Exodus 25–27. "Parsha" refers to the sections of the Torah that are read each Saturday, with each "parsha" being read once yearly.

6. The *Tallit* is the tasselled shawl that is wore by Jewish men during prayer and the *Tefillah* (also called "phylacteries") is the small black box containing scriptural texts, worn on the forehead during weekday prayer.

7. See Spiegelman in Schneider, 2010: 23.

8. Berger references the comment that Vladek makes to Artie during an interview in the Catskills: "[In Auschwitz] God did not come. We were all on our own" (189).

9. Sleep disturbances in Holocaust survivors have been the subject of many studies. See Rosen et al, "Sleep Disturbances in Survivors of the Nazi Holocaus'" (1991); Kuch et al., "Symptoms of PTSD in 124 Survivors of the Holocaust" (1992); and Barel et al., "Surviving the Holocaust: A Meta-Analysis of the Long-term Sequelae of a Genocide" (2010).

10. No substantial research has been conducted in the area of nightmares in witnesses of conflict trauma. However, other types of trauma have been considered. For more information, see Fernandez et al., "Cognitive-Behavioral Treatment of Trauma-Related Nightmare Experienced by Children" (2012); Kilpatrick, "Post-Traumatic Stress Disorder in Child Witnesses to Domestic Violence" (1998); and Boulanger, "From Voyeur to Witness: Recapturing Symbolic Function After Massive Psychic Trauma" (2012).

11. Masking is described by McCloud as the use of simplistic characters, often juxtaposed with detailed verisimilar backgrounds. This is most commonly used to allow readers to place themselves in the narrative—a type of projective identification. One of the most famous uses of this technique is Hergé's *Tintin* series.

Chapter Four

1. The most comprehensive text on transgenerational trauma is *The International Handbook of Multigenerational Legacies of Trauma*, edited by Yael Danieli, which addresses a wide range of traumatic events, including the Cambodian genocide, the Holocaust, the Japanese atomic bombs, children of Nazi commanders, the war in the Balkans, and the legacy of slavery in America. There are also many narrower psychological and psychiatric studies that concentrate on specific events or groups, including Coffey, *Unspeakable Truths and Happy Endings* (1998); Degruy, *Post Traumatic Slave Syndrome* (2005), and Fossion et al., "Family Approach to Grandchildren of Holocaust Survivors" (2003).
2. Although I focus on conflict trauma, these phenomena are also seen in the parenting experiences of survivors of personal trauma, including rape, and violent non-conflict traumata.
3. For information on current clinical thought, see Gottesman et al., "Severe Mental Disorders in Offspring with 2 Psychiatrically Ill Parents" (2010) and Göpfert et al., *Parental Psychiatric Disorders: Distressed Parents and Their Families* (2004).
4. Although this sign appears to be written in German, the grammar and sentence construction are not accurate. However, the translation I offer is an approximation of what the sign aims to say.
5. Obsessive Compulsive Disorder is a psychiatric condition characterized by "recurrent obsessions or compulsions ... that are severe enough to be time-consuming or cause marked distress or significant impairment" (DSM-V: 456). Often, compulsions are repetitive behaviors (such as handwashing, touching certain items, or repeating certain words) that must be completed to reduce anxiety. Scrupulosity is recognized as a form of OCD, in which the individual experiences pathological guilt regarding moral and religious issues, leading them to commit certain repetitive acts in order to assuage this guilt (Santa, 1999).
6. The reader assumes that conversations in the family narrative part of the book are in Vietnamese. Whenever French is being spoken, the dialogue is encased in guillemets, the standard French punctuation mark used to indicate speech.
7. In 1987, the US Supreme Court ruled that Jews can be classed as a race for the purposes of certain anti-discrimination laws. However, the term "race" refers to people of shared ancestry and genetic traits. These are not required for one to convert to Judaism. Many (mostly American) secular Jews consider their "Jewishness" a matter of culture and ethnicity. For them, Judaism is a matter of food, language, and cultural values. Much of this is derived from Ashkenazic Jewish culture; Ashkenazi Jews originate in Central and Eastern Europe. Thus, Judaism cannot be considered a race but can be considered a cultural or ethnic group.

Chapter Five

1. I would argue that this is the most important distinction between comics and film. In a film, all information is presented in the same space; we watch the entire sequence of events unfolding on one screen. The physical-spatial relationship is lacking.

2. Perhaps the most extreme disruption of personal time that can occur in the wake of a traumatic event is catatonia, in which the individual experiences an extreme loss of motor skills, among other things. Some catatonic patients hold rigid poses for hours at a time, as if they are paused. However, this does not occur in all traumatized individuals. Some studies suggest that it affects less than 2 percent of traumatised individuals but these statistics are debated (FDA, 2010).

3. Analepsis is defined as "evocation after the fact of an event that took place earlier in the point of the story" (flashback) (Genette, 1972: 40). Similarly, prolepsis is defined as "any narrative manoeuvre that consists in narrating or evoking in advance an event that will take place" (flash-forward) (Genette, 1972: 40). See Chapter 3 for the definition of metalepsis.

4. Bakhtin uses the example of the Greek "novel of ordeal" (including *Aethiopica*, *Clitophon and Leucippe*, and *Ephesiaca*) to show how the road forms the basic structure of the novel (1978: 495). He writes that as "the action of the plot unfolds against a broad geographical background," movement of time and space becomes inextricably linked and, thus, the novel's structure is formed entirely around this spatial movement (1978: 500).

5. The term *ligne claire* comes from Dutch cartoonist Joost Swarte (originally rendered *klare lijn*) and his 1977 exhibition in Rotterdam (Miller, 2007: 18). However, the style is synonymous with the Franco-Belgian *bandes-dessinées* tradition and, more specifically, Belgian comics artist Hergé. This style "privileges smooth, continuous linework, simplified contours and bright, solid colors, while avoiding frayed lines, exploded forms and expressionistic rendering" (Hatfield, 2005: 60). *Ligne claire* has not been widely used in American comics, although some artists do employ it and to good effect. Recent examples include Daniel Clowes's *Ghost World* (1997) and Jason Lutes's series *Berlin* (2008).

6. Here is the inclusion of another "actual" event into the story arc of *The 'Nam*. Operation Cedar Falls was a search-and-destroy mission that ran from January 8–28, 1967. The objective was to eradicate the "Iron Triangle," an area of south Vietnam, close to Saigon, that was a Viet Cong stronghold. Many thousands of Vietnamese saw their homes destroyed, and the US used Agent Orange to destroy crops.

7. Thomas's character provides much comic relief, and most of the characters lament him ever being drafted into the army. He left Vietnam by helicopter, after falling into said helicopter face first.

8. Verzyl is the subject of a short comic entitled "Tunnel Rat" that appears alongside other issues of *The 'Nam*. After being attacked by a nest of rats in a Viet Cong tunnel, Verzyl is traumatized. When his commanding officer tries to force him back into the tunnel to continue looking for VC soldiers, Verzyl shoots him and then enters a stage of extreme catatonia. This return to him in hospital, bound and silent, is the only other mention of this character in the series.

9. In my article for *Comics Forum*, "The Whites of their Eyes: Implied Violence and Double Frames in *Blazing Combat* and *The 'Nam*," I talk about this image of Frank Verzyl in relation to his wide-eyed stare. I contend that "the way an eye is drawn and its relationship to the rest of the image is in fact an acutely important representational tool and one that allows violence to be implicit, dependent on the reader's imagination" (Earle, 2015: n.p.) I continue, suggesting that "it is in the representation of the trauma of violence, rather than the violence itself that the true power of these comics is felt. Violence is universal but trauma is uniquely human and its displays are more likely to stir something in us. It is when we begin to consider trauma that the difference between seeing and understanding becomes heightened" (Earle, 2015: n.p.).

10. According to the *New York Times* archives in 2003.

11. "Suu" is in reference to Vo Suu, a fellow photographer.

12. Aeder was an eighteen-year-old private who was often shown reading comics. He died in Issue 31.

Chapter Six

1. Various interpretations include postmodernism as the result, aftermath, development, denial, or rejection of modernism (Appignanesi and Garratt, 2006: 4).

2. The word that is translated as "traditional" is "BD"—a term used as equivalent to "mainstream" in the Franco-Belgian tradition.

3. In his 1982 article on the Vietnam War, Michael Mandelbaum boldly states that "the Vietnam War was the first to be televised" (1982: 157). *Dispatches*, Michael Herr's 1977 memoir of his time as a war correspondent in Vietnam, gives detailed descriptions of soldiers playing up to television crews, suggesting that the Vietnam War was not only televised but also manipulated due to its televised status. Some critics think that 9/11 marks another shift in representation, especially due to the development of the internet and its shift in methods of news transmission and consumption.

4. And also Bakhtin's chronotope of *Madame Bovary*—time that oozes and clots in space. See Chapter 5.

5. However, this is not to say that postmodernist techniques are not seen in comics at all, as I discuss later in this chapter.

6. See Reed, *Manet, Flaubert, and the Emergence of Modernism: Blurring Genre Boundaries*, 2003.

7. Furthermore, enough time has seemingly passed for Nazism to become a source of parody and (black) humor. Consider Quentin Tarantino's 2009 black comedy film *Inglourious Basterds*.

8. See the section on "traumatic representation" in the introduction.

9. In his essay on this text, "The Holocaust Without Ink," Brad Prager suggests another reason for the lack of ink in this comic. He reminds us that, typically, comics are drawn in pencil and then "inked," with the pencil traces being completely erased. The absence of ink

echoes the absence of a camp tattoo, "the mark of victimhood," that Kubert does not bear (Prager, 2010: 118).

10. The Greek root "allo" translates as "other" or "different."

11. Another type of allohistory, and one that is much more common, shows a more wide-ranging situation. For example, "What if the Nazis won the Second World War?" or "What if Nixon had served a third term as president?" This second question forms the basis of Alan Moore and Dave Gibbons's 1986 comic *Watchmen*.

Excursus

1. I have called this final chapter an "excursus" in order to highlight its difference to the chapters that have come before it. I take the name from Jürgen Habermas's *Philosophical Discourse of Modernity* (1985).

2. Cestac's comic reads "43rd Festival and only one woman elected as *Grand Prix*!" The men respond with "Oh yeah?" and "Are you sure?" The caption reads: "Yes, it doesn't even come into their minds!"

3. See Lamothe (2015), "Marine Experiment Finds Women Get Injured More Frequently, Shoot Less Accurately than Men," *Washington Post*. This article includes an executive summary of the findings of the study, but at this point I have been unable to access a full report.

4. In an article on rape in the US military, journalist Kathleen Parker writes: "Male soldiers and officers have confided that many men resent women because they've been forced to pretend that women are equals, and men know they're not. The lie breeds contempt, which leads to a simmering rage that sometimes finds expression in aggression toward those deemed responsible. . . . It's also not the women's fault that they've been put in this untenable situation—exposed both to combat and to the repressed fury of sexually charged young men" (2007: n.p.).

5. The regiment was later known as the 46th "Taman" Guards Night Bomber Aviation Regiment. "Night Witches" is an English translation of *Nachthexen*, the German nickname for the regiment. As the pilots flew in wood-and-canvas Polikarpov Po-2 biplanes, the noise of the engines made stealth a serious problem. To combat this, the Night Witches cut the engine as they neared the target and glided to the bomb release point. Only wind noise gave them away—a sound which the German soldiers likened to broomsticks.

6. *Feldwebel* is a German noncommissioned officer rank that is roughly equivalent to sergeant in the US and UK armies.

7. "*Jobnik*" is an Israeli slang term for a noncombatant soldier whose military service role involves secretarial or office clerk duties. It is generally used as a derogatory term.

8. *Tznuit* is the Hebrew term for modesty of dress, such as that which is required and expected of Orthodox Jewish women.

9. Naturally, there was much outcry over the "women in refrigerators" list when it was first published, with many fans claiming that male characters had it just as bad as female characters—or worse. The compilers of the original list released a statement, introducing "Dead Men Defrosting," which suggested that, while it was accurate that male characters

did go through horrific injuries and events, they "usually come back even better than before, either power-wise or in terms of character development/relevancy to the reader" (WiR Website). When heroes do die and are not brought back to life, their death is considered "heroic or touching" (WiR). The same certainly cannot be said for female characters.

10. This statistic comes from Graphic Policy, a website that considers representation and social impact in the comics world. By measuring Facebook user information, interaction with comics publishers, and "likes," this number was reached. Facebook is becoming a useful tool for market research, as noted on the Graphic Policy website. This is the clearest study on readership statistics that I have been able to find; very few academic studies have been conducted. The full report can be found here: http://graphicpolicy.com/2015/09/01/demo-graphics-comic-fandom-on-facebook-14/.

Conclusion

1. deviantART is an online art community. Users can create profiles and post their artwork—traditional and digital media, photography and creative writing—to the site for others to view and comment on. The site also has links to other websites that allow users to buy prints of the artwork.

2. The Cerebus Syndrome can be seen in tandem with another similar cultural phenomenon. Comics (and also other popular forms, such as animation and film) is a highly self-aware form and uses audience perceptions to its advantage; if comics isn't expected to be anything other than provide cheap entertainment, it can do anything it chooses because there are no preconceived ideas. This phenomenon is most clearly demonstrated by a quotation from long-running animated series *The Simpsons*, which is a good example of a self-aware series that uses its "low" form to make bold statements: "Cartoons don't have messages, Lisa. They're just a bunch of hilarious stuff, like people getting hurt and stuff" (Groening et al., 1995). Unfortunately, neither of these phenomena has received any substantial critical interest and, as such, there are no academic studies available.

Bibliography

Primary Texts

Bendis, Brian Michael, and Scott Morse. 2002. "Moment of Silence: A True Story." In *A Moment of Silence*. 2002. New York: Marvel. pp. 9–16.

Boyd, Ron. 2001. "Ayekah." In *9/11: Artists Respond*. 2002. Milwaukee: Dark Horse Comics. pp. 168–69.

Eisner, Will. 2000. *Last Day in Vietnam: A Memory*. Milwaukee: Dark Horse Comics.

Ennis, Garth, and Russell Braun. 2009. *Battlefields Volume 1: The Night Witches*. Runnemede: Dynamite.

———. 2011. *Battlefields Volume 6: Motherland*. Runnemede: Dynamite.

———. 2013. *Battlefields Volume 8: The Fall & Rise of Anna Kharkova*. Runnemede: Dynamite.

Fields, Gary. 2001. "Untitled." In *9/11: The World's Finest Comic Book Writers and Artists Tell Stories to Remember*. 2002. New York: DC Comics. p. 59.

Giffen, Keith, and William Wray. 2002. "Dust." In *9/11: The World's Finest Comic Book Writers and Artists Tell Stories to Remember*. New York: DC Comics. pp. 111–13.

Kelly, Joe, Scott Kollins, and Dan Panosian. 2002. "Wake Up." In *9/11: The World's Finest Comic Book Writers and Artists Tell Stories to Remember*. New York: DC Comics. pp. 19–23.

Kubert, Joe. 2002a. "Untitled." In *Heroes: The World's Greatest Super Hero Creators Honor The World's Greatest Heroes 9-11-2001*. New York: Marvel. p. 4.

———. 2002b. "What of Tomorrow?" In *9/11: The World's Finest Comic Book Writers and Artists Tell Stories to Remember*. 2002. New York: DC Comics. pp. 212–15.

———. 2003. *Yossel April 19, 1943*. New York: DC Comics.

Libicki, Miriam. *Jobnik! An American Girl's Adventures in the Israeli Army*. Coquitlam: Real Gone Girl Studios.

Loeb, Jeph, Carlos Pacheco, and Jesús Merino. 2001. "A Hard Day's Night." In *9/11: The World's Finest Comic Book Writers and Artists Tell Stories to Remember*. 2002. New York: DC Comics. pp. 71–73.

Murray, Doug, and Mike Golden. 1990. "Back in the Real World." *The 'Nam #41*. New York: Marvel.

———. 1991a. "The Punisher invades The 'Nam Part 1." *The 'Nam #52*. New York: Marvel.

———. 1991b. "The Punisher invades The 'Nam Part 2." *The 'Nam #53*. New York: Marvel.

———. 1992a. "The Punisher invades The 'Nam Part 1." *The 'Nam #67*. New York: Marvel.
———. 1992b. "The Punisher invades The 'Nam Part 2." *The 'Nam #68*. New York: Marvel.
———. 1992c. "The Punisher invades The 'Nam Part 3." *The 'Nam #69*. New York: Marvel.
———. 2009. *The 'Nam Volume 1*. New York: Marvel.
———. 2010. *The 'Nam Volume 2*. New York: Marvel.
———. 2011. *The 'Nam Volume 3*. New York: Marvel.
Pak, Greg, and Carmine Di Giandomenico. 2009. *X-Men: Magneto Testament*. New York: Marvel.
Sacco, Joe. 2001. *Palestine*. Seattle: Fantagraphics.
———. 2009. *Footnotes in Gaza*. Seattle: Fantagraphics.
Sale, Tim. 2002. "Untitled." In *9/11: The World's Finest Comic Book Writers and Artists Tell Stories to Remember*. New York: DC Comics. p. 70.
Seagle, Steven, Duncan Rouleau, and Aaron Sowd. 2002. "Unreal." In *9/11: The World's Finest Comic Book Writers and Artists Tell Stories to Remember*. New York: DC Comics. 2002. New York: Marvel. pp. 15–16.
Sim, Dave. 2008. *Judenhass*. Kitchener: Aardvark-Vanaheim.
Spiegelman, Art. 2003. *Maus: A Survivor's Tale*. London: Penguin.
Strom, Kellie. 2002. "Untitled." In *9/11: Artists Respond*. 2002. Milwaukee: Dark Horse Comics. pp. 142–43.
Torres, Alissa, and Sungyoon Choi. 2008. *American Widow*. New York: Villard.
Tran, GB. 2011. *Vietnamerica: A Family's Journey*. New York: Villard.
Tyler, C. 2009. *You'll Never Know Book 1: A Good and Decent Man*. Seattle: Fantagraphics.
———. 2010. *You'll Never Know Book 2: Collateral Damage*. Seattle: Fantagraphics.
———. 2012. *You'll Never Know Book 3: Soldier's Heart*. Seattle: Fantagraphics.
Various. 2002a. *9/11: Artists Respond*. Milwaukee: Dark Horse Comics.
———. 2002b. *9/11: The World's Finest Comic Book Writers and Artists Tell Stories to Remember*. New York: DC Comics.
———. 2002c. *A Moment of Silence*. New York: Marvel.
———. 2002d. *Heroes: The World's Greatest Super Hero Creators Honor The World's Greatest Heroes 9-11-2001*. New York: Marvel.

Secondary Sources

Aarseth, Espen. 1997. *Cybertext: Perspectives on Ergodic Literature*. Baltimore: Johns Hopkins University Press.
Abraham, Nicolas, and Maria Torok. 1994. *The Shell and the Kernel: Renewals of Psychoanalysis*. Chicago: University of Chicago Press.
Abrams, M. H., and Stephen Greenblatt. 2002. "Beowulf." *Norton Anthology of English Literature: The Middle Ages*. New York: W. W. Norton. pp. 28–31.
Adams, Eddie. *Saigon Execution*. 1968. Photograph. Library of Congress, Washington, DC.
———. 1969. *Saigon Execution: An Interview*. Dolph Briscoe Center for American History Archives. Available at: http://www.cah.utexas.edu/db/dmr. Accessed January 8, 2013.

Adams, Jeff. 2000. "Working Out Comics." *Journal of Art and Design Education* 19 (3). pp. 304–312.
Akhtar, Salman. 2009. *The Comprehensive Dictionary of Psychoanalysis*. London: Karnac.
American Psychiatric Association. 2013. *Diagnostic and Statistical Manual of Mental Disorders Fifth Edition*. Washington: American Psychiatric Association Press.
Antonov-Ovseenko, Anton. 1981. *The Time of Stalin: Portrait of a Tyranny*. New York: Harper & Row.
Appignanesi, Richard, and Chris Garratt. 2006. *Introducing Postmodernism*. Cambridge: Icon.
Aristotle. 1984. *Poetics*. Trans. Ingram Bywater. New York: Modern Library College Editions.
———. 1991. *The Art of Rhetoric*. Trans. Hugh Lawson-Tancred. London: Penguin.
Arnheim, Rudolf. 1973. *The Genesis of a Painting: Picasso's Guernica*. Berkeley: University of California Press.
Askin, Kelly Dawn. 1997. *War Crimes Against Women: Prosecution in International War Crimes Tribunals*. Leiden: Martinus Nijhoff.
Attridge, Derek. 2011. "Once More with Feeling: Art, Affect and Performance." *Textual Practice* 25 (2). pp. 329–43.
Auerbach, Erich. 1988. *Mimesis: Dargestellte Wirklichkeit in der Abendlandischen Literatur*. Tübingen: Francke.
Axe, David. 2010. *War is Boring: Bored Stiff, Scared to Death in the World's Worst War Zone*. New York: New American Library.
———. 2013. "Inside the Israeli Army in a Time of Terror—War Is Boring." *Medium*. Available at: https://medium.com/war-is-boring/inside-the-israeli-army-in-a-time-of-terror-f68423ce9b17#.wg6w6c244. Accessed February 10, 2016.
Baker, Steven. 1993. *Picturing the Beast: Animals, Identity and Representation*. Manchester: Manchester University Press.
Bakhtin, Mikhail. 1978. "The Forms of Time and the Chronotopos in the Novel: From the Greek Novel to Modern Fiction." *Journal of Descriptive Poetics and Theory of Literature* 3. pp. 493–528.
Balaev, Michelle. 2014. *Contemporary Approaches in Literary Trauma Theory*. London: Palgrave Macmillan.
Barel, Efrat et al. 2010. "Surviving the Holocaust: A Meta-analysis of the Long-term Sequelae of a Genocide." *Psychological Bulletin* 136 (5). pp. 677–98.
Bar-On, Dan, and Gûlyā Čayṭîn. 2001. *Parenthood and the Holocaust*. Jerusalem: Yad Vashem.
Barrett, Deirdre. 1996. *Trauma and Dreams*. Cambridge: Harvard University Press.
———. 2013. "Content of Dreams from World War Two Prisoners Of War." *Imagination, Cognition and Personality* 33 (2). pp. 193–204.
Barthes, Roland. 1967. *Elements of Semiology*. London: Jonathan Cape.
———. 1974. *S/Z*. London: Jonathan Cape.
———. 1977. *Image, Music, Text*. London: Fontana.
———. 2007. *Mythologies*. Paris: Éditions Du Seuil.
Baudrillard, Jean. 2004. *The Consumer Society: Myths and Structures*. London: Sage.

BD Égalité. 2016. "The International Festival of Comics (Angouleme): Women Banned From Comics." Available at: http://bdegalite.org/wp-content/uploads/2016/01/grandprix-fibd-ENG.gif. Accessed January 16, 2016.

Beaty, Bart. 2012. *Comics Versus Art: Comics in the Art World*. Toronto: University of Toronto Press.

Beidler, Philip. 1991. *Rewriting America*. Athens: University of Georgia Press.

Bender, Hy. 1999. *The Sandman Companion*. New York: Vertigo.

Bendis, Brian Michael, and Marko Djurdjevic. 2010. *The New Avengers: Siege*. New York: Marvel.

Bennett, Jill. 2005. *Empathic Vision: Affect, Trauma and Contemporary Art*. Stanford: Stanford University Press.

Berger, Alan. 1998. "Bearing Witness: Theological Implications of Second Generation Literature in America." In *Breaking Crystal: Writing Memory after Auschwitz*. Ed. Efraim Sicher. Chicago: University of Illinois Press. pp. 200–205.

Berger, John. 1969. *The Moment of Cubism*. New York: Pantheon.

——. 1973. *Ways of Seeing*. New York: Viking Press.

Bergman, Lucy. 2010. *Religion, Death, and Dying*. Santa Barbara: Praeger.

Bibby, Michael. 1999. "The Post-Vietnam Condition." In *The Vietnam War and Postmodernity*. Ed. Michael Bibby. Amherst: University of Massachusetts Press. pp. 143–72.

The Bible: New Revised Standard Version. 1995. Oxford: Oxford University Press.

Blaine, Adam. 2013. "Discussion on the Experience of Vietnam Veterans." Personal communication. September 16, 2013.

Bolhafner, J. Stephen. 1991. "Art for Art's Sake: Spiegelman Speaks on RAW's Past, Present and Future." *Comics Journal* 145. pp. 96–97.

Bosmajian, Hamida. 1998. "The Orphaned Voice in Art Spiegelman's *Maus*." *Literature and Psychology* 44 (1.2). pp. 1–22.

Boulanger, Ghislaine. 2012. "From Voyeur to Witness: Recapturing Symbolic Function After Massive Psychic Trauma." *Psychoanalytic Psychology* 22 (1). pp. 21–31.

Brady, Matt. 2008. "Interview with Garth Ennis on Battlefields: Night Witches." Newsarama. Available at: http://www.newsarama.com/812-garth-ennis-on-battlefields-night-witches.html. Accessed February 8, 2016.

Brett E. A., and R. Ostroff. 1985. "Imagery and Post-traumatic Stress Disorder: An Overview." *American Journal of Psychiatry* 142 (4). pp. 417–24.

Brokaw, Tom. 2001. "Breaking News on September 11th." *NBC News*.

Brownmiller, Susan. 1975. *Against Our Will: Men, Women, and Rape*. New York: Bantam.

Bull, Malcolm. 1999. *Seeing Things Hidden: Apocalypse, Vision, and Totality*. London: Verso.

Calder, Angus. 2004. *Disasters and Heroes: On War, Memory and Representation*. Cardiff: University of Wales Press.

Carpenter, Lucas. 2003 "'It Don't Mean Nothin'": Vietnam War Fiction and Postmodernism." *College Literature* 30 (2). pp. 30–50.

Carrier, David. 2001. *The Aesthetics of Comics*. University Park: Pennsylvania State University Press.

Caruth, Cathy. 1995. *Trauma: Explorations in Memory*. Baltimore: Johns Hopkins University Press.

———. 1996. *Unclaimed Experience: Trauma, Narrative, and History*. Baltimore: Johns Hopkins University Press.

Childs, Peter. 2005. *Modernism*. London: Routledge.

Chute, Hillary. 2008. "Comics as Literature? Reading Graphic Narrative." *PMLA* 123 (2). pp 452–65.

———. 2010. *Graphic Women: Life, Narrative and Contemporary Comics*. New York: Columbia University Press.

———. 2011. "Comics Form and Narrating Lives." *Profession* 2011. pp. 107–117.

———. 2016. *Disaster Drawn: Visual Witness, Comics, and Documentary Form*. Cambridge: Harvard University Press.

Chute, Hillary, and Marianne Dekoven. 2012. "Comic Books and Graphic Novels." In *The Cambridge Companion to Popular Fiction*. Eds. David Glover and Scott McCracken. Cambridge: Cambridge University Press. pp. 175–95.

Clark, Spencer. 2013. "Encounters with Historical Agency: The Value of Nonfiction Graphic Novels in the Classroom." *History Teacher* 46 (4). pp. 489-508.

Clark, T. J. 2013. *Picasso and Truth: From Cubism to Guernica*. Princeton: Princeton University Press.

Coffey, R. 1998. *Unspeakable Truths and Happy Endings*. Brooklandville: Sidran Press.

Collectif. 2006. *Le Coup de Grâce*. Brussels: La Cinquième Couche.

Comic Book Legal Defense Fund. 2012. Available at: http://www.cbldf.org. Accessed May 15, 2013.

"Conflict." *The Oxford English Dictionary*. 2012. Oxford: Clarendon Press. Available at: http://www.oed.com/conflict. Accessed July 7, 2012.

Cooper, Simon, and Paul Atkinson. 2008. "Graphic Implosion: Politics, Time and Value in Post-9/11 Comics." In *Literature after 9/11*. Eds. Ann Keniston and Jeanne Follansbee Quinn. New York: Routledge. pp. 60–81.

Cottington, David. 2004. *Cubism and its Histories*. Manchester: Manchester University Press.

Crane, Stephen. 1994. *The Red Badge of Courage*. London: Penguin.

Crosthwaite, Paul. 2009. *Trauma, Postmodernism and World War II*. Basingstoke: Palgrave Macmillan.

Danieli, Yael. 1998. *The International Handbook of Multigenerational Legacies of Trauma*. Berlin: Springer.

Dasberg, Haim. 2003. "Late Onset of Post-traumatic Reactions in Holocaust Survivors at Advanced Age." In *Das Schweigen Brechen*. Eds. H. Rossberg and J. Lansen. Berlin: Peter Lang. pp. 311–48.

Davis, J. L. et al. 2007. "Characteristics of Chronic Nightmares in a Trauma-exposed Treatment-seeking Sample." *Dreaming* 17 (2). pp. 187–98.

Dawes, James. 2005. *The Language of War: Literature and Culture in the US from the Civil War through World War II*. Cambridge: Harvard University Press.

Dean, Chuck. 2000. *Nam Vet: Making Peace with Your Past*. New York: WordSmith.

DeGroot, G. J. 1997. "Whose Finger on the Trigger? Mixed Anti-Aircraft Batteries and the Female Combat Taboo." *War in History* 4 (4). pp. 434–53.

Degruy, J. 2005. *Post Traumatic Slave Syndrome: America's Legacy of Enduring Injury and Healing*. Oakland: Uptone Press.

Deleuze, Gilles, and Félix Guattari. 1987. *A Thousand Plateaus: Capitalism and Schizophrenia*. Trans. Brian Massumi. Minneapolis: University of Minnesota Press.

———. 1994. *What Is Philosophy?* Trans. Hugh Tomlinson and Graham Burchell. New York: Columbia University Press.

"Demo-Graphics: Comic Fandom." 2015. Graphic Policy. Available at: https://graphicpolicy.com/2015/09/01/demo-graphics-comic-fandom/. Accessed January 4, 2016.

Derf. 2012. *My Friend Dahmer*. New York: Abrams.

Diekmann, Irene, and Julius Schoeps. 2002. *Das Wilkomirski-Syndrom*. Zurich: Pendo.

Diehl, Jörg. 2007. "Hitler's Destruction of Guernica: Practicing Blitzkrieg in Basque Country." *Der Spiegel* online. Available at: http://www.spiegel.de/international/europe/hitler-s-destruction-of-guernica-practicing-blitzkrieg-in-basque-country-a-479675.html. Accessed September 1, 2013.

Dobbs, David. 2009. "Soldiers' Stress: What Doctors Get Wrong about PTSD." *Scientific American* 300 (4). pp. 64–69.

Domsch, Sebastian. 2012. "Growing Complexity; or, the Cerebus Effect." In *Cerebus the Barbarian Messiah: Essays on the Epic Graphic Satire of Dave Sim and Gerhard*. Ed. Eric Hoffman. Jefferson: McFarland. pp. 65–96.

Dougall, Alastair. 2009. *The Marvel Comics Encyclopedia*. London: Dorling Kindersley.

Drew, Richard, and Peter Howe. 2010. "Richard Drew." The Digital Journalist. Available at: http://digitaljournalist.org/issue0110/drew.htm. Accessed September 22, 2013.

Duncan, Randy, and Matthew J. Smith. 2009. *The Power of Comics: History, Form and Culture*. New York: Continuum.

Earle, Harriet. 2014. "My Friend Dahmer: The Comic as Bildungsroman." *Journal of Graphic Novels and Comics* 5 (2). pp. 429–40.

———. 2015. "The Whites of their Eyes: Implied Violence and Double Frames in *Blazing Combat* and *The 'Nam*." Comics Forum. Available at: http://comicsforum.org/2015/05/13/the-whites-of-their-eyes-implied-violence-and-double-frames-in-blazing-combat-and-the-nam. Accessed April 4, 2015.

———. 2016. "Trans/Forming Literature: Comics and Migrations." With S. Knowles and J. Peacock. *Journal of Postcolonial Writing* 52 (4). pp. 1–12.

Eco, Umberto. 1997. *The Role of the Reader: Explorations in the Semiotics of Texts*. Bloomington: Indiana University Press.

Eisner, Will. 2008a. *Comics and Sequential Art*. New York: W. W. Norton.

———. 2008b. *Graphic Storytelling and Visual Narrative*. New York: W. W. Norton.

Ellenberger, Henri. 1970. *The Discovery of the Unconscious: The History and Evolution of Dynamic Psychiatry*. New York: Basic.

Elmwood, Victoria. 2004. "'Happy, Happy Ever After': The Transformation of Trauma Between the Generations in Art Spiegelman's *Maus: A Survivor's Tale*." *Biography* 27 (4). pp. 691–720.

Ewing, Al, and PJ Holden. 2008. *Murderdrome*. Available at: http://www.pauljholden.com/murderdrome. Accessed April 10, 2014.

Farr, Michael. 2001. *Tintin: The Complete Companion*. London: John Murray.

Ferguson, Margaret, Mary Salter, and Jon Stallworthy, eds. 2005. *The Norton Anthology of Poetry*. New York: Norton.

Fernandez, Shantel et al. 2013. "Cognitive-Behavioural Treatment of Trauma-Related Nightmares Experienced by Children." *Clinical Case Studies* 12 (1). pp. 39–59.

Festival International de la Bande Dessinée d'Angoulême. 2016. "The Angoulême Festival Loves Women . . . But Cannot Revise the History of Comics." Available at: http://www.bdangouleme.com/936,the-angouleme-festival-loves-women-but-cannot-revise-the-history-of-comics. Accessed January 13, 2016.

Fingeroth, Danny. 2008. *The Rough Guide to Graphic Novels*. London: Rough Guides.

Fink, Bruce. 1995. *The Lacanian Subject: Between Language and Jouissance*. Princeton: Princeton University Press.

Fiske, John. 1982. *Introduction to Communication Studies*. London: Routledge.

Fossion et al. 2003. "Family Approach with Grandchildren of Holocaust Survivors." *American Journal of Psychotherapy* 57 (4). pp. 519–27.

Fowler, Alastair. 1989 *The History of English Literature*. Cambridge: Harvard University Press.

Franklin, Thomas. 2001. *Raising the Flag at Ground Zero or Ground Zero Spirit*. Photograph. Washington, DC: Library of Congress.

Freud, Sigmund. 1961. *Totem and Taboo*. London: Routledge and Kegan Paul.

———. 1991. *The Interpretation of Dreams*. In *The Standard Edition of the Complete Psychological Works of Sigmund Freud, Vol. IV and V*. Ed. James Strachey. London: Vintage.

———. 2000. With Joseph Breuer. *Studies on Hysteria*. In *The Standard Edition of the Complete Psychological Works of Sigmund Freud, Vol. II*. Ed. James Strachey. London: Vintage.

———. 2001a. *Moses and Monotheism*. In *The Standard Edition of the Complete Psychological Works of Sigmund Freud, Vol. XXIII*. Ed. James Strachey. London: Vintage.

———. 2001b. *Introductory Lectures on Psychoanalysis*. In *The Standard Edition of the Complete Psychological Works of Sigmund Freud, Vol. XV*. Ed. James Strachey. London: Vintage.

———. 2001c. *Pre-Psycho-Analytical Publications*. In *The Standard Edition of the Complete Psychological Works of Sigmund Freud, Vol. I*. Ed. James Strachey. London: Vintage.

———. 2001d. *An Infantile Neurosis and Other Works*. In *The Standard Edition of the Complete Psychological Works of Sigmund Freud, Vol. XVII*. Ed. James Strachey. London: Hogarth Press.

———. 2002. *On the History of the Psychoanalytic Movement*. In *The Standard Edition of the Complete Psychological Works of Sigmund Freud, Vol. XIV*. Ed. James Strachey. London: Vintage.

———. 2003. *Beyond the Pleasure Principle*. In *The Standard Edition of the Complete Psychological Works of Sigmund Freud, Vol. XVIII*. Ed. James Strachey. London: Vintage.

Friedman, Susan. 1981. *Psyche Reborn: The Emergence of H. D.* Bloomington: Indiana University Press.

Frow, John. 1997. *Time and Commodity Culture: Essays in Cultural Theory and Postmodernity.* Oxford: Clarendon.

Garland, Caroline. 1998. *Understanding Trauma: A Clinical Approach.* London: Duckworth.

Genette, Gérard. 1972. *Narrative Discourse.* Oxford: Blackwell.

Giddens, Anthony. 1990. *The Consequences of Modernity.* Stanford: Stanford University Press.

Glover, David, and Scott McCracken, eds. 2012. *The Cambridge Companion to Popular Fiction.* Cambridge: Cambridge University Press.

Goggin, Joyce, ed. 2010. *The Rise and Reason of Comics and Graphic Literature: Critical Essays on the Form.* Jefferson: McFarland.

Golding, John. 1968. *Cubism: A History and Analysis, 1907–1914.* London: Faber and Faber.

———. 1994. *Visions of the Modern.* London: Thames and Hudson.

Gonshak, Henry. 2009. "Beyond Maus: Other Holocaust Graphic Novels." *Shofar: An Interdisciplinary Journal of Jewish Studies* 28 (1). pp. 55–79.

Göpfert, Michael et al. 2004. *Parental Psychiatric Disorders: Distressed Parents and Their Families.* Cambridge: Cambridge University Press.

Gordon, Andrew. 2004. "Jewish Fathers and Sons in Spiegelman's Maus and Roth's Patrimony." *ImageTexT: Interdisciplinary Comics Studies* 1 (1). Available at: http://www.english.ufl.edu/imagetext/archives/v1_1/gordon/index.shtml. Accessed March 13, 2012.

Gottesman, Irving et al. 2010. "Severe Mental Disorders in Offspring with 2 Psychiatrically Ill Parents." *Arch Gen Psychiatry* 67 (3). pp. 252–57.

Gottlieb, Sherry Gershon. 1991. *Hell No, We Won't Go!: Resisting the Draft During the Vietnam War.* New York: Viking.

Graziosi, Barbara. 2002. *Inventing Homer: The Early Reception of Epic.* Cambridge: Cambridge University Press.

Gray, Richard J. 2011. *After the Fall: American Literature since 9/11.* Chichester: Wiley-Blackwell.

Greenberg, Clement. 1961. *Art and Culture.* Boston: Beacon Press.

Groening, Matt et al. 1995. "Lisa the Vegetarian." *The Simpsons* (episode 133). Los Angeles: Fox Broadcasting.

———. 2001. "Homer the Moe." *The Simpsons* (episode 272). Los Angeles: Fox Broadcasting.

Groensteen, Thierry. 2007. *The System of Comics.* Jackson: University Press of Mississippi.

———. 2013. *Comics and Narration.* Jackson: University Press of Mississippi.

Grove, Laurence. 2010. *Comics in French: The European Bande Dessinée in Context.* Oxford: Berghahn.

Gunning, Tom. 2014. "The Art of Succession: Reading, Writing, and Watching Comics." *Critical Inquiry* 40 (3). pp. 36–51.

Hacking, Ian. 2013. "Lost in the Forest: Review of *DSM-5.*" *London Review of Books* 35 (15). pp. 7–8.

Halkin, Hillel. 1992. "Inhuman Comedy." *Commentary.* pp. 55–56.

Hamblen, Jessica. 2011. "What is PTSD?" National Center for PTSD. Available at: http://www.ptsd.va.gov/professional/ptsd101/. Accessed October 10, 2013.

Harris, William. 2007. "Homer the Hostage." Middlebury College Online. Available at: http://community.middlebury.edu/~harris/hostage.html.

Hartmann, Ernest. 1996. "Who Develops PTSD Nightmares and Who Doesn't." In *Trauma and Dreams*. Ed. Deirdre Barrett. Cambridge: Harvard University Press. pp. 100–113.
Harvey, Robert. 2008. *The Art of the Comic Book*. Charlotte: Baker and Taylor.
Hatfield, Charles. 2005. *Alternative Comics: An Emerging Literature*. Jackson: University Press of Mississippi.
Heaney, Seamus. 1999. *Beowulf*. London: Faber.
Heberle, Mark A. 2001. *A Trauma Artist: Tim O'Brien and the Fiction of Vietnam*. Des Moines: University of Iowa Press.
Hefti, Sebastian. 2002. *Alias Wilkomirski: Die Holocaust-Travestie*. Berlin: Jüdische Verlagsanstalt.
Heinze, Rüdiger. 2007. "Trauma, Morality & Conformity: American (Super)Heroes After 9/11." *Erfurt Electronic Studies in English* 13. Available at: http://webdoc.gwdg.de/edoc/ia/eese/artic27/heinze/6_2007.html. Accessed April 20, 2012.
Heller, Joseph. 2011. *Catch-22*. London: Vintage Classic.
Hemingway, Ernest. 2004. *A Farewell to Arms*. London: Arrow.
Hergé. 1999. *Les Aventures De Tintin: Reporter Du Petit Vingtième Au Pays Des Soviets*. Paris: Casterman.
Herman, Judith. 1992. *Trauma and Recovery*. New York: HarperCollins.
Herr, Michael. 1991. *Dispatches*. London: Picador.
Hewitt, John. 1980. *After Suicide*. Philadelphia: Westminster.
Hirsch, Marianne. 1993. "Family Pictures: *Maus*, Mourning and Post-Memory." *Discourse: Theoretical Studies in Media and Culture* 15 (2). pp. 3–29.
Hobsbawm, E. J. 1987. *The Age of Empire, 1875–1914*. London: Abacus.
Holloway, David. 2008. *Cultures of the War on Terror: Empire, Ideology, and the Remaking of 9/11*. Montréal: McGill University Press.
Homer. 2003. *The Iliad*. London: Penguin.
Hughes, Mark. 2013. "Top 10 Highest Grossing Superhero Films Of All Time." *Forbes*. Available at: http://www.forbes.com/sites/markhughes/2013/06/09/top-10-highest-grossing-superhero-films-of-all-time/. Accessed September 22, 2013.
Hutcheon, Linda. 1988. *The Poetics of Postmodernism*. London: Routledge.
———. 2002. *The Politics of Postmodernism*. London: Taylor and Francis.
Huyssen, Andreas. 1986. *After the Great Divide: Modernism, Mass Culture, Postmodernism*. Bloomington: Indiana University Press.
Irving, Washington. 1998. "Rip Van Winkle." In *The Complete Tales of Washington Irving*. London: Penguin. pp. 28–42.
James, William, and Carl Georg Lange. 1922. *The Emotions*. Baltimore: Williams & Wilkins.
Jameson, Fredric. 1991. *Postmodernism: Or, The Cultural Logic of Late Capitalism*. London: Verso.
———. 1998. *The Cultural Turn: Selected Writings on the Postmodern, 1983–1998*. London: Verso.
———. 2002. *The Political Unconscious: Narrative as a Socially Symbolic Act*. London: Routledge.
Jason. 2008. "SSHHHH!" In Will Eisner. *Comics and Sequential Art*. New York: W. W. Norton. p. 19.

Jensen, Minna Skafte. 1980. *The Homeric Question and the Oral-Formulaic Theory*. New York: Appleton.

Jones, Gerard. 2006. *Men of Tomorrow: Geeks, Gangsters, and the Birth of the Comic Book*. London: Arrow.

Kaplan, Arie. 2006. *Masters of the Comic Book Universe Revealed!* Chicago: Chicago Review Press.

Kaplan, E. Ann. *Motherhood and Representation: The Mother in Popular Culture and Melodrama*. New York: Routledge, 2013.

Kaplan, Elizabeth, and Ban Wang. 2004. *Trauma and Cinema: Cross-Cultural Explorations*. Hong Kong: Hong Kong University Press.

Karnow, Stanley. 2008. *Vietnam: A History*. New York: Viking Press.

Keniston, Ann, and Jeanne Follansbee Quinn. 2008. *Literature after 9/11*. New York: Routledge.

Kermode, Mark. 2011. *The Good, the Bad and the Multiplex: What's Wrong with the Modern Movies?* London: Random House.

Khoury, Jorge. 2008. "The 'Nam Veterans Day Interview." Comic Book Resources. Available at: http://www.comicbookresources.com/?page=article&id=18745. Accessed April 29, 2013.

Kibedi, Aron Varga. 1989. *Discours, Récit, Image*. Liège: Pierre Mardaga.

Kilpatrick, Kym. 1998. "Post-Traumatic Stress Disorder in Child Witnesses to Domestic Violence." *Child Abuse and Neglect* 22 (4). pp. 319–30.

Kopf, Martina. 2005. *Trauma und Literatur*. Frankfurt: Brandes & Apsel.

Kozol, Wendy. 2012. "Complicities of Witnessing in Joe Sacco's Palestine." In *Theoretical Perspectives on Human Rights and Literature*. Eds. Elizabeth Swanson Goldberg and Alexandra Schultheis Moore. London: Routledge. pp. 165–79.

Kubert, Joe. 2010. *Dong Xoai, Vietnam 1965*. New York: DC Comics.

Kübler-Ross, Elisabeth. 1997. *On Death and Dying*. New York: Scribner.

Kuch, K, and BJ Cox. 1992. "Symptoms of PTSD in 124 Survivors of the Holocaust." *American Journal of Psychiatry* 149 (3). pp. 337–40.

Kunzle, David. 2007. *Father of the Comic Strip: Rodolphe Töpffer*. Jackson: University Press of Mississippi.

Lacan, Jacques. 1977. *The Four Fundamental Concepts of Psychoanalysis*. London: Hogarth.

———. 1988. *The Ego in Freud's Theory and in the Technique of Psychoanalysis*. Cambridge: Cambridge University Press.

LaCapra, Dominick. 1994. *Representing the Holocaust: History, Theory, Trauma*. Ithaca: Cornell University Press.

———. 1998. *History and Memory After Auschwitz*. Ithaca: Cornell University Press.

———. 2001. *Writing History, Writing Trauma*. Baltimore: Johns Hopkins University Press.

Lamothe, Dan. 2015. "Marine Experiment Finds Women Get Injured More Frequently, Shoot Less Accurately than Men." *Washington Post*. Available at: https://www.washingtonpost.com/news/checkpoint/wp/2015/09/10/marine-experiment-finds-women-get-injured-more-frequently-shoot-less-accurately-than-men/. Accessed February 8, 2016.

Lander, Ben. 2005. "Graphic Novels as History: Representing and Reliving the Past." *Left History* 10 (2). pp. 113–25.

Lane, Christopher. 2007. *Shyness: How Normal Behavior Became a Sickness*. New Haven: Yale University Press.

Laplanche, Jean, and J. B. Pontalis. 1973. *The Language of Psychoanalysis*. New York: W. W. Norton.

Latour, Bruno. 2002. "What is Iconoclash? Or Is There a World Beyond the Image Wars?" In *Iconoclash: Beyond the Image-Wars in Science, Religion and Art*. Eds. Peter Weibel and Bruno Latour. Cambridge: MIT Press. pp. 14–37.

Lavie, Peretz, and Hanna Kaminer. 1996. "Sleep, Dreaming and Coping Style in Holocaust Survivors." In *Trauma and Dreams*. Ed. Deirdre Barrett. Cambridge: Harvard University Press. pp. 114–24.

Lawrence, Bruce B., and Aisha Karim. 2007. *On Violence: A Reader*. Durham: Duke University Press.

Levithan, David. 2009. *Love is the Higher Law*. New York: Random House.

Lidz, Theodore. 1985. *Schizophrenia and the Family*. New York: International Universities Press.

Lifton, Robert Jay. 1996. "Dreaming Well: On Death and History." In *Trauma and Dreams*. Ed. Deirdre Barrett. Cambridge: Harvard University Press. pp. 125–39.

Lorah, Michael. 2008. "9/11's Legacy—Alissa Torres, *American Widow*." Newsarama. Available at: http://www.newsarama.com/994-9-11-s-legacy-alissa-torres-american-widow.html. Accessed January 20, 2016.

Lovett, Lisetta. 2012. "A Psychiatrist's Opinion of the Neuronovel." In *Diseases and Disorders in Contemporary Fiction: The Syndrome Syndrome*. Eds. T. J. Lustig and James Peacock. New York: Routledge. pp. 169–182.

Lustig, T. J. 2001. "Moments of Punctuation: Metonymy and Ellipsis in Tim O'Brien." *Yearbook of English Studies* 31. pp. 74–92

———. 2013. *Knight Prisoner: Thomas Malory Then and Now*. Eastbourne: Sussex Academic Press.

Lustig, T. J., and James Peacock, eds. 2013. *Diseases and Disorders in Contemporary Fiction: The Syndrome Syndrome*. New York: Routledge.

Lyotard, Jean-François. 1991. *The Postmodern Condition: A Report on Knowledge*. Manchester: Manchester University Press.

Madden, Matt. 2006. *99 Ways to Tell a Story: Exercises in Style*. London: Jonathan Cape.

Maechler, Stefan. 2001. *The Wilkomirski Affair: A Study in Biographical Truth*. Berlin: Schocken.

Maier, Klaus. 1975. *Guernica April 1937: Die Deutsche Intervention in Spanien und der Fall Guernica*. Freiburg: Rombach.

Mailer, Norman. 2006. *The Naked and the Dead*. London: Harper Perennial.

Malory, Thomas. 1889. *Le Morte D'Arthur*. London: MacMillan.

Mandelbaum, Michael. 1982. "Vietnam: The Television War." *Daedalus* 111 (4). pp. 157–69.

"Manipulation." *The Oxford English Dictionary*. 2012. Oxford: Clarendon Press. Available at: http://www.oed.com/manipulation. Accessed July 7, 2012.

Martin, Russell. 2004. *Picasso's War*. New York: Pocket Books.
Mason, Pierre. 1985. *Lire la Bande Dessinée*. Lyon: Presses Universitaires de Lyon.
McCloud, Scott. 1994. *Understanding Comics: The Invisible Art*. New York: HarperPerennial.
———. 2010. "That Hand on Your Shoulder." Available at: http://www.scottmccloud.com. Accessed March 2, 2013.
McCubbin, Laurenn. 2016. "The Not-so-Secret History of Comics Drawn by Women." Available at: http://www.theguardian.com/books/2016/jan/10/women-comics-not-so-secret-history. Accessed February 6, 2016.
McKevitt, Greg. 2009. "NI Comics Heroes Find US Success." *BBC Online*. Available at: http://news.bbc.co.uk/1/hi/northern_ireland/8074611.stm. Accessed April 2, 2014.
McKinney, Mark, ed. 2011. *History and Politics in French Language Comics and Graphic Novels*. Jackson: University Press of Mississippi.
McNally, Richard. 2003. "Progress and Controversy in the Study of Posttraumatic Stress Disorder." *Annual Review of Psychology* 54. pp. 229–52.
Médecins Sans Frontières International. 2016. *Rape as a Weapon of War*. Available at: http://www.msf.org/article/rape-weapon-war. Accessed February 9, 2016.
Melley, Timothy. 2003. "Postmodern Amnesia: Trauma and Forgetting in Tim O'Brien's *In the Lake of the Woods*." *Contemporary Literature* 44 (1). pp. 106–31.
Meskin, Aaron, and Roy Cook. 2012. *The Art of Comics: A Philosophical Approach*. Chichester: Wiley-Blackwell.
Milbank, Alison. 1998. *Dante and the Victorians*. Manchester: Manchester University Press.
Miles, Donna. 2011. "Vietnam's Legacy Shapes Today's Military Leaders." US Department of Defense. Available at: http://www.defense.gov/News/NewsArticle.aspx?ID=63744. Accessed July 19, 2013.
Miller, Ann. 2007. *Reading Bande Dessinée: Critical Approaches to the French-language Comic Strip*. Bristol: Intellect.
Murray, Christopher. 2007. "Holy Hypertexts!: The Pose of Post-modernity in Comics and Graphic Novels of the 1980s." In *Reflections on Creativity*. Ed. H. van Koten. Dundee: Duncan of Jordanstone College.
"Naming of World War Two." US Department of State. Available at: http://www.ibiblio.org/pha/policy/post-war/450911a.html. Accessed July 22, 2013.
Neal, Arthur G. 2005. *National Trauma and Collective Memory: Extraordinary Events in the American Experience*. Armonk: M. E. Sharpe.
Neale, Stephen. 2000. *Genre and Hollywood*. London: Routledge.
O'Brian, Patrick. 2012. *Picasso: A Biography*. London: HarperCollins.
O'Brien, Tim. 1991. *The Things They Carried*. London: Flamingo.
———. 2006. *If I Die In A Combat Zone*. London: Harper Perennial.
O'Reilly, James. 2012. "Discussion on the Experience of Vietnam Veterans." Personal communication. June 11, 2012.
O'Sullivan, Simon. 2001. "The Aesthetics of Affect: Thinking Art Beyond Representation." *Angelaki: Journal of the Theoretical Humanities* 6 (3). pp. 125–35.

Oksman, Tahneer. 2016. *"How Come Boys Get to Keep Their Noses?": Women and Jewish American Identity in Contemporary Graphic Memoirs*. New York: Columbia University Press.

Owen-Crocker, Gale R. 2000. *The Four Funerals in Beowulf: And the Structure of the Poem*. Manchester: Manchester University Press.

Parker, Kathleen. 2016. "The Fog of Rape." Townhall. Available at: http://townhall.com/col umnists/kathleenparker/2007/03/28/the_fog_of_rape/page/full. Accessed February 23, 2016.

Patterson, Ian. 2007. *Guernica and Total War*. Cambridge: Harvard University Press.

Payne, Robert. 1962. *The Civil War in Spain, 1936-1939*. New York: Putnam.

Peacock, James. 2014. "Risk, Disappointment and Distraction in Keith Gessen's *All the Sad Young Literary Men*." *European Journal of American Studies* 1. pp. 1–13.

Peeters, Benoît, and Jacques Samson. 2010. *Chris Ware: La Bande Dessinée Réinventée*. Brussels: Les Impressions Nouvelles.

Picasso, Pablo. 1937a. *The Dream and Lie of Franco*. New York: The Metropolitan Museum of Art.

———. 1937b. *Guernica*. Madrid: Museo Nacional Centro de Arte Reina Sofía.

Porro, Simona. 2012. "Postmodern, or Else? The Case of *Maus*." *CoSMo: Comparative Studies in Modernism* 1. pp. 10–111.

Postman, Neil. 1985. *Amusing Ourselves to Death: Public Discourse in the Age of Show Business*. New York: Viking.

Prager, Brad. 2010. "The Holocaust Without Ink." In *The Jewish Graphic Novel: Critical Approaches*. Eds. Samantha Baskin and Ranen Omer-Sherman. New Brunswick: Rutgers University Press. pp. 111–28.

Pratt, George. 1998. *Enemy Ace: War Idyll*. New York: DC Comics.

Radstone, Susannah. 2007. "Trauma Theory: Contexts, Politics, Ethics." *Paragraph* 20 (1). pp. 9–29.

Raeburn, Daniel. 2004. *Chris Ware*. New Haven: Yale University Press.

Randall, Martin. 2011. *9/11 and the Literature of Terror*. Edinburgh: Edinburgh University Press.

Reed, Arden. 2003. *Manet, Flaubert, and the Emergence of Modernism: Blurring Genre Boundaries*. Cambridge: Cambridge University Press.

Reynolds, Paul. 2007. "Declining Use of War on Terror." *BBC Online*. Available at: http://news.bbc.co.uk/1/hi/uk_politics/6562709.stm. Accessed July 22, 2013.

Ricciardi, Alessia. 2003. *The Ends of Mourning: Psychoanalysis, Literature, Film*. Stanford: Stanford University Press.

Ricœur, Paul. 1985. *Temps Et Récit*. Paris: Éditions Du Seuil.

———. 1994. *Oneself as Another*. Chicago: University of Chicago Press.

Roberts, Garyn. 2004. "Understanding the Sequential Art of Comic Strips and Comic Books and Their Descendants in the Early Years of the New Millennium." *Journal of American Culture* 27 (2). pp. 210–17.

Rosen, Jules et al. 1991. "Sleep Disturbances in Survivors of the Nazi Holocaust." *American Journal of Psychiatry* 148 (1). pp. 62–66.

Ross, Christine. 2006. *The Aesthetics of Disengagement: Contemporary Art and Depression*. Minneapolis: University of Minnesota Press.

Roth, M. 2010. "*Jobnik!*: Sex, Guns, and Hot Israeli Soldiers (An Interview)." My Jewish Learning. Available at: http://www.myjewishlearning.com/mixed-multitudes/jobnik-sex-guns-and-hot-israeli-soldiers-an-interview/#. Accessed February 10, 2016.

Rothberg, Michael. 2000. *Traumatic Realism: The Demands of Holocaust Representation*. Minneapolis: University of Minnesota Press.

———. 2009. *Multidirectional Memory*. Stanford: Stanford University Press.

Sabin, Roger. 2001. *Comics, Comix and Graphic Novels: A History of Graphic Novels*. London: Phaidon.

Salmi, Charlotta. 2016. "Reading Footnotes: Joe Sacco and the Graphic Human Rights Narrative." *Journal of Postcolonial Writing* 52 (4).

Scarry, Elaine. 1985. *The Body in Pain: The Making and Unmaking of the World*. Oxford: Oxford University Press.

Scherr, Rebecca. 2013. "Shaking Hands with Other People's Pain: Joe Sacco's *Palestine*." *Mosaic* 46 (1). pp. 19–36.

Schjeldahl, Peter. 2005. "Words and Pictures: Graphic Novels Come of Age." *New Yorker*. Available at: http://www.newyorker.com/archive/2005/10/17/05. Accessed September 30, 2012.

Schneider, Ruth. 2010. "Interview: Art Spiegelman." *Exberliner*. Available at: http://www.exberliner.com/interview-art-spiegelman/. Accessed May 1, 2013.

Schwab, Gabriele. 2010. *Haunting Legacies: Violent Histories and Transgenerational Trauma*. New York: Columbia University Press.

Scott, Suzanne. 2013. "Fangirls in Refrigerators: The Politics of (In)visibility in Comic Book Culture." *Transformative Works and Cultures* 13. Available at: http://testjournal.transformativeworks.org/index.php/twc/article/view/460/384. Accessed February 10, 2016.

Scott, Wayne. 2001. *Posttraumatic Stress: A Vietnam Veteran's Experience*. Kirwan: Vietnam Veterans Counselling Service.

Searle, William, ed. 1988. *Search and Clear: Critical Responses to Selected Literature and Films of the Vietnam War*. Bowling Green: Bowling Green University Press.

Seltzer, Mark. 1998. *Serial Killers: Death and Life in America's Wound Culture*. Hove: Psychology Press, 1998.

Shakespeare, William. 2008. *Henry IV, Part 1*. Oxford: Oxford University Press.

"Shoot." *The Oxford English Dictionary*. 2012. Oxford: Clarendon Press. Available at: http://www.oed.com/shoot. Accessed July 7, 2012.

Simon, Joe, and Jack Kirby. 2005. *Marvel Masterworks Presents Golden Age Captain America Comics*. New York: Marvel Comics.

Smith, Philip, and Mitchel Goodrum. 2011. "'We Have Experienced a Tragedy Which Words Cannot Properly Describe': Representations of Trauma in Post-9/11 Superhero Comics." *Literature Compass* 8 (8). pp. 487–98.

Smith, Tyler et al. 2008. "New Onset and Persistent Symptoms of Post-Traumatic Stress Disorder Self-Reported after Deployment and Combat Exposures: Prospective Population based US Military Cohort Study." *British Medical Journal* 336 (7640). Available at: http://www.bmj.com/content/336/7640/366.pdf%2Bhtml. Accessed September 23, 2013.

Sontag, Susan. 2004a. *Regarding the Pain of Others*. London: Penguin.

———. 2004b. "The Truth of Fiction Evokes Our Common Humanity." Presentation at Los Angeles Public Library. Available at: http://www.uiowa.edu/~co8goo1d/Sontag_LA_Library.pdf. Accessed September 22, 2013.

Sousa, Cynthia. 2012. *X-Men Guernica*. Theamat deviantART Gallery. Available at: http://theamat.deviantart.com/art/X-Men-Guernica-308308234. Accessed March 11, 2014.

Spiegelman, Art. 2011a. *MetaMaus*. New York: Pantheon.

———. 2011b. "Holiday Interview with Art Spiegelman." *Comics Reporter*. Available at: http://www.comicsreporter.com/index.php/art_spiegelman/. Accessed June 6, 2013.

Stocks, Claire. 2007. "Trauma Theory and the Singular Self: Rethinking Extreme Experiences in the Light of Cross-Cultural Identity." *Textual Practice* 21 (1). pp. 71–92.

Straczynski, J. Michael, and John Romita Jr. 2001. *The Amazing Spiderman #36*. New York: Marvel.

Tabachnick, Stephen. 2004. "The Religious Meaning of Art Spiegelman's *Maus*." *Shofar: An Interdisciplinary Journal of Jewish Studies* 22 (4). pp. 1–13.

———. 2014. *The Quest for Jewish Belief and Identity in the Graphic Novel*. Tuscaloosa: University of Alabama Press.

Tal, Kalí. 1995. *Worlds of Hurt: Reading the Literature of Trauma*. Cambridge: Cambridge University Press.

Tambling, Jeremy. 2001. *Becoming Posthumous: Life and Death in Literary and Cultural Studies*. Edinburgh: Edinburgh University Press.

Tatum, James. 2004. *The Mourner's Song: War and Remembrance from the Iliad to Vietnam*. Chicago: University of Chicago Press.

Taylor, A. J. P. 1979. *How Wars Begin*. London: Hamilton.

Tew, Philip. 2007. *The Contemporary British Novel*. London: Continuum.

Tolkien, J. R. R. 1937. *Beowulf: The Monsters and the Critics*. Oxford: Oxford University Press.

Topffer, Rodolphe, and David Kunzle. 2007. *Rodolphe Topffer: The Complete Comic Strips*. Jackson: University Press of Mississippi.

Torres, Alissa. 2002. "Wrath of a Terror Widow." *Salon*. Available at: http://www.salon.com/2002/03/15/widow_wrath/. Accessed February 2, 2012.

Tran, GB. 2014. "Discussion on Bilingualism and Second-Generation Language Abilities." Personal communication. January 17, 2014.

Trump, Donald. 2013. "26,000 unreported sexual assaults [sic] in the military-only 238 convictions. What did these geniuses expect when they put men & women together?" Available at: https://twitter.com/realdonaldtrump/status/331907383771148288?lang=en-gb&lang=en-gb. Accessed February 5, 2016.

United Nations Security Council. 2016. "Resolution 1820." Available at: http://www.un.org/press/en/2008/sc9364.doc.htm. Accessed February 9, 2016.

Uphaus, Robert W. 1988. *The Idea of the Novel in the Eighteenth Century*. East Lansing: Colleagues.

"U.S. Department of Labor—Office of Workers' Compensation Programs-Division of Federal Employees' Compensation." United States Department of Labor. Available at: http://www.dol.gov/owcp/dfec/. Accessed February 13, 2012.

Van der Kolk, B. et al. 1984. "Nightmares and Trauma: A Comparison of Nightmares after Combat with Lifelong Nightmares in Veterans." *American Journal of Psychiatry* 141 (2). pp. 187–90.

Van Hensbergen, Gijs. 2013. *Guernica: The Biography of a Twentieth-Century Icon*. London: Bloomsbury.

Varvin, Sverre et al. 2012. "Traumatische Träume: Streben nach Beziehung." *Traum: Theorie und Deutung* 9. pp. 937–67.

Vernon, Alex. 2004. *Soldiers Once and Still: Ernest Hemingway, James Salter & Tim O'Brien*. Des Moines: University of Iowa Press.

Versaci, Rocco. 2008. *This Book Contains Graphic Language: Comics as Literature*. London: Continuum.

Vice, Sue. 1997. *Introducing Bakhtin*. Manchester: Manchester University Press.

Vonnegut, Kurt. 1991. *Slaughterhouse-Five: Or, The Children's Crusade: A Duty-Dance with Death*. London: Vintage.

Walker, Mort. 2000. *The Lexicon of Comicana*. Bloomington: iUniverse.

Walker, Tristram. 2010. "Graphic Wound: The Comics Journalism of Joe Sacco." *Journeys* 11 (1). pp. 69–88.

Walsh, Jeffrey. 1982. *American War Literature: 1914 to Vietnam*. London: Macmillan.

Ware, Chris. 2012. *Building Stories*. London: Pantheon.

Watkin, William. 2004. *On Mourning: Theories of Loss in Modern Literature*. Edinburgh: Edinburgh University Press.

Watt, Ian P. 2001. *The Rise of the Novel: Studies in Defoe, Richardson and Fielding*. Berkeley: University of California Press.

Watterson, Bill. 1987. *Calvin and Hobbes*. Kansas City: Andrews McMeel.

Weil, Simone, and James P. Holoka. 2003. *The Iliad, Or, The Poem of Force: A Critical Edition*. New York: P. Lang.

Weiner, Stephen. 2003. *Faster than a Speeding Bullet: The Rise of the Graphic Novel*. New York: NBM.

Whitehead, Anne. 2004. *Trauma Fiction*. Edinburgh: Edinburgh University Press.

Whitlock, Gillian. 2006. "Autographics: The Seeing 'I' of Comics." *Modern Fiction Studies* 52 (4). pp. 965–79.

———. 2007. *Soft Weapons: Autobiography in Transit*. Chicago: University of Chicago Press.

Whitman, Walt. 2008. "Old War Dreams." *Leaves of Grass*. Oxford: Oxford University Press. p. 246.

Wieseltier, Leon. 2002. "A Year Later." *New Republic*. Available at: http://www.newrepublic.com/articles/year-later. Accessed February 4, 2012.

Williams, Paul, and James Lyons. 2010. *The Rise of the American Comics Artist*. Jackson: University Press of Mississippi.

Wilmer, Harry. 1996. "The Healing Nightmare: War Dreams of Vietnam Veterans." In *Trauma and Dreams*. Ed. Deirdre Barrett. Cambridge: Harvard University Press. pp. 85–99.

Wolk, Douglas. 2007. *Reading Comics: How Graphic Novels Work and What They Mean*. Cambridge: Da Capo Press.

Woolf, Virginia. 2008. "The New Biography." *Selected Essays*. Oxford: Oxford University Press.

World Health Organization. 1992. *International Statistical Classification of Diseases and Related Health Problems Tenth Revision*. Geneva: World Health Organization Press.

Wright, Bradford W. 2003. *Comic Book Nation: The Transformation of Youth Culture in America*. Baltimore: Johns Hopkins University Press.

Zelizer, Barbie. 2003. "Photography, Journalism and Trauma." In *Journalism after September 11*. Ed. Stuart Allan. London: Routledge.

Žižek, Slavoj. 2006. *How to Read Lacan*. New York: W. W. Norton.

Index

Aarseth, Espen, 149–50
Abraham, 71
Abraham, Nicolas, 27, 99
acceptance, 61, 62, 65, 69
A Contract with God, 23–24
"acting out," 40
Action Comics #1, 11
action-to-action transitions, 48, 71
"actual" information, 136
Adams, Eddie, 138, 139–43
Aeder, 134, 146
A Farewell to Arms, 15
affect (philosophy), 42–45, 46, 121, 165, 168, 169
Against Our Will: Men, Women and Rape, 178–79
À la Recherche du Temps Perdu, 14
"allohistory," 162, 164
American Revolutionary War, 97, 120–21
American Widow, 26, 48–49, 59, 61–69, 73–74, 91–93, 127, 138–39, 140, 143, 175–76
analepsis, 125, 128–29, 130–31, 162
anger, 61, 64
Anna Kharkova, 176, 177–78
"Answering the Question: What Is Postmodernism?," 152, 170
anticipatory fear, 130, 144–45, 146, 148
Apel, Dora, 116
Apple App Store, 192
Aristotle, 42
arthrology, 47, 157
Asher, 181, 182–83

Askin, Kelly Dawn, 178
aspect-to-aspect transitions, 71, 159
Astérix, 50–51
Atkinson, Paul, 69–70, 147
Attridge, Derek, 44, 45
Auerbach, Erich, 14, 15
"Auld Acquaintance," 134–36
"authentic social history," 10, 11
"autobiofictionalography," 19
"autobiographical pact," 20
autobiography, 18–21, 24, 68, 117, 168, 175, 180
"Avant-Garde and Kitsch," 42
Aviazione Legionaria, 3
awakening, 80–81, 91–94
Axe, David, 3, 185
"Ayekah," 70–72, 73–74
Azzarello, Brian, 192

Backderf, Derf, 118
"Back in the Real World," 145–46
Baker, Steven, 115
Bakhtin, Mikhail, 27, 125, 126–27
Balaev, Michelle, 25, 29, 32–33, 67, 76, 79–80
bargaining, 61, 64–65, 69
Bar-On, Dan, 99–100
Barry, Lynda, 19, 175
Barthes, Roland, 137, 157, 169
Batman, 5, 11, 23, 194
Battlefields, 173, 175, 176–78, 179–80, 185–86
Baudrillard, Jean, 160–61
Bay, Michael, 13

225

BD Égalité, 171
Bendis, Brian Michael, 128
Bennett, Jill, 9–10, 37, 61, 67, 90, 120, 196
Beowulf, 26, 57–58, 59, 69
Berger, Alan, 88
Berger, John, 187
Best American Comics, The, 187
Beyond the Pleasure Principle, 33–34
Beyond Time and Again, 24
Bibby, Michael, 153
Binky Brown, 13, 111
birth narratives, 62–63
Blaine, Adam, 75
Blankets, 24
"blank parody," 193
bleeds, 49–50, 53, 62, 63, 87, 92–93, 139, 140
blink-gutters, 63
Blood Meridian, 44
Bloodstar, 24
"body/text gap," 19
Bosmajian, Hamida, 102
Boyd, Ron, 72
Braque, Georges, 164
Braun, Russell, 173, 175, 176
Breuer, Joseph, 130
Bricken, Rob, 186–87
brokenness, 28, 157, 158, 188
Brown, L. S., 30
Brownmiller, Susan, 178–79, 180
Bruchstück, 19–20, 21
bubbles, 50–52, 53, 62, 63, 90, 126, 128, 131, 142, 183
Building Stories, 152–53
Bull, Malcolm, 6–7, 39, 158, 164

candles, 71–72
Capa, Robert, 136
Captain America, 12, 70, 145–46, 147
Captain Marvel, 188
Carpenter, Lucas, 153–54
Caruth, Cathy, 10, 26, 29, 30–32, 35, 37, 39, 76, 80, 91, 124, 158

Catch-22, 15
Cavell, Stanley, 6–7
Çaytîn, Gûlyâ, 99–100
CCA (Comics Code Authority), 12, 125, 131, 153, 192
"Cerebus Syndrome," 194, 196
Cerebus the Aardvark, 194
Cestac, Florence, 171, 172
Chandler: Red Tide, 24
Childs, Peter, 5
Choi, Sungyoon, 48, 61, 92
chronotope, 27, 125, 126–28, 135–36, 138–39, 143, 144
Chute, Hillary, 16–17, 24, 117, 174–75
Clark, 134
Clark, Spencer, 17–18
"classic" trauma model, 29, 30–38, 52
closure, 46–47, 48, 57, 69, 73, 192
Clowes, Daniel, 24
CMAA (Comic Magazine Association of America), 12
coercive reading/viewing, 136
collective mourning, 62, 66–67, 69–70
"collectivization" of trauma, 66–67
Comic Book Resources, 189
Comics Journal, 115–16
Comics Should Be Good, 189
communal grief, 62, 66–67, 69–70
condensation stage, 81, 86
"Condor Legion," 3, 4
"conspiracy of silence," 100, 104
Cooper, Simon, 69–70, 147
Corben, Richard, 24
Crane, Stephen, 15
Crumb, Robert, 10, 175
Cubism, 6, 8, 164, 165
"cultural coping," 41
cultural identity, 98, 111–16
Cyclops, 190, 191

Danielewski, Mark, 150
Dante, 14
Dark Horse Comics, 66

Index

DC Comics, 11, 47, 66, 144, 195
D-Day landings, 136
"Death of the Author, The," 157, 169
de Sade, Marquis, 192
deferred action, 35–36, 124
Deleuze, Gilles, 43
denial, 61, 62
depression, 61, 63
Der Spiegel, 4
devastation, 5, 55–57
deviantART, 189
Di Giandomenico, Carmine, 161
Diehl, Jörg, 4
digital comics, 192–93
Disaster Drawn: Visual Witness, Comics, and Documentary Form, 16–17
Dismemberment of Orpheus, The, 150–51
distortion stage, 81, 86
Doctorow, E. L., 155
"documentary comics," 17
double-frame format, 142
Dream and Lie of Franco, The, 8–9
"dream of the burning boy," 37, 80–81, 87, 91, 92
Dreamwork, 26, 76, 79, 81–83, 86
Dresden bombing, 46, 127, 136
Drew, Richard, 138–39
DSM (*Diagnostic and Statistical Manual of Mental Disorders*), 38
Duchamp, Marcel, 164
duck/rabbit image, 6–7
"Dust," 53, 64, 71

Eco, Umberto, 27–28, 125, 146, 147
Ed Marks, 26, 131–34
Eisner, Will, 23–24, 50, 51
El Refaie, Elisabeth, 20
Elmwood, Victoria, 104, 107
"Enemy Ace," 195
Ennis, Garth, 173, 175, 176–77, 178
Episodic Paroxysmal Anxiety, 75
ergodic literature, 149–50
experimentation, 6, 196

Exposition Internationale des Arts et Techniques dans la Vie Moderne, 4
extradiegetic narrative level, 83, 142, 143
Extremely Loud and Incredibly Close, 45

Fall and Rise of Anna Kharkova, The, 176
Falling Man, The, 138–39, 140, 143
Fantagraphics Books, 22–23
female comics artists, 171–73, 174–75, 176, 186, 187–88
female narratives, 28, 172–73, 174–88
female representations, 12, 28, 186–88; in combat, 173–74, 175–80, 183, 185–86; and comics form, 178, 182–83, 185, 188; and sexuality, 180–83, 185
Fingeroth, Danny, 11, 12, 13
Finnegans Wake, 5
Fiske, John, 137
"Five Stage Model" of grief, 26, 61–62, 63, 64–65, 69
flashbacks, 31, 34, 82, 128–29, 130–31, 162
Flaubert, Gustave, 128
Foer, Jonathan Safran, 45, 139
Footnotes in Gaza, 27, 117, 120
form, 5–6; and brokenness, 28, 157, 158, 188; and experimentation, 6, 196; and female representations, 178, 182–83, 185, 188; and identity, 105, 113; and modernism, 7; and mourning narratives, 60–61, 63–66, 67–68, 71, 73; multi-aspectival viewing, 6–7, 164–65, 189; panelization, 7–9, 149, 165, 189; and physicality of comics, 59–61, 85, 123; and postmodernism, 149, 150, 151, 153, 157, 159, 165, 168; and representing trauma, 10–11, 46–53, 196; and temporal representation, 27–28, 125–26, 128–31, 135–36, 139, 140, 142, 148; and traumatic dreaming, 77, 83, 85–87, 88, 89–90, 91–93, 94
fragmentation of narrative, 14–15
framed narratives, 125, 128–34
Franco, Francisco, 8
Frank Castle, 145

Frank T. Verzyl, 135
Freud, Sigmund: and anticipatory fear, 130, 144; and deferred action, 124; Freudian trauma theory, 25, 29, 30, 31, 33–37, 39, 40; and identity, 27, 102; and "incubation period," 133; and mourning, 55, 59, 73; and postmodernism, 151, 158, 165; and traumatic dreaming, 26, 76, 79–80, 81–83, 86, 87
Friedman, Susan, 5
"From Cedar Falls, with Love," 131, 132–33, 134
"funny animal" comics, 114–15

Gaiman, Neil, 6, 24
Ganzfried, Daniel, 19
Garland, Caroline, 39
Generalized Anxiety Disorder, 75
Genette, Gérard, 83, 86
Gernika (Guernica) bombing, 3–4, 8, 9, 190
Gibbons, Dave, 23
Gibson, William, 158
Giddens, Antony, 153
Giffen, Keith, 53
Gitelman, Lisa, 17
Gloeckner, Phoebe, 175
glorification of conflict, 13–14
Golden, Mike, 142
Golding, John, 8–9
Goodrum, Mitchel, 47
Gordon, Andrew, 114
Goscinny, René, 50
Graf, 177, 179
"graphic novels," 13, 23–25
Graphic Women: Life Narrative and Contemporary Comics, 174–75
Great Escape, The, 13
Green, Justin, 111
Greenberg, Clement, 42–43
Green Lantern, 186
Gregory of Tours, 14
Groening, Matt, 149
Groensteen, Thierry, 7, 47, 68, 125–26, 153, 157

Grove, Laurence, 130
Guardian, 118
Guattari, Félix, 43
Guernica, 4–5, 6, 7–9, 10, 149, 189, 190–91, 192, 193
guilt, 40, 73, 102, 164
Guitar, The, 164
Gunning, Tom, 123
gutter transitions, 46–49, 53, 71, 91, 93

Habermas, Jürgen, 28
Hacking, Ian, 38
Halkin, Hillel, 115
Hamlet, 37
Hartmann, Ernest, 77–78
Harvey, Robert, 114
Hassan, Ihab, 150–51
Hatfield, Charles, 6
Haunting Legacies: Violent Histories and Transgenerational Trauma, 27
Hector, 56–57, 58
Heller, Joseph, 15
Hemingway, Ernest, 15
Henri, Yazier, 67
Henry IV, Part I, 29
Hergé, 130
Herman, Judith, 25, 30, 31, 35, 53, 76–77, 97, 156
Heroes, 70
high culture, 150, 162, 168, 193–94
Historia Francorum, 14
historiography, 17–18, 39–40, 158–60
history/historical events, 136–48, 155–56, 158–64
Hitler, Adolf, 12, 103, 109–11
Holloway, David, 62, 66, 67
Holocaust, 19–20, 23, 28, 41, 73, 89–90, 98, 99–101, 102–4, 107, 109, 113, 115, 159, 160–64, 165–68
"Holokitsch," 160–61
"Homage to Joe Sacco," 16
Homer, 14, 15, 56–57, 58–59, 195
Honor Lost, 21

Index

horror genre, 11, 12
House of Leaves, 150
"house style," 52, 125, 131, 153
Hurt Locker, The, 13, 15
Hutcheon, Linda, 149, 151–52, 158–60, 164
Huyssen, Andreas, 193
hyperpanels, 126, 142, 144

Ice Haven, 24
Iceman, 134, 146
identity, 97–98, 120–21; and autobiography, 20; and comics form, 105, 113; and journalistic distance, 27, 98, 117–20, 121; nationality and cultural identity, 27, 98, 111–16; and parent-child relationships, 27, 89, 98–100, 101–11, 121
Iliad, 26, 56–59, 69, 195
Imp, 24
incest-victim narratives, 41
"incubation period," 133
Inferno, 14
International Comics Festival, 171–72
Interpretation of Dreams, The, 76, 79, 81
intradiegetic narrative level, 83, 86
Iron Man, 145–46
Irving, Washington, 97
Isaac, 71

James, William, 43
Jameson, Fredric, 14, 15, 149, 150, 153, 154–56, 158, 193
Jastrow, Joseph, 6–7
Jobnik!, 175, 180–86
John Paul II (pope), 165
Johnson, BS, 150
journalistic distance, 27, 98, 117–20, 121
Journal of Postcolonial Writing, 188
Judenhass, 165–68
"juvenile delinquents," 12

Kaplan, E. Ann, 179
Karnow, Stanley, 101
Kermode, Mark, 13

Khouri, Norma, 21
Kibedi, Aron Varga, 157
Kirby, Jack, 12
Kitsch, 42–43, 160–61
Kominsky-Crumb, Aline, 174–75
Kozol, Wendy, 118
Kubert, Joe, 70, 147, 161–63, 164
Kübler-Ross, Elisabeth, 26, 61–62, 63, 64, 65, 69

Lacan, Jacques, 25, 26, 29, 36–37, 39, 79–80, 91, 155
LaCapra, Dominick, 25, 39, 40, 45
La Chanson de Roland, 14
Lander, Ben, 17–18
Laplanche, Jean, 33
Latour, Bruno, 137
Lecigne, Bruno, 130
Le Corbusier, 4
Le Coup de Grâce, 152
Lee, Stan, 190
Lejeune, Philippe, 20
Le Lotus Bleu, 130
Le Morte d'Arthur, 26, 57, 58, 59, 69
Les Aventures de Tintin, 5, 130
Levithan, David, 55
Leys, Ruth, 32
Libicki, Miriam, 175, 180–85
Lidz, Theodore, 108
Lifton, Robert Jay, 32
ligne claire, 128, 129–31
linking motifs, 53, 64
Loan, General Nguyen Ngoc, 140, 142
long distance chronology, 134–36
low culture, 150, 162, 168, 193–94
Lustig, Timothy, 58, 156
Lyotard, Jean-François, 149, 151–52, 153, 154, 164, 170

Madame Bovary, 128
Maechler, Stefan, 20
Malory, Sir Thomas, 58
manipulation, 60–61

Marcellinus, Ammianus, 14
Marvel Comics, 66, 124–25, 131, 144, 145, 159, 160
Mason, Pierre, 157
materiality, 60–61
Maus, 13, 23, 26, 27, 59, 68, 72, 73, 88–90, 94, 95, 98, 101–4, 107, 113–16, 175–76
Max Eisenhardt, 159
McCarthy, Cormac, 44
McCloud, Scott, 46–47, 48, 51, 71, 91, 126
Médecins Sans Frontières, 178
mediation, 36, 104, 106–7, 121, 142, 158, 165, 169, 176
medicalization of trauma, 38
melancholia, 73
Melley, Timothy, 158, 165
memorialization, 59–60, 71–72
memory, 20, 55, 67, 107, 130, 132–33, 137, 158, 165
metadiegetic narrative level, 83, 86, 142–43
metalepsis, 83, 85, 86, 125, 142
Metzger, George, 24
Milbank, Alison, 14
Miller, Frank, 14, 23, 49, 71, 192
Mimesis: Dargestellte Wirklichkeit in Der Abendländischen Literatur, 14
modernism, 5, 7, 14–15, 150–53, 154, 160, 164, 168, 193
"Moment of Silence: A True Story," 128
moment-to-moment transitions, 48
Moore, Alan, 23
Morse, Scott, 128
Moses and Monotheism, 27, 35, 124
Motherland, 176
mourning narratives, 26, 55; case studies, 56–59; collective mourning, 62, 66–67, 69–70; and comics form, 60–61, 63–66, 67–68, 71, 73; and rituals, 26, 60, 61, 69–72, 73; shrines and memorialization, 59–60, 69–70, 71–72; structured grief, 61–69
Ms. Marvel, 188
multi-aspectival viewing, 6–7, 164–65, 189

multiple analepsis, 125, 131
Murderdrome, 192
Murray, Doug, 142
My Friend Dahmer, 118
My Lai, 75
"Myth of Superman, The," 27–28, 125, 146, 147

'Nam, The, 26, 27, 28, 84, 85–88, 90, 93, 95, 124–25, 131–35, 140–43, 145–46, 148, 159
Narrative Discourse, 83
Nation, The, 24
National Allied Publications, 11
nationality, 98, 111–16
New Avengers, 147
Newsweek, 168
New Yorker, 10
New York Times, 68–69, 138
nightmares. *See* traumatic dreaming
Night Witches, The, 176, 179–80, 185–86
9/11 attacks, 9, 45, 61, 62, 65–67, 127, 138–39, 144
9/11 charity comics, 26, 27, 47–48, 60, 66, 69–71, 73–74, 93–94, 127–28, 146–48, 191
non sequiturs, 48, 91
North, Sterling, 11–12, 192
"Notes from the World," 131, 133–34
Nude Descending a Staircase No. 2, 164

O'Brien, Tim, 15, 16, 21, 55
Odyssey, 14
Oedipus complex, 151
Oksman, Tahneer, 180, 183
"Once More With Feeling," 44, 45
On Death and Dying, 61–62
100 Bullets, 192
One! Hundred! Demons!, 19
On Mourning, 60
Operation Cedar Falls, 131–32
O'Reilly, James "Bud," 22
O'Sullivan, Simon, 43
over-determination, 81, 86
Owen-Crocker, Gale, 58

Pak, Greg, 159, 161
Palestine, 27, 117, 118, 119
panelization, 7–9, 149, 165, 189
Panic Disorder, 75
paranoia, 151
parent-child relationships, 27, 89, 98–100, 101–11, 121
Parenthood and the Holocaust, 99–100
parody, 193–94
Parshas Truma, 88, 89, 94, 95
pastiche, 159, 193
Peacock, James, 156
Pearl Harbor, 13
Persepolis, 24, 168, 194–95
"personal trauma," 41
Petraeus, General David, 22
"Philosophical Discourse of Modernity," 28
photographs, 68, 70, 105, 125, 136–43
physicality of comics, 59–61, 85, 123
Picasso, Pablo, 4–5, 8–9, 10, 42, 189, 190–92, 193
"pleasure principle," 35, 36
"pluralistic" trauma model, 29–30, 37, 42
"Poem of Force, The," 195
Poetics, 42
Poetics of Postmodernism, The, 158
Politics of Postmodernism, The, 193
Popova, Nadezhda, 178
pornographic comics, 12
post-Freudian theories, 25, 26, 38–42
postmodernism, 28, 169–70; and authorship, 169; and comics form, 149, 150, 151, 153, 157, 159, 165, 168; and ergodic literature, 149–50; and history/historical events, 155–56, 158–64; and modernism, 150–53, 154, 160, 164, 168; and multi-aspectual viewing, 164–65; parody and pastiche, 193; and postmodernity, 153–54; and temporal representation, 149, 154–56, 158–64
Postmodernism, 153
postmodernity, 153–54
Prager, Brad, 162

Pratt, George, 195
"Prisoner on the Hell Planet," 26, 72–73, 107, 108–9
Proust, Marcel, 14
psychoanalytical models/theories, 37, 42, 75–76
PTSD (Post-Traumatic Stress Disorder), 38, 75, 77–78, 101
Punisher, 145, 186–87
"Punisher invades The 'Nam, The," 145

quadrillage, 7, 125

radical constructivism, 39–40
Raeburn, Daniel, 24
Ragtime, 155
rape, 174, 178–80, 186
Raw Magazine, 13
Red Badge of Courage, The, 15
Reed, Arden, 160
"repetition compulsion," 31, 34, 37, 40, 53, 81–82, 158, 165, 168
Repin, Illya, 42
representation stage, 81–82, 83, 86
representing conflict, 13–18
Reservoir Dogs, 192
Ricoeur, Paul, 97
Rip Van Winkle, 97, 120–21
rituals, 26, 60, 61, 69–72, 73
Rob Little, 131, 133, 134–35
Rosh Hashanah, 70–72
Ross, Christine, 38
Rothberg, Michael, 45

Sabin, Roger, 23
Sacco, Joe, 27, 98, 117–20, 121, 136
Said, Edward, 16, 117
Saigon Execution, 138, 139–43
Sale, Tim, 147
Salmi, Charlotta, 120
Salon, 67
Sandman, 6
Satrapi, Marjane, 24, 168, 194–95

Saving Private Ryan, 136
Scarry, Elaine, 121
schizophrenia, 151, 155–56, 157
"schizophrenogenic parent," 108
Schjeldahl, Peter, 10
Schueffel, Wolfram, 100
Schwab, Gabriele, 27
Scott, Wayne, 101
secondary revision stage, 81, 82–83
"secondary witnesses," 10, 39, 90–91
Second Intifada, 183, 185
Seduction of the Innocent, 12
Seltzer, Mark, 119
semiotic breaks, 68
sexual assault, 174, 175, 178
Shakespeare, William, 29
Shell and the Kernel, The, 27
shiva, 72
shrines, 59–60, 69–70, 71–72
silent comics, 52–53, 128
Sim, Dave, 165, 168, 194
Simon, Joe, 12
Simone, Gail, 186
Simpsons, The, 194
Sin City, 71, 192
Slaughterhouse-Five, 46, 128
Smith, Philip, 47
Smithsonian Magazine, 171
Sontag, Susan, 123, 137
Sousa, Cynthia, 189–91
space-time relationships, 17, 19, 123, 125–28, 129–30, 135–36, 138–39
Spanish Civil War, 3, 192
"spatio-topical system," 125–26
Speer, George, 3, 4
Spiegelman, Anja, 72, 88, 89, 107, 108–9, 115, 116, 173, 176
Spiegelman, Art, 13, 22, 23, 26, 27, 68, 72–73, 88–90, 95, 98, 102–4, 107, 108–9, 113–16, 148, 161
Spiegelman, Françoise, 26, 89, 95, 103, 115
Spiegelman, Vladek, 26, 73, 88–90, 94–95, 102–4, 107, 108–9, 113–16, 176

Spurgeon, Tom, 172
Steranko, Jim, 24
Stocks, Claire, 32, 38–39
structured grief, 61–69
Studies in Hysteria, 35, 81, 130
suicide, 32, 72–73, 107
superheroes, 144–48, 159–60, 186–87, 191
Superman, 5, 11, 47–48, 146, 147
surrealism, 8
survival, 31–32, 35, 81, 102, 104, 162, 164
System of Comics, The, 125

Tabachnick, Stephen, 89, 182
Tal, Kalí, 25, 39, 41–42, 45, 168–69
Tarver, 134–35
Tatum, James, 56–57, 195
temporal representation, 27–28, 31, 46, 124; and chronotope, 27, 125, 126–28, 135–36, 138–39, 143, 144; and comics form, 27–28, 125–26, 128–31, 135–36, 139, 140, 142, 148; and deferred action, 35–36, 124; and framed narratives, 125, 128–34; and history/historical events, 136–44, 147–48, 155–56, 158–64; long distance chronology, 134–36; and photographs, 125, 136–43; and postmodernism, 149, 154–56, 158–64; space-time relationships, 17, 19, 123, 125–28, 129–30, 135–36, 138–39; theories of time, 125–28
"testamentary," 17
Thackeray, William, 15
"theatre of war," 10–11
Thelma and Louise, 127–28
Things They Carried, The, 15
Thompson, Craig, 24
Thor, 145–46
"Three Day Pass," 84, 85–88, 90, 93, 95
300, 14, 49
"Tijuana Bibles," 12
Times, 3
Tolkien, J. R. R., 57, 58
Tolmie, Jane, 19, 173, 187
Tolstoy, Leo, 15

Torok, Maria, 27, 99
Torres, Alissa, 26, 48, 50, 61, 62–69, 73–74, 91–93, 138–39, 140, 143, 176
Torres, Luis Eduardo "Eddie," 61, 62, 63, 64, 68, 69, 73, 91–92, 139
To the Lighthouse, 14
Tran, Dzung, 102, 103, 106–7, 111–12, 128, 176
Tran, GB, 22, 27, 49–50, 68, 98, 102, 103, 106–7, 111–13, 116, 124–25, 128, 130
Tran, Tri, 98, 102, 103, 106–7, 112–13, 128–31, 176
"transgenerational phantom," 99
Trauma: A Genealogy, 32
Trauma and Recovery, 30
"trauma by proxy," 66, 90–91, 95, 101
trauma theory: "classic" model, 29, 30–38, 52; formal techniques for representing trauma, 46–53, 196; Freudian, 25, 29, 30, 31, 33–37, 39, 40; "pluralistic" model, 29–30, 37, 42; post-Freudian theories, 25, 26, 38–42
traumatic dreaming, 26–27, 75–76; and awakening, 80–81, 91–94; and comics form, 77, 83, 85–87, 88, 89–90, 91–93, 94; dreams of traumatic experience, 83, 85–90, 95; dreams of traumatic loss, 83, 90–95; and dreamwork, 26, 76, 79, 81–83, 86; neuropsychology and psychoanalysis, 76–85; and traditional nightmares, 77–79, 82–83
"traumatic neurosis," 34–35, 76, 79, 81–82, 124, 148
"traumatic realism," 45
"traumatogenic parent," 108–9
Trump, Donald, 174
Tyler, Carol, 98, 102, 104–6, 109–11
Tyler, Chuck, 104, 105–6, 110–11, 176
Tyler, Julia, 111

Uderzo, Alberto, 50
"unclaimed" experience/trauma, 10, 30, 33, 37
"underground comix," 12–13, 22–23

Unfortunates, The, 150
"Unreal," 47–48, 49, 146–47
"Untitled," 26, 72, 93
Uphaus, Robert, 15

van der Kolk, Bessel, 77, 85, 86
Vanity Fair, 15
Versaci, Rocco, 118
Vice, Sue, 127–28
Vidor, King, 179
Vietnamerica, 27, 49–50, 68, 98, 101–2, 103, 106–7, 112–13, 124–25, 128–31, 175–76
Vietnam War, 15, 22, 41, 49–50, 75, 84, 85–88, 100–101, 103, 106–7, 112–13, 124–25, 128–29, 131–35, 139–43, 145–46, 153–54
Vonnegut, Kurt, 46, 127, 147
VVA (Vietnam Veterans of America), 101

"Wake Up," 93, 94–95
Walker, Tristram, 119–20
War and Peace, 15
Ware, Chris, 152, 187
Waste Land, The, 5
Watchmen, 23
Watkin, William, 60–61
Watterson, Bill, 189
Ways of Seeing, 187
Weil, Simone, 137, 195
Weltwoche, 19
Wertham, Fredric, 12, 192
West Point Military Academy, 194–95
"What Is an Emotion," 43
"What Is Philosophy," 43
Whitlock, Gillian, 18, 21, 117
Whitman, Walt, 75
Wieseltier, Leon, 66
Wilkomirski, Binjamin, 19–20, 21, 161
Wilmer, Harry, 76
Wolk, Douglas, 24
Women in Refrigerators, 186, 187
Women's Armed Services Integration Act (1948), 174
Wonder Woman, 11

Woolf, Virginia, 14, 20
"working through," 40
World's Fair (1937), 4
Worlds of Hurt: Reading the Literature of Trauma, 41, 168–69
"wound culture," 119–20
Wray, Bill, 53
Writing History, Writing Trauma, 39

X-Men: Guernica, 189–92, 193
X-Men: Magneto Testament, 159–60, 161, 164, 178

Yom Kippur, 26
Yossel, 161–63, 164
You'll Never Know, 27, 98, 101–2, 104–6, 109–11, 175–76

Zero Dark Thirty, 15

www.ingramcontent.com/pod-product-compliance
Lightning Source LLC
Chambersburg PA
CBHW070315240426
43661CB00057B/2648